Treatise on Law

Other Titles of Interest from St. Augustine's Press

Thomas Aquinas, *Commentary on Aristotle's Nicomachean Ethics*

Thomas Aquinas, *Commentary on Aristotle's De Anima*

Thomas Aquinas, *Commentary on Aristotle's Metaphysics*

Thomas Aquinas, *Commentary on Aristotle's Posterior Analytics*. Translated by Richard Berquist

Thomas Aquinas, *Commentary on Aristotle's Physics*

Thomas Aquinas, *Disputed Questions on Virtue*. Translated by Ralph McInerny

Thomas Aquinas, *Commentary on the Epistle to the Hebrews*. Translated by Chrysostom Baer, o. praem.

Thomas Aquinas, *Commentaries on St. Paul's Epistles to Timothy, Titus, and Philemon*. Translated by Chrysostom Baer, o. praem.

John of St. Thomas, *Introduction to the Summa Theologiae of Thomas Aquinas*. Translated by Ralph McInerny.

John Poinsot [John of St. Thomas], *Tractatus de Signis Poinsot: The Semiotic of John Poinsot*.

St. Augustine, *On Order [De Ordine]*. Translated by Silvano Borruso.

St. Augustine, *The St. Augustine LifeGuide: Words to Live by from the Great Christian Saint*. Translated by Silvano Borruso,

Plato, *The Symposium of Plato: The Shelley Translation*. Translated by Percy Bysshe Shelley.

Aristotle, *Aristotle – On Poetics*. Translated by Seth Benardete and Michael Davis

Aristotle, *Physics, Or Natural Hearing*. Translated by Glen Coughlin.

Peter Kreeft, *Socratic Logic: A Logic Text Using Socratic Method, Platonic Questions, and Aristotelian Principles*

Josef Pieper, *Happiness and Contemplation*

Josef Pieper, *Scholasticism: Personalities and Problems*

Josef Pieper, *The Silence of St. Thomas*

Josef Pieper, *Enthusiasm and Divine Madness: On the Platonic Dialogue Phaedrus*

Francisco Suarez, *On Creation, Conservation, & Concurrence: Metaphysical Disputations 20–22*. Translated by A.J. Freddoso

Francisco Suarez, *Metaphysical Demonstration of the Existence of God*. Translated by John P. Doyle

Jacques Maritain, *Natural Law: Reflections on Theory and Practice*

Fulvio di Blasi, *God and the Natural Law: A Rereading of Thomas Aquinas*

Joseph Bobik, *Veritas Divina: Aquinas on Divine Truth*

Joseph Owens, c.ss.r., *Aristotle's Gradations of Being in Metaphysics E–Z*

Treatise on Law
The Complete Text

Thomas Aquinas

Translated by Alfred J. Freddoso

St. Augustine's Press
South Bend, Indiana

Manufactured in the United States of America

2 3 4 5 6   19 18 17 16 15 14

Library of Congress Cataloging in Publication Data
Thomas, Aquinas, Saint, 1225?–1274.
[Summa theologica. English. Selections]
Treatise on law: the complete text / Thomas Aquinas;
translated by Alfred J. Freddoso.
p. cm.
Includes index.
ISBN-13: 978-1-58731-880-1 (paperbound : alk. paper)
ISBN-10: 1-58731-880-6 (paperbound : alk. paper)
1. Natural law. 2. Law – Philosophy. 3. Christianity and law.
I. Freddoso, Alfred J. II. Title.
K447.T45A36713 2009
340'.1 – dc22   2009002013

∞ *The paper used in this publication meets the minimum requirements of the
American National Standard for Information Sciences – Permanence of
Paper for Printed Materials, ANSI Z39.48-1984.*

ST. AUGUSTINE'S PRESS
www.staugustine.net

Table of Contents

QUESTION 90

The Essence of Law

We next have to consider the exterior principles of acts. Now the exterior principle that inclines us toward evil is the devil, whose temptations were discussed in the First Part (*ST* 1, q. 114). On the other hand, the exterior principle that moves us toward the good is God, who both instructs us with law and assists us with grace. Hence, we must first discuss law (questions 90–108) and then grace (questions 109–114).

On the topic of law, we must first consider law itself in general (questions 90–92) and then the parts of law (questions 93–108).

Now there are three things to consider about law in general: first, the essence of law (question 90); second, the different kinds of law (question 91); and, third, the effects of law (question 92).

On the first topic there are four questions: (1) Is law something that belongs to reason? (2) What is the end or purpose (*finis*) of law? (3) What is the cause of law? (4) What about the promulgation of law?

Article 1

Is law something that belongs to reason?

It seems that law is not something that belongs to reason (*non sit aliquid rationis*):

Objection 1: In Romans 7:23 the Apostle says, "I see another law in my members . . . ." But in those members [of the body] there is nothing that belongs to reason, since reason does not use a corporeal organ. Therefore, law is not something that belongs to reason.

Objection 2: Nothing exists in reason which is not either a power, a habit, or an act. But law is not the very *power* of reason itself. Likewise, law is not a *habit* of reason, since the habits of reason are the intellectual virtues that were discussed above (q. 57). Nor, again, is law an *act* of reason, since if it were, then law would cease to exist when reason ceased to act, e.g., in those who are asleep. Therefore, law is not something that belongs to reason.

Objection 3: Law moves those who are subject to the law to act in an upright way (*ad recte agendum*). But as is clear from what was said above

(q. 9, a. 1), it is properly speaking the role of the will to move one to act. Therefore, law has to do not with reason but rather with the will, in keeping with what [Justinian] the Legal Expert says [in *Digestum Vetus* 1]: "Whatever pleases the ruler (*princeps*) has the force of law."

But contrary to this: It is law's function to command and forbid. But as was established above (q. 17, a. 1), commanding belongs to reason. Therefore, law is something that belongs to reason.

I respond: Law is a certain rule and measure of acts in accord with which one is either induced to act or restrained from acting. For 'law' (*lex*) is derived from 'to bind' (*ligare*), since law obligates (*obligare*) one to act. Now the rule and measure of human acts is reason, which, as is clear from what was said above (q. 1, a. 1), is the first principle of human acts. For it belongs to reason to order things to their end—where, according to the Philosopher, the end is the first principle in matters of action (*in agendis*). But in every genus, that which is the principle is the measure and rule of that genus. For instance, *one* is the measure in the genus *number*, and the first motion is the measure in the genus *motion*. Hence, it follows that law is something that belongs to reason.

Reply to objection 1: Since law is a rule and measure, there are two ways in which it is said to exist in something.

First, law exists in that which measures and regulates. And since this is proper to reason, law taken in this sense exists in reason alone.

Second, law exists in that which is regulated and measured. And this is how law exists in all the things that are inclined in any way by any kind of law. As a result, any inclination that stems from any kind of law can itself be called a law—not by its essence but, as it were, by participation. And it is in this sense that the very inclination of the members [of the body] toward sensual desire is called 'the law of the members'.

Reply to objection 2: Just as in the case of exterior acts one must consider both the action (*operatio*) and the thing that is done (*operatum*)—e.g., the act of building and the thing built—so too in the works of reason one must consider (a) the very acts of reason, i.e., the act of understanding and the act of discursive reasoning, and (b) what is constituted by acts of this sort. In the case of speculative reason, the constituted things are, first, the definition; second, the proposition (*enunciatio*); and, third, the syllogism or argument.

Now, as was explained above (q. 76, a.1) in keeping with what the Philosopher teaches in *Ethics* 7, practical reason likewise uses a certain type of syllogism with respect to things that can be done (*operabilia*).

Hence, in the case of practical reason there is something that is related to the actions (*operationes*) in the same way that the proposition is related to the conclusions in the case of speculative reason. These universal propositions of practical reason, which are ordered toward actions, have the character of law. At certain times these propositions are actually being considered, and at other times reason possesses them as habits.

Reply to objection 3: As was explained above (q. 17, a. 1), it is from the will that reason has its power to effect movement. For it is because someone wills the end that his reason issues commands regarding what is ordered toward the end. However, for an act of will about what is commanded to have the character of law, it must be regulated in some way by reason (*aliqua ratione regulata*). And this is how to understand the claim that the ruler's will has the force of law; otherwise, the ruler's will would constitute wickedness (*esset iniquitas*) rather than law.

Article 2

Is law always ordered toward the common good as its end?

It seems that law is not always ordered toward the common good (*bonum commune*) as its end:

Objection 1: It is law's function to command and forbid. But precepts are ordered toward certain individual goods (*singularia bona*). Therefore, law does not always have the common good as its end.

Objection 2: Law directs a man toward acting. But human acts have to do with particular matters. Therefore, law is likewise ordered toward a certain particular good (*particulare bonum*).

Objection 3: In *Etymologia* Isidore says, "If law is founded upon reason, then law will consist of everything that is founded upon reason." But it is not just what is ordered toward the common good that is founded upon reason, but also what is ordered toward one's private good (*bonum privatum*). Therefore, law is ordered not only toward the common good, but also toward one's private good.

But contrary to this: In *Etymologia* 5 Isidore says, "Law is formulated not for any private advantage, but for the common benefit of the citizens."

I respond: As has been explained (a. 1), by virtue of the fact that law is a rule and measure, it has to do with the principle of human acts. Now just as reason is the principle of human acts, so too within reason itself there is something which is the principle with respect to everything else. Hence, this must be what law is chiefly and especially concerned with.

Now in actions, which practical reason is concerned with, the first principle is the ultimate end. But, as was established above (q. 2, a. 7), the ultimate end of human life is happiness or beatitude. Hence, law must have to do mainly with an ordering that leads to beatitude.

Again, since (a) every part is ordered toward its whole in the way that what is incomplete (*imperfectum*) is ordered toward what is complete (*perfectum*), and since (b) a man is part of a complete community, law must properly be concerned with the ordering that leads to communal happiness (*ad felicitatem communem*). Hence, in the definition of legal affairs alluded to above, the Philosopher makes mention of both happiness and political communion. For in *Ethics* 5 he says, "The laws (*legalia*) we call 'just' are those that effect and conserve happiness and its elements within the political community." For as *Politics* 1 puts it, a city is a complete community.

Now in every genus, the genus is especially predicated of the thing that serves as the principle of the others, and the genus is predicated of the others because of their relation to that thing. For instance, fire, which is maximally hot, is a cause of the heat in mixed bodies, which are called 'hot' to the extent that they participate in fire. Hence, since 'law' is predicated especially in relation to the common good, it must be the case that any other precept about a particular act has the character of law only to the extent that it is ordered toward the common good. And so every law is ordered toward the common good.

Reply to objection 1: 'Precept' implies the application of law to the things that are regulated by the law. But an ordering toward the common good, which law is concerned with, is applicable to individual ends. Accordingly, precepts are likewise handed down with respect to certain particular matters.

Reply to objection 2: Actions are, to be sure, concerned with particular matters. However, those particular matters can be referred back to the common good—not, indeed, because they share with it a common genus or species, but rather because they share with it a common final cause. This is why the common good is called a common end.

Reply to objection 3: Just as nothing is firmly established through speculative reason except by being traced back to first indemonstrable principles, so too nothing is firmly established through practical reason except by being ordered to the ultimate end, which is the common good. But what is founded upon reason in this way has the character of law.

Article 3

Whose reason is it that makes law?

It seems that everyone's reason makes law:

Objection 1: In Romans 2:14 the Apostle says, "When the Gentiles, who do not have the Law, do by nature those things that are of the Law, they, not having the Law, are a law unto themselves." But he says this in general about everyone. Therefore, everyone is able to make law for himself.

Objection 2: As the Philosopher says in *Ethics* 2, the lawmaker's intent is to lead men to virtue. But every man is capable of leading another to virtue. Therefore, every man's reason can make law.

Objection 3: Just as the ruler (*princeps*) of a city is the one who governs (*gubernator*) the city, so too every father of a family (*paterfamilias*) is the one who governs the household. But the ruler of a city is able to make law in the city. Therefore, every father of a family is able to make law in his own household.

But contrary to this: In the *Etymologia* Isidore says (and *Decretals*, dist. 2 repeats this), "A law is an ordinance (*constitutio*) of the people, by which the elders (*maiores*), along with the common people (*plebes*), have sanctioned something." Therefore, it is not just anyone's role to make law.

I respond: Law has to do properly, primarily, and principally with an ordering toward the common good. Now to order something toward the common good is the role either of the whole multitude or of someone who is acting in place of the whole multitude. Therefore, establishing a law is something that belongs either to the whole multitude or to a public personage who is in charge of (*habet curam*) the whole multitude. For in all other cases as well, ordering something to an end is the role of someone for whom that end is his own.

Reply to objection 1: As was explained above (a. 1), when law exists in something, it exists not only in that which regulates, but also, by participation, in that which is regulated. And everyone is a law unto himself in the sense that he participates in the order established by that which does the regulating. This is why the Apostle adds immediately in the same place, ". . . who show the work of the law that is written in their hearts."

Reply to objection 2: A private person cannot efficaciously lead anyone to virtue. For he can only issue a warning, and if his warning is not heeded, he does not have the sort of coercive power (*vim coactivam*) which, according to the Philosopher in *Ethics* 10, law must have in order to lead someone efficaciously to virtue. Now, as will be explained below (q. 92, a. 2), this coercive power is had by the multitude or by a public personage whose role it is to inflict punishments. Only someone like this is in a position to make laws.

Reply to objection 3: Just as a man is part of a household, so a household is part of a city and, as *Politics* 1 puts it, a city is a complete community (*communitas perfecta*). And so just as the good of a single man is not the ultimate end, but is instead ordered toward the ultimate end, so too the good of a single household is ordered toward the good of a single city, which is a complete community. Hence, the one who governs a family can, to be sure, make certain precepts and statutes, but these do not, properly speaking, have the character of law.

Article 4

Is promulgation part of the nature of law?

It seems that promulgation is not part of the nature of law:

Objection 1: Natural law especially has the nature of law. But natural law does not require promulgation. Therefore, it is not part of the nature of law that it be promulgated.

Objection 2: Properly speaking, law plays the role of obligating someone to do or not to do something. But it is not just those to whom a law is promulgated who are obligated to fulfill the law; the others are obligated as well. Therefore, promulgation is not part of the nature of law.

Objection 3: The obligatory force of law extends even into the future, since, as jurists say, laws impose necessity on future transactions. But promulgation is made [only] to those who exist at present. Therefore, law does not require promulgation.

But contrary to this: *Decretals*, dist. 4, says, "Laws are instituted when they are promulgated."

I respond: As has been explained (a. 1), law is imposed on others in the manner of a rule and measure. But a rule or measure is imposed by being applied to the things that are ruled and measured. Hence, in order for a law to acquire the power to obligate, which is proper to law, it must be applied to the men who are supposed to be regulated by it. Now this sort of application is accomplished by the law's being brought to their knowledge through its promulgation. Hence, promulgation is necessary in order for law to have its power.

And so from the four traits that have been mentioned, we can put together a definition of law: Law is (a) an ordinance (*ordinatio*) of reason, (b) for the common good, (c) made by one who is in charge of the community, and (d) promulgated.

Reply to objection 1: The promulgation of the law of nature consists in God's having instilled it in the minds of men in order that they might know it naturally.

Reply to objection 2: Those who are such that the law is not promulgated in their presence are obligated to follow the law insofar as it is or can be brought to their knowledge through others, once the promulgation has been made.

Reply to objection 3: A present promulgation extends into the future by reason of the permanence of writing, which in some sense continually promulgates the law. Hence, in *Etymologia* 2 Isidore says, "'Law' (*lex*) is derived from reading (*legendo*), because it is written."

QUESTION 91

The Different Kinds of Law

We next have to consider the different kinds of law. On this topic there are six questions: (1) Is there such a thing as eternal law? (2) Is there such a thing as natural law? (3) Is there such a thing as human law? (4) Is there such a thing as divine law? (5) Is there just a single [divine] law, or more than one? (6) Is there such a thing as 'the law of sin'?

Article 1

Is there such a thing as eternal law?

It seems that there is no such thing as eternal law:

Objection 1: Every law is imposed on someone. But there was no one on whom law could have been imposed from eternity, since God alone existed from eternity. Therefore, there is no such thing as eternal law.

Objection 2: Promulgation is part of the nature of law. But there could not have been a promulgation from eternity, since nothing existed from eternity to which the law might have been promulgated. Therefore, there cannot be any such thing as eternal law.

Objection 3: Law implies an ordering to an end. But there is nothing eternal that might be ordered to an end, since the ultimate end alone is eternal. Therefore, there is no such thing as eternal law.

But contrary to this: In *De Libero Arbitrio* 1 Augustine says, "The law that is called the 'highest ideal plan' (*summa ratio*) cannot but seem unchangeable and eternal to anyone who understands it."

I respond: As was explained above (q. 90, a. 4), law is nothing other than a certain dictate (*dictamen*) of practical reason on the part of a ruler who governs some complete community. But once we assume, as was established in the First Part (*ST* 1, q. 22, a. 1), that the world is governed by divine providence, it is obvious that the entire community of the universe is governed by divine reason. Therefore, the very nature of the governance of things that exists in God as the ruler of the universe has the character of law. And since, as Proverbs 8:23 puts it, God's reason does not conceive of anything temporally but instead has an eternal conception, it follows that a law of this kind must be called eternal law.

Reply to objection 1: Those things that do not exist in themselves exist in God's presence (*apud Deum*) insofar as they are foreknown and preordained by Him—this according to Romans 4:17 ("He calls the things that are not in the same way as those that are"). So, then, the eternal conception of God's law has the character of an eternal law, since it is ordered by God toward the governance of the things foreknown by Him.

Reply to objection 2: Promulgation is accomplished by both the spoken word (*verbum*) and the written word (*scriptum*), and the eternal law has both sorts of promulgation on the part of God who promulgates it. For God's Word is eternal (see *ST* 1, q. 34), and the writing in the book of life is eternal (see *ST* 1, q. 24).

On the other hand, as far as the creature who hears or reads is concerned, the promulgation cannot be eternal.

Reply to objection 3: Law implies an ordering to an end in the *active* sense—viz., in the sense that certain things are ordered to the end through law.

However, law does not imply an ordering to an end in the *passive* sense, i.e., in the sense that the law itself is ordered to an end—except, incidentally, in the case of a governor whose end lies outside himself and is such that his law, too, must be ordered to it. By contrast, the end of divine governance is God Himself, and His law is not distinct from Himself. Hence, the eternal law is not ordered toward any further end.

Article 2

Is there any such thing as natural law in us?

It seems that there is no such thing as natural law in us:

Objection 1: Man is sufficiently governed by eternal law, since, as Augustine says in *De Libero Arbitrio* 1, "Eternal law is the law by which it is just that all things should be well ordered." But nature does not abound in what is superfluous, just as it is not deficient in what is necessary. Therefore, there is no such thing as natural law for man.

Objection 2: As was established above (q. 90, a.1), it is through law that man is ordered to the end in his acts. But the ordering of human acts to their end does not stem from nature in the way that this occurs in non-rational creatures, which act for the sake of an end by natural appetite alone; instead, man acts for the sake of an end through his reason and will. Therefore, there is no law that is natural to man.

Objection 3: The more free someone is, the less subject he is to law. But man is more free than all the [other] animals because of the power of free choice (*liberum arbitrium*), which he has in contrast to all the other animals. Therefore, since the other animals are not subject to a natural law, neither is man subject to any natural law.

But contrary to this: The Gloss on Romans 2:14 ("For when the Gentiles, who do not have the Law, do by nature those things that are of the Law . . .") says, "Even if they do not have the written Law, they nonetheless have the natural law, by which everyone understands and knows within himself what is good and what is evil."

I respond: As was explained above (q. 90, a. 1), since law is a rule and a measure, there are two senses in which it can exist in something: first, in the sense of existing in that which regulates and measures and, second, in the sense of existing in that which is regulated and measured. For a thing is measured and regulated to the extent that it has some participation in the rule and measure. So since, as is clear from what was said above (a. 1), all the things subject to divine providence are regulated and measured by eternal law, it is clear that all things in some way participate in eternal law. More precisely, because eternal law is imprinted on them, they have inclinations toward their own proper acts and ends.

Now among all creatures, the rational creature is subject to divine providence in a more excellent manner, because he himself participates in providence, providing for himself and for others. Hence, in him, too, there is a participation in eternal reason through which he has a natural inclination to his due act and end. And the rational creature's mode of participation in the eternal law is called natural law.

Hence, after the Psalmist (Psalm 4:6) has said, "Offer up the sacrifice of justice," he adds, as if someone were asking what the works of justice are, "Many say, 'Who is there to show us good works?'" In reply to this question he says, "The light of Your countenance, Lord, is imprinted on us"—as if to say, the light of natural reason, by which we discern what is good and what is evil. This has to do with natural law, which is nothing other than the imprint of God's light within us.

Hence, it is clear that natural law is nothing other than a participation in eternal law on the part of a rational creature.

Reply to objection 1: This argument assumes that natural law is something different from eternal law. However, as has been explained, natural law is nothing other than a certain kind of participation in eternal law.

Reply to objection 2: As was established above (q. 10, a. 1), every operation of reason and will in us is derived from what is in accord with nature. For every instance of discursive reasoning stems from principles that are naturally known to us, and every desire for things that are ordered to an end stems from a natural desire for the ultimate end. And so, likewise, the initial ordering of our acts to their end (*prima directio actuum nostrorum ad finem*) must be brought about through natural law.

Reply to objection 3: Non-rational animals participate in the eternal law in their own way, just as rational creatures do. However, since a rational creature participates in natural law in an intellectual and rational way, a rational creature's participation in the eternal law is itself properly called a law. For as was explained above (q. 90, a. 1), law belongs to reason. By contrast, a non-rational creature does not participate in the eternal law in a rational way, and so its participation cannot be called law except by way of a likeness (*per similitudinem*).

Article 3

Is there any such thing as human law?

It seems that there is no such thing as human law:

Objection 1: As has been explained (a. 2), natural law is a participation in eternal law. But as Augustine says in *De Libero Arbitrio* 1, all things are completely ordered through eternal law. Therefore, natural law is sufficient for ordering all human affairs. Therefore, it is unnecessary for there to be any such thing as human law.

Objection 2: As has been explained (q. 90, a. 1), law has the character of a measure. But human reason is not the measure of things; just the opposite, as *Metaphysics* 10 insists. Therefore, there cannot be a law that proceeds from human reason.

Objection 3: As *Metaphysics* 10 says, a measure should be absolutely fixed (*certissima*). But human reason's dictates about things to be done are not fixed, since according to Wisdom 9:14, "The thoughts of mortal men are fearful and our counsels uncertain." Therefore, there cannot be a law that proceeds from human reason.

But contrary to this: In *De Libero Arbitrio* 1 Augustine posits two kinds of law, one eternal and the other temporal, and the latter he calls 'human law'.

I respond: As was explained above (q. 90, a. 4), law is a dictate of practical reason. Now practical reason and speculative reason proceed in similar ways, since, as was established above (q. 90, a. 1), both proceed from given principles to given conclusions. Accordingly, then, just as, in the case of speculative reason, conclusions in the diverse sciences, which are not naturally known to us but are instead discovered by the activity of reason, are brought forth from naturally known indemonstrable principles, so too from the precepts of natural law, which are, as it were, common and indemonstrable principles, human reason must proceed to determine certain matters in a more particular way. And these particular determinations, devised by human reason, are called human laws—assuming the preservation of all the other conditions, described above (q. 90, a. 4), that are relevant to the nature of law.

Thus, in his *Rhetorica* Tully says, "The beginnings of justice came from nature; next, certain things came to be customs because of their advantageous nature; afterwards, fear and reverence sanctioned both what had come from nature and what had been approved by custom."

Reply to objection 1: Human reason is incapable of participating fully in the dictates of divine reason (*non potest participare plenum dictamen rationis divinae*); rather, it participates in its own way and incompletely. And so just as, in the case of speculative reason, there exists in us, through our natural participation in God's wisdom, a cognition of certain common principles, but not a proper cognition of every truth as there is in God's wisdom, so too, in the case of practical reason, man naturally participates in eternal law with respect to certain general principles, but not with respect to the particular determination of singular acts, even though the latter are contained within the eternal law. This is why it is necessary for human reason to proceed further to the particular sanctions contained in laws.

Reply to objection 2: Human reason is not in its own right (*secundum se*) a rule with respect to things; instead, it is the principles naturally instilled in human reason that are general rules and measures of all the things which are to be done by man and with respect to which natural reason is the rule and measure—even though it is not a measure of what stems from nature.

Reply to objection 3: Practical reason is concerned with actions (*operabilia*), which are singular and contingent, and not with necessary things like those which speculative reason is concerned with. And so human laws cannot have the sort of infallibility that the demonstrated conclusions of the sciences do. Nor is it necessary that every measure should be in every way infallible and fixed; rather, it should be as fixed as is possible within its own genus.

Article 4

Was it necessary for there to be such a thing as divine law?

It seems to have been unnecessary for there to be such a thing as divine law:

Objection 1: As has been explained (a. 2), natural law is within us a kind of participation in eternal law. But as has been said (a. 1), eternal law is a divine law. Therefore, it is unnecessary for there to be a divine law in addition to natural law and the human laws that stem from it.

Objection 2: Ecclesiasticus 15:14 says, "God left man in the hand of his own counsel." But as was established above (q., 14, a. 1), counsel is an act of reason. Therefore, man was left to the governance provided by his own reason. But as has been explained (a. 3), a dictate of human reason is human law. Therefore, it is unnecessary for man to be governed by some other divine law.

Objection 3: Human nature is more self-sufficient than non-rational creatures. But a non-rational creature does not have any divine law in addition to the natural inclination that has been instilled in it. Therefore, *a fortiori*, a rational creature should not have any divine law in addition to natural law.

But contrary to this: David asked God for a law to be imposed on him, saying, "Set before me for a law the way of Your justifications, O Lord" (Psalm 118:33).

I respond: In addition to natural law and human law, it was necessary for us to have divine law in order to direct human life—and this for four reasons:

First, through law man is directed to his own proper acts in relation to the ultimate end. And if man were ordered just to an end that is not disproportionate to man's natural power, then it would not be necessary for man to have any directive from reason in addition to natural law and the humanly posited law that stems from it. However, since, as was established above (q. 5, a. 5), man is ordered to the end of eternal beatitude, which is disproportionate to natural human power, it was necessary that, in addition to natural law and human law, he should also be directed to his end by a law that is divinely given.

Second, due to the uncertainty of human judgment, especially about contingent and particular matters, different people can make diverse judgments about human acts, and these diverse judgments lead to diverse and contrary laws. Therefore, in order that man might be able to know without any hesitation what he should do and what he should avoid doing, it was necessary that he be directed in his proper acts by a law that is divinely given and is clearly such that it cannot be mistaken.

Third, man is able to make law with respect to those things which he is in a position to make judgments about. However, human judgments cannot encompass interior movements, which are hidden, but can encompass only exterior acts, which are observable. Yet for the perfection of virtue it is required that a man be upright with respect to both sorts of acts. So human law could not adequately restrain and order interior acts, and divine law had to be added for this purpose.

Fourth, as Augustine says in *De Libero Arbitrio* 1, human law is incapable of prohibiting or punishing all evil deeds. For if it tried to do away with all evils, many goods would also be destroyed as a result, and the promotion of the common good, which is necessary for human living, would be impeded. Therefore, in order that no evil remain unforbidden and unpunished, it was necessary that there should be, in addition, a divine law by which all sins are prohibited.

These four reasons are touched on in Psalm 118:8, where it says, "The law of the Lord is unspotted . . . ," i.e., does not permit any foulness of sin; ". . . converting souls . . . ," since it directs not just exterior acts, but interior acts as well; ". . . the testimony of the Lord is faithful . . . ," because of the certitude of what is true and upright; ". . . giving wisdom to the little ones," because it orders man to his supernatural and divine end.

Reply to objection 1: Natural law participates in eternal law in a way proportioned to the power of human nature. But man has to be directed in a deeper way to his ultimate supernatural end. And so there is, in addition, a divinely given law, through which eternal law is participated in more deeply.

Reply to objection 2: Counsel is a certain sort of inquiry, and so it must proceed from given principles. But it is not enough that it should proceed from naturally instilled principles, i.e., from the precepts of the natural law—and this for the [four] reasons explained above. Rather, certain other principles must be added, viz., the precepts of divine law.

Reply to objection 3: Non-rational creatures are not ordered to an end higher than the end that is proportioned to their natural power. And so the arguments are not parallel.

Article 5

Is there just a single divine law?

It seems that there is just a single divine law:

Objection 1: A single king in a single kingdom has a single law. But the whole human race is related to God as to a single king—this according to Psalm 46:8 ("God is king of all the earth"). Therefore, there is just a single divine law.

Objection 2: Every law is ordered toward the end that the lawmaker intends in those for whom he makes the law. But what God intends in all men is one and the same thing—this according to 1 Timothy 2:4 ("He wills that all men be saved and come to knowledge of the truth"). Therefore, there is just a single divine law.

Objection 3: To the extent that the revelation of grace is higher than natural cognition, divine law seems to be closer to eternal law, which is a single law, than is natural law. But natural law is a single law for all men. Therefore, *a fortiori*, so is divine law.

But contrary to this: In Hebrews 7:12 the Apostle says, "For the priesthood having been changed, it is necessary for the law to be changed." But as is explained in the same place, there are two kinds of priesthood, the Levitical priesthood and Christ's priesthood. Therefore, there are two laws, viz., the Old Law and the New Law.

I respond: As was explained in the First Part (*ST* 1, q. 30, a. 3), distinction is a cause of number. Now there are two ways in which things can be distinct from one another. First, they are distinct in the sense of being altogether diverse in species, e.g., a horse and an ox. Second, they are distinct in the sense that the one is perfect and the other imperfect within the same species, e.g., a man and a boy. It is in this latter sense that the divine law is divided into the Old Law and the New Law. Hence, in Galatians 3:24–25, the Apostle compares the status of the Old Law to the status of a child under the tutelage of a pedagogue, while he compares the status of the New Law to a full-grown man who is no longer under the tutelage of a pedagogue.

Now perfection and imperfection apply to these laws relative to three of those elements pertaining to law that were noted above.

First, as was noted above (q. 90, a. 2), law is ordered toward the common good as its end. But there are two kinds of common good. The first is a *sensible and earthly good* (*bonum sensibile et terrenum*), and it is to this sort of good that the Old Law directly ordered [the people]; hence, in Exodus 3:8–17, at the very initiation of the Old Law, the people are invited into the earthly kingdom of the Canaanites. The second is an *intelligible and heavenly good* (*bonum intelligibile et caeleste*), and it is to this sort of good that the New Law orders [the people]; hence, at the very beginning of His teaching Christ issued an invitation to the kingdom of heaven, saying, "Repent, for the kingdom of heaven is at hand" (Matthew 4:17). Thus, in *Contra Faustum* 4 Augustine says, "Promises of temporal things were contained in the Old Testament, and this is why it is called 'old'; by contrast, the New Testament has to do with the promise of eternal life."

Second, law has to do with directing human acts in accord with the order of justice. On this score, too, the New Law outstrips the Old Law by ordering the interior acts of the soul—this according to Matthew 5:20, "Unless your justice exceeds that of the Scribes and Pharisees, you will not enter into the kingdom of heaven." For this reason it is said that the Old Law restrains the hand, whereas the New Law restrains the mind.

Third, law has the role of inducing men to obey the commandments. The Old Law did this through the fear of punishment, whereas the New Law does it through the love that is infused into our hearts by Christ's grace, which is conferred under the New Law but was prefigured under the Old Law. This is why in *Contra Adimantum Manichaei Discipulum* Augustine says, "In brief, the difference between the Law and the Gospel is this: fear and love."

Reply to objection 1: Just as the father of a household issues different commands to children and to adults, so too the one king God, within His single kingdom, gives one law to men who are still imperfect and another more perfect law to those who have already been led by the hand through the prior law to a greater capacity for divine things.

Reply to objection 2: The salvation of men was impossible except through Christ—this according to Acts 4:12 ("There is no other name given to men, whereby we must be saved"). And so a law that leads all men perfectly to salvation could not have been given prior to Christ's coming. Before that, the people from whom Christ was to be born had to be given a preparatory law for receiving Christ, and in this law certain rudiments of salvific justice were contained.

Reply to objection 3: The natural law directs man in accord with certain general precepts which are shared by both perfect and imperfect men, and this is why there is a single natural law for everyone. In addition, however, the divine law directs man in certain particulars with respect to which the perfect and the imperfect are not similarly positioned. And as has already been explained, this is why it was necessary for there to be two divine laws.

Article 6

Is there such a thing as a 'law of the stimulant [to sin]'?

It seems that there is no such thing as a 'law of the stimulant [to sin]' (*lex fomitis [peccati]*):

Objection 1: In *Etymologia* 5 Isidore says, "The law is founded upon reason." But the stimulant to sin does not consist in reason, but rather it deviates from reason. Therefore, the stimulant to sin does not have the character of law.

Objection 2: Every law is obligatory in the sense that anyone who does not keep it is called a transgressor. But the stimulant to sin does not render anyone a transgressor by virtue of his not following it; to the contrary, he is rendered a transgressor if he does follow it. Therefore, the stimulus to sin does not have the character of law.

Objection 3: As was established above (q. 90, a. 2), law is ordered toward the common good. But the stimulant to sin inclines one not toward the common good, but instead toward his own private good. Therefore, the stimulant to sin does not have the character of law.

But contrary to this: In Romans 7:23 the Apostle says, "I see another law in my members, fighting against the law of my mind."

I respond: As was explained above (a. 2), law exists in an essential way in that which rules and measures, whereas it exists by way of participation in that which is measured and ruled—so that, as is clear from what was said above, every inclination or ordering that is found in things subject to the law is itself called 'law' by way of participation.

Now there are two ways in which an inclination stemming from the lawmaker can be found in things that are subject to the law: (a) in one way, insofar as such an inclination *directly* inclines what is subject to it toward something, and sometimes diverse subjects to diverse acts, in the way that military law (*lex militum*) can be said to be different from business law (*lex mercatorum*); (b) in another way, *indirectly*, viz., insofar as the fact that the lawmaker takes away some office (*dignitas*) from one who is subject to him results in the latter's passing into another order and, as it were, into another law. For instance, if a soldier is discharged from the army, then he will pass into rural law (*lex rusticorum*) or business law.

So, then, under God the Lawmaker different creatures have different natural inclinations, with the result that what is in some way law for one is contrary to what is law for another. For instance, *being fierce* is in a certain sense the law for a dog, whereas it is contrary to the law for a sheep or some other gentle animal.

Thus, the law for man, which is given by divine ordination according to man's proper condition, is that he should act in accord with reason. This law was, to be sure, so strong in man's initial state that nothing either beyond reason or contrary to reason could take man unawares (*posset sub-repere hominem*). But once man turned away from God, he fell into being carried away by the impetus of sensuality; and this happens in a particular way to each man the more he recedes from reason, so that he becomes in a certain sense like the beasts, which are carried away by the impetus of sensuality—this according to Psalm 48:21 ("Man, when he existed in honor, did not understand: he has been put on the same footing as senseless beasts and been made similar to them").

So, then, this inclination toward sensuality, which is called the 'stimulant' (*fomes*), has the character of law absolutely speaking in the case of the other animals—yet in the manner in which it can be called 'law' in such animals, viz., as a direct inclination. In men, by contrast, the stimulant does not have the character of law in this way, but is rather a deviation from the law of reason. Yet insofar as man was stripped of original justice and of vigorous reason through God's justice, this impetus to sensuality which leads him on has the character of law in the sense that it is a punishment and follows from God's law, which strips man of his proper dignity (*hominem destituente propria dignitate*).

Reply to objection 1: This argument proceeds from the stimulant considered by itself, insofar as it inclines one to evil. For, as has been explained, it does not in this sense have the character of law. Instead, it has the character of law insofar as it follows from the justice of God's law—in the way that one might call it a law that a nobleman should, because of some sin, be subjected to the work of a servant.

Reply to objection 2: This objection proceeds on the assumption that the stimulant is a law in the sense of a rule and measure; for those who deviate from the law in this sense are rendered transgressors. However, the stimulant is not a law in this sense, but is instead a law by participation of a certain sort, in the way explained above.

Reply to objection 3: This argument proceeds from the stimulant's proper inclination and not from its origin. Yet if the inclination toward sensuality is considered as it exists in other animals, then it is indeed ordered to the common good, i.e., to the conservation of nature in the species and in the individual. And this is also true in the case of man, to the extent that sensuality is subject to reason. However, the name 'stimulant' is used for it insofar as it departs from the order of reason.

QUESTION 92

The Effects of Law

We next have to consider the effects of law. On this topic there are two questions: (1) Is it an effect of law to make men good? (2) Are the effects of law, as the Jurist [Gratian] claims, to command, to forbid, to permit, and to punish?

Article 1

Is it the role of law to make men good?

It seems that it is not the role of law to make men good:

Objection 1: Men are good through virtue, since as *Ethics* 2 puts it, "Virtue is what makes the one who has it good." But virtue comes to man only from God, since He "works it in us without us," as was explained when we defined virtue (q. 55, a. 4). Therefore, it is not the role of law to make men good.

Objection 2: Law does a man no good unless he obeys the law. But the very fact that a man obeys the law stems from his goodness. Therefore, a man's goodness is presupposed in relation to law. Therefore, it is not law that makes men good.

Objection 3: As was explained above (q. 90, a. 2), law is ordered toward the common good. But there are some men who act well in matters pertaining to the common good and yet do not act well in their own proper affairs. Therefore, it is not the role of law to make men good.

Objection 4: As the Philosopher points out in *Politics* 3, some laws are tyrannical. But a tyrant aims only at his own advantage and not at the goodness of his subjects. Therefore, it is not the role of law to make men good.

But contrary to this: In *Ethics* 2 the Philosopher says, "Every lawmaker intends to make the citizens good."

I respond: As was explained above (q. 90, a. 1), law is nothing other than a dictate of reason which exists in the one who is in charge (*in praesidente*) and by which his subjects are governed. Now, in general, the virtue of what is subordinate lies in its being subordinated in the right way to that by which it is governed; for instance, we see that the virtue of the irascible and concupiscible [parts of the soul] consists in their being obedient in the right way to reason. Similarly, as the Philosopher puts it in *Politics* 1, "The virtue of any subject lies in his being subjected to his ruler in the right way (*ut bene subiiciatur principanti*)."

Now each law is ordered toward being obeyed by those subject to it. Hence, it is clear that it is a property of law that it should lead its subjects toward their own proper virtue. Therefore, since virtue is what makes the one who has it good, it follows that a proper effect of law is to make those to whom it is given good, either *absolutely speaking* or *relatively speaking.*

For if the lawmaker's intention is directed toward the true good, i.e., the common good regulated in accord with divine justice, then it follows that through his law men become good *absolutely speaking.*

On the other hand, if the lawmaker's intention is not directed toward the good absolutely speaking, but is instead directed toward a good which is advantageous or pleasant for himself or which is incompatible with divine justice, then his law makes men good not absolutely speaking, but only *relatively speaking*, viz., in relation to that sort of regime. This is the sense in which the good exists even in things that are *per se* evil, as when someone is said to be a good thief because he operates in a way that is appropriate for his end.

Reply to objection 1: As is clear from what was said above (q. 63, a. 2), there are two kinds of virtue, viz., *acquired* virtue and *infused* virtue. The regularity (*assuetudo*) of the actions plays a role in both kinds of virtue, but in different ways. For this regularity is in fact a *cause* of acquired virtue, whereas it [merely] *disposes* one for infused virtue and then conserves and promotes that virtue once it is already possessed. Since law is given in order to direct human acts, law makes men good to the extent that human acts contribute to virtue. Hence, the Philosopher like-wise says in *Politics* 2, "Lawmakers make men good by habituating them."

Reply to objection 2: It is not always the case that someone obeys the law because of his perfect goodness in virtue. Rather, he sometimes obeys because of his fear of punishment, and at other times simply because of the dictate of reason, which, as was explained above (q. 63, a. 1), is in some sense the principle of virtue.

Reply to objection 3: The goodness of a part is seen in relation to its whole. Hence, as Augustine says in *Confessiones* 3, "Any part that does not fit in with its whole is bad (*turpis*)." Therefore, since every man is part of a political community (*pars civitatis*), it is impossible that any man should be good without being related in the right way to the common good; nor can the whole consist appropriately of anything except parts that are proportioned to it.

Hence, it is impossible for the common good of the political community to fare well unless at least the citizens who are the rulers are virtuous. However, as far as the good of the community is concerned, it is enough that the other citizens be virtuous to the extent that they obey the commands of the rulers. This is why in *Politics* 3 the Philosopher says, "The virtue of a ruler is the same as the virtue of a good man, whereas the virtue of a common citizen is not the same as the virtue of a good man."

Reply to objection 4: Since a tyrannical law is not in accord with reason, it is not a law absolutely speaking, but is instead a kind of perversion of law. And yet to the extent that it retains something of the character of law, it aims at the citizens' being good. For it has nothing of the character of law except to the extent that (a) it is a dictate of someone who is in charge of the subjects and that (b) it intends that the subjects obey the law in the right way, i.e., that they be good—not absolutely speaking, but in relation to that regime.

Article 2

Are the acts of law correctly enumerated when one says that the acts of law are to command, to forbid, to permit, and to punish?

It seems that the acts of law are not correctly enumerated when one says that the acts of law are to command, to forbid, to permit, and to punish:

Objection 1: As the Jurist [Gratian] says [in *Decretum* 3], law consists in all of the general precepts. But to command is the same as to issue a precept. Therefore, the other three acts are superfluous.

Objection 2: As was explained above (a. 1), the effect of law is to lead its subjects to the good. But a counsel concerns a better good than a precept does. Therefore, law has more to do with giving counsel than with issuing precepts.

Objection 3: Just as a man is spurred on toward the good by punishments, so too he is spurred on toward the good by rewards. Therefore, just as punishing is counted as an effect of law, so rewarding should be counted as well.

Objection 4: As was explained above (a. 1), the lawmaker's intention is to make men good. But one who obeys the law solely out of fear of punishment is not a good man; for as Augustine says, "Even if one does something *good* out of servile fear, i.e., the fear of punishment, he still has not done anything *well*." Therefore, to punish does not seem to be a property of law.

But contrary to this: In *Etymologia* 5 Isidore says, "Every law either *permits* something (e.g., that a brave man may seek a reward), or it *prohibits* something (e.g., that no one is permitted to seek marriage with a consecrated virgin), or it *punishes* something (e.g., someone who has committed murder shall be put to death)."

I respond: Just as a spoken proposition (*enunciatio*) is a dictate of reason in the mode of *asserting* (*enuntiandi*), so too a law is a dictate of reason in the mode of *issuing a precept* (*praecipiendi*).

Now it is proper to reason to go from one thing to another. Hence, in the case of the demonstrative sciences, reason induces assent to the conclusion by means of certain principles; in the same way, it induces assent to a precept of the law by means of something. Now as was explained above (q. 90, a. 1), the precepts of the law concern human acts, which the law directs, and there are three different kinds of human acts:

As was explained above (q. 18, a. 8), some acts, viz., the acts of the virtues, are *good by their genus* (*boni ex genere*), and the act of law that is posited with respect to such acts is *to command* or *to issue a precept*. For as *Ethics* 5 says, law commands all the acts of the virtues.

By contrast, some acts, such as the acts of the vices, are *evil by their genus* (*mali ex genere*), and it is characteristic of law *to forbid* these acts.

On the other hand, some acts are *indifferent by their genus* (*indifferentes ex genere*), and it is characteristic of law *to permit* these acts. In addition, all acts that have either just a little goodness or just a little badness can likewise be called indifferent.

Finally, it is through *fear of punishment* that the law induces obedience to itself, and in this regard *to punish* is counted as an effect of law.

Reply to objection 1: Just as ceasing to do evil has a certain type of goodness, so too a prohibition is a certain type of precept. Accordingly, if 'precept' is taken broadly, a law may in general be called a 'precept'.

Reply to objection 2: To give counsel is not an act proper to law, but can also be the act of a private person who does not have the role of making law. Thus it is that in 1 Corinthians 7:12, when he is giving counsel on a certain matter, the Apostle says, "It is I speaking, and not the Lord." This is why giving counsel is not posited among the effects of law.

Reply to objection 3: Once again, to reward can be the role of any-one, whereas to punish pertains only to a minister of the law, by whose authority the punishment is inflicted. And this is why only punishing, and not rewarding, is counted as an act of law.

Reply to objection 4: Given that someone begins to be accustomed to avoiding evil and doing good because of his fear of punishment, he is sometimes led to enjoy doing good and to do it of his own will. Accordingly, it is also by punishing that the law leads to men being good.

QUESTION 93

The Eternal Law

We next have to consider each type of law individually. We will consider, first, the eternal law (question 93); second, the natural law (question 94); third, human law (questions 95–97); fourth, the Old Law (questions 98–105); and, fifth, the New Law, i.e., the Law of the Gospel (questions 106–108). As for the law of the stimulant to sin (*lex fomitis*), enough was said above during the discussion of Original Sin (questions 81–83).

On the first topic there are six questions: (1) What is the eternal law? (2) Is the eternal law known to everyone? (3) Does every law flow from the eternal law? (4) Are necessary things subject to the eternal law? (5) Are natural contingent things subject to the eternal law? (6) Are all human affairs subject to the eternal law?

Article 1

Is the eternal law the highest conception or plan existing in God?

It seems that the eternal law is not the highest conception or plan (*ratio summa*) existing in God:

Objection 1: The eternal law is a single law only. But there are many conceptions (*rationes*) in God's mind, since in *83 Quaestiones* Augustine says, "God made individual things by means of conceptions that are proper to each of them." Therefore, the eternal law does not seem to be the same as a conception existing in God's mind.

Objection 2: As was explained above (q. 90, a. 4), it is part of the nature of law that it be promulgated by a spoken word (*verbum*). But as was established in the First Part (*ST* 1, q. 34, a. 1), 'Word' (*verbum*) is predicated of a person in God, whereas 'conception' (*ratio*) is predicated of the divine essence. Therefore, the eternal law is not the same as God's conception.

Objection 3: In *De Vera Religione* Augustine says, "It is clear that above our mind there is a law, which is called truth." But the law that exists above our mind is the eternal law. Therefore, the eternal law is truth. But the nature of truth is not the same as the nature of a conception. Therefore, the eternal law is not the same as the highest conception.

But contrary to this: In *De Libero Arbitrio* 1 Augustine says, "The eternal law is the highest conception, which must always be conformed to."

I respond: Just as a conception (*ratio*) of the things made through his craft exists beforehand in a craftsman's mind, so too in anyone who governs there must exist beforehand a conception of the ordering of the things to be done by those who are subject to the governor's rule. And just as the conception of the things to be made through a craft is called an *artistic conception* (*ars*) or *exemplar* (*exemplar*) of the artifacts, so too the conception had by one who governs the acts of his subjects takes on the character of *law*, given the presence of all the other elements we described above as belonging to the nature of law (q. 90).

Now as was established in the First Part (*ST* 1, q. 14, a. 8), it is through His wisdom that God is the *creator* of the totality of things, and He is related to those things in the way a craftsman is related to his artifacts. As was likewise established in the first part (*ST* 1, q. 22, a. 2 and q. 103, a. 5), God is also the *governor* of all the acts and motions found in each creature. Hence, just as the divine wisdom's conception has the character of an *artistic conception* or *exemplar* because all things are created through it, so too the divine wisdom's conception has the character of *law* insofar as it moves all things to their appropriate ends. Accordingly, the eternal law is nothing other than the divine wisdom's conception insofar as it directs all acts and movements.

Reply to objection 1: Augustine is speaking here about the ideal conceptions (*rationes ideales*) that relate to the proper natures of singular things, and so, as was established in the First Part (*ST* 1, q. 15, a. 2), among these conceptions there is distinction and plurality corresponding to their diverse relations to the things.

However, as was explained above (q. 90, a. 2), law directs acts in relation to the common good. But things that are diverse in themselves are counted as one insofar as that they are ordered to something common. And this is why there is a single eternal law, which is the conception of this ordering.

Reply to objection 2: There are two things that can be considered with respect to any word, viz., (a) the word itself and (b) what is expressed by the word. For a spoken word is a certain sound emanating from a man's mouth, and this word expresses the things that are signified by human words. The same holds for a man's mental word (*de verbo hominis mentali*), which is none other than something which is conceived by the mind and by which a man mentally expresses the things he is thinking about.

In God, then, the Word, which is the conception of the Father's intellect, is predicated of a person, but, as is clear from Augustine in *De*

Trinitate 15, this Word expresses each thing that is contained in the Father's knowledge—regardless of whether it has to do with the divine persons, the divine essence, or even the works of God. And among the other things expressed by this Word, the eternal law itself is also expressed by this Word. Nor does it follow from this that 'eternal law' is predicated of a person in God. However, it is appropriated to the Son because of the consonance between a conception and a word (see *ST* 1, q. 39, aa. 7–8).

Reply to objection 3: God's intellectual conception is related to things in a way different from the way in which the human intellect's conception is.

For human understanding *is measured by* the things, so that a man's conception is not true by virtue of itself, but is instead called 'true' by virtue of the fact that it fits (*consonat*) the things. For a belief (*opinio*) is true or false by virtue of the fact that the thing is or is not such-and-such.

By contrast, God's understanding *is the measure of* the things, since, as was explained in the First Part (*ST* 1, q. 16, a. 1), each thing is true insofar as it is like (*imitatur*) God's understanding of it. And so God's understanding is true by virtue of itself, and thus His conception is truth itself.

Article 2

Is the eternal law known to everyone?

It seems that the eternal law is not known to everyone:

Objection 1: As the Apostle says in 1 Corinthians 2:11, "So the things also that are of God, no man knows, but the Spirit of God." But the eternal law is a certain conception existing in God's mind. Therefore, it is not known to anyone except God alone.

Objection 2: In *De Libero Arbitrio* Augustine says, "The eternal law is that by which it is fitting for all things to be very well ordered." But not everyone knows the way in which all things are very well ordered. Therefore, not everyone knows the eternal law.

Objection 3: In *De Vera Religione* Augustine says, "The eternal law is something upon which men cannot pass judgment." But as *Ethics* 1 says, "Each one judges best the things that he knows." Therefore, the eternal law is not known to us.

But contrary to this: In *De Libero Arbitrio* Augustine says, "Knowledge of the eternal law has been imprinted upon us."

I respond: There are two ways in which a thing can be known. First, it can be known in itself. Second, it can be known in its effect, where some likeness of the thing is found; for instance, someone who does not see the sun in its substance knows it in what radiates from it (*in irradiatione*).

So, then, no one except the blessed in heaven, who see God through His essence, can know the eternal law as it is in itself. However, every rational creature knows the eternal law with respect to more or less of what radiates from it. For any cognition of the truth is a sort of radiation from and participation in the eternal law, which is unchangeable truth, as Augustine says in *De Vera Religione*. But everyone knows the truth in some sense, at least with respect to the common principles of the natural law. As for other matters, some participate to a greater degree and some to a lesser degree in the cognition of the truth and, accordingly, they know more or less of the eternal law.

Reply to objection 1: The "things that are of God" cannot be known by us in themselves, but they are nonetheless made manifest to us in their effects—this according to Romans 1:20 ("The invisible things of God . . . are clearly seen, being understood through the things that are made.")

Reply to objection 2: Even if everyone knew the eternal law to the limit of his capacity in the way explained above, no one would be able to comprehend it, since it cannot be made totally manifest through its effects. And so one who knows the eternal law in the way explained above need not know the entire order by which all things are very well ordered.

Reply to objection 3: There are two possible ways to understand what it is to pass judgment upon something.

In the first way, a cognitive power makes a judgment about its own proper object—this in accord with Job 12:11 ("Does not the ear judge words, and the palate of him who eats, the taste?"). And it is about this mode of judgment that the Philosopher says, "Each one judges best the things he knows," viz., by judging whether what is proposed to him is true.

In the second way, through a certain kind of practical judgment someone higher judges, with respect to something lower, whether or not it ought to be such-and-such. This is the sense in which no one can pass judgment upon the eternal law.

Article 3

Does every law flow from the eternal law?

It seems that not every law flows from (*derivatur*) the eternal law:

Objection 1: As was explained above (q. 91, a. 6), there is a certain law of the stimulant to sin (*lex fomitis*). But this law does not flow from God's law, i.e., the eternal law, since it involves the "prudence of the flesh," about which the Apostle says in Romans 8:7 that "it is not subject to the law of God." Therefore, not every law flows from the eternal law.

Objection 2: Nothing wicked can proceed from the eternal law, since, as has been explained (a. 2), "the eternal law is that by which it is fitting for all things to be very well ordered." But some laws are wicked—this according to Isaiah 10:1 ("Woe to those who make wicked laws"). Therefore, not every law proceeds (*procedit*) from the eternal law.

Objection 3: In *De Libero Arbitrio* 1 Augustine says, "Law written in order to rule the people correctly permits many things that are avenged through God's providence." But as has been explained (a. 1), the plan (*ratio*) of divine providence is the eternal law. Therefore, not even all the upright laws proceed from the eternal law.

But contrary to this: In Proverbs 8:15 God's wisdom says, "By me kings reign, and lawgivers decree just things." But as has been explained (a. 1), the plan of God's wisdom is the eternal law. Therefore, all laws proceed from the eternal law.

I respond: As was explained above (q. 90, aa. 1–2), 'law' implies a certain plan that directs acts to their end. Now in every case involving ordered movers, the power of a secondary mover flows from the power of the first mover, since a secondary mover moves only insofar as it is moved by the first mover. Hence, we see the same thing in the case of all those who govern as well, viz., that the plan of governance flows from the first governor to the secondary governors. For instance, the plan of things to be done in a city flows by way of command (*per praeceptum*) from the king to the lower administrators. In the case of artifacts, too, the plan for the acts involved in making the artifacts flows from the architect to the lower craftsmen who work by hand.

Therefore, since the eternal law is the plan of governance that exists in the highest governor, all the plans of governance found in the lower governors must flow from the eternal law. Now these plans of the lower governors consist in all the kinds of law besides eternal law. Hence, all laws flow from the eternal law to the extent that they participate in right reason. This is why Augustine says in *De Libero Arbitrio* 1, "There is nothing just or legitimate in temporal law except what men have drawn from the eternal law."

Reply to objection 1: The stimulant to sin (*fomes*) has the character of law in man to the extent that it is a punishment that follows upon God's justice, and on this score it clearly flows from the eternal law. However, as is clear from what was said above (q. 91, a. 6), to the extent that the stimulant inclines one toward sin, it is contrary to God's law and does not have the character of law.

Reply to objection 2: Human law has the character of law to the extent that it is in accord with right reason and, so understood, it clearly flows from the eternal law.

However, to the extent that human law departs from reason, it is called 'unjust law' (*lex iniqua*) and has the character not of law but of a certain sort of violence. Yet to the extent that some likeness to law is preserved in this unjust law because it is ordained by the power of a lawmaker, in this respect it, too, flows from the eternal law. For as Romans 13:1 says, "All power is from the Lord God."

Reply to objection 3: Human law is said to permit certain things not in the sense that it approves of them, but rather in the sense that it is incapable of directing them. However, there are many things directed by God's law that cannot be directed by human law, since there are more things subject to a higher cause than to a lower cause. Hence, the very fact that human law does not intrude into matters that it cannot direct flows from the order of the eternal law. (It would be different if human law were to approve of things that the eternal law condemns.) Thus, it does not follow from this that human law does not flow from the eternal law; rather, all that follows is that human law does not perfectly measure up to the eternal law.

Article 4

Are necessary and eternal things subject to the eternal law?

It seems that necessary and eternal things are subject to the eternal law:

Objection 1: Everything reasonable (*rationabile*) is subject to a plan (*subditur ratione*). But God's will is reasonable, since it is just. Therefore, it is subject to a plan. But the eternal law is God's plan. Therefore, God's will is subject to the eternal law. But God's will is something eternal. Therefore, even eternal and necessary things are subject to the eternal law.

Objection 2: Whatever is subject to the king is subject to the king's law. But as 1 Corinthians 15:24 and 28 says, "the Son will be subject to

God and the Father . . . when He has handed over the kingdom to Him." Therefore, the Son, who is eternal, is subject to the eternal law.

Objection 3: The eternal law is the plan of divine providence. But many necessary things, e.g., the permanence of incorporeal substances and of the celestial bodies, are subject to divine providence. Therefore, even necessary things are subject to the eternal law.

But contrary to this: Things that are necessary are such that it is impossible for them to be otherwise, and so they do not need to be restrained. By contrast, as is clear from what was said above (q. 92, a. 2), law is imposed on men in order to restrain them from evil. Therefore, necessary things are not subject to law.

I respond: As was explained above (a. 1), the eternal law is the plan of divine governance. Therefore, whatever is subject to divine governance is likewise subject to the eternal law, and whatever is not subject to eternal governance is likewise not subject to the eternal law.

Now the distinction between these two sorts of things can be understood on the basis of what we are familiar with. For things that *can be done by men* are subject to human governance, whereas things that *belong to man's nature*—e.g., that a man has a soul or hands or feet—are not subject to human governance. So, then, whatever exists in the things created by God—whether it be contingent or necessary—is subject to the eternal law, whereas whatever pertains to God's own nature or essence is not subject to the eternal law, but is in reality the eternal law itself.

Reply to objection 1: We can speak of God's will in two ways.

First, we can speak of the *will itself*, and if we are speaking in this way, then since God's will is His very essence, it is not subject either to divine governance or to the eternal law; instead, it is just the same as the eternal law.

Second, we can speak of the divine will *in relation to what God wills concerning creatures*. The things He wills concerning creatures are subject to the eternal law insofar as a plan for them exists in God's wisdom. It is in relation to these things that God's will is called reasonable. On the other hand, in virtue of its very self, God's will should instead be called the plan itself.

Reply to objection 2: The Son of God is not made by God, but is instead naturally generated by Him. And so He is not subject to divine providence or to the eternal law, but, as is clear from *De Vera Religione*, is rather Himself the eternal law through a certain appropriation (cf. *ST* 1, q. 39, aa. 7–8). However, He is said to be subject to the Father by reason of

His human nature, in accord with which the Father is also said to be greater than He is.

Reply to objection 3: We concede the third objection, since it has do with necessary things that are created.

Reply to argument for the contrary: As the Philosopher says in *Metaphysics* 5, certain necessary things have a cause of their necessity, and so they depend on another for the very fact that it is impossible for them to be otherwise. And this in itself is a certain kind of efficacious restraint. For things that are restrained are said to be restrained to the extent that they are unable to act differently from the way in which they are determined to act (*aliter facere quam de eis disponatur*).

Article 5

Are natural contingent things subject to the eternal law?

It seems that natural contingent things are not subject to the eternal law:

Objection 1: As was explained above (q. 90, a. 4), promulgation is part of the nature of law. But promulgation can be made only to rational creatures, to whom a pronouncement can be made. Therefore, only rational creatures are subject to the eternal law. Therefore, natural contingent things are not subject to it.

Objection 2: As *Ethics* 1 says, "Things that obey reason somehow participate in reason." But as was explained above (a. 1), the eternal law is the highest conception or plan. Therefore, since natural contingent things do not in any way participate in reason but are instead completely non-rational (*penitus irrationabilia*), it seems that they are not subject to the eternal law.

Objection 3: The eternal law is absolutely efficacious. But defects occur among natural contingent things. Therefore, they are not subject to the eternal law.

But contrary to this: Proverbs 8:29 says, "When He set the border around the sea and gave a law to the waters, lest they pass their limits . . ."

I respond: What we say about the eternal law, i.e., the law of God, has to differ from what we say about the law of man. For the law of man reaches only the rational creatures who are subject to man. The reason for this is that law directs the acts of those who are subject to someone's governance, and so no one, properly speaking, imposes a law on his own acts. Now whatever is done by way of using the non-rational things that are subject to man is done through the act of man himself moving things of this sort; for as was explained above (q. 1, a. 2), these non-rational creatures do not move themselves (*non agunt seipsas*) but are instead acted upon by others. And so man cannot impose law on non-rational creatures, no matter how much they are subject to him. By contrast, he can impose law on the rational beings who are subject to him, because by his command or by some other pronouncement he imprints upon their mind a rule that serves as a principle of acting.

Now just as, by means of a pronouncement, one man imprints (*imprimit*) an interior principle of acting on another man who is subject to him, so God imprints on the whole of nature principles with respect to their proper acts. It is in this sense that God is said to command the whole of nature, according to Psalm 148:6 ("He has commanded and His command will not pass away"). And this is also the sense in which all the movements and acts of the whole of nature are subject to the eternal law.

Hence, non-rational creatures are subject to the eternal law in a way different from rational creatures, viz., insofar as they are moved by divine providence, and not, as with rational creatures, through an understanding of God's precept.

Reply to objection 1: The imprinting of an active intrinsic principle plays the same role with respect to natural things that the promulgation of the law plays with respect to men. For as has been explained, a principle that directs human acts is imprinted on men through the promulgation of law.

Reply to objection 2: Non-rational creatures do not participate in or obey *human* reason, but they do participate in *divine* reason in the mode of obedience. For the power of God's plan extends to more things than does the power of human reason. And just as the members of the human body are moved at the command of reason and yet do not participate in reason (for they do not have any apprehension related to reason), so also non-rational creatures are moved by God and yet are not thereby rational.

Reply to objection 3: Even though the defects that occur in natural things lie outside the order of particular causes, they do not lie outside the order of universal causes or, especially, outside the order of the first cause, viz., God, whose providence nothing can undermine. This was explained in the First Part (*ST* 1, q. 22, a. 2). And since, as has been explained (a. 1), the eternal law is the plan of divine providence, it follows that the defects in natural things are subject to the eternal law.

Article 6

Are all human affairs subject to the eternal law?

It seems that not all human affairs are subject to the eternal law:

Objection 1: In Galatians 5:18 the Apostle says, "If you are led by the Spirit, you are not under the law." But according to Romans 8:14 ("Those who are acted on by the Spirit of God are the sons of God"), the just, who are sons of God by adoption, are acted on by the Spirit of God. Therefore, not all men are under the eternal law.

Objection 2: In Romans 8:7 the Apostle says, "Prudence of the flesh is the enemy of God, since it is not subject to the law of God." But there are many men in whom prudence of the flesh is dominant. Therefore, not all men are subject to the eternal law.

Objection 3: In *De Libero Arbitrio* 1 Augustine says, "It is the eternal law by which the wicked merit unhappiness and the good merit the life of beatitude." But men who are either already beatified or already damned are not in a position to merit. Therefore, they are not subject to the eternal law.

But contrary to this: In *De Civitate Dei* 19 Augustine says, "Nothing in any way evades the laws of the most high creator and governor by whom the peace of the universe is administered."

I respond: As is clear from what was said above (a. 5), there are two ways for a thing to be subject to the eternal law: first, insofar as eternal law is participated in through the mode of cognition; and second, through the mode of acting and being acted upon, insofar as eternal law is participated in as a moving principle. As has been explained (a. 5), it is in this second way that non-rational creatures are subject to the eternal law.

However, since rational nature, in addition to what it shares in common with all creatures, has something proper to itself because it is rational, it is subject to the eternal law in both ways. For as was explained above (a. 2), in one way or another a rational nature has knowledge of the eternal law and, in addition, each rational creature has within itself a natural inclination toward what is consonant with the eternal law. For as *Ethics* 2 says, "We are naturally prone toward having the virtues."

Yet both these modes are imperfect and in some sense corrupted in bad people, in whom (a) the natural inclination toward virtue is perverted by vice (*per habitum vitiosum*) and (b) the natural cognition of the good is darkened by passions and sinful habits. By contrast, in good people both of the modes are more perfect, since (a) in addition to the natural cognition of the good, they also have the cognition provided by faith and wisdom, and (b) in addition to the natural inclination toward the good, they also have the interior movement of grace and virtue.

So, then, good people are perfectly subject to the eternal law to the extent that they always act in accord with it. By contrast, bad people are, though subject to the eternal law, imperfectly subject to it in their actions, since they have imperfect knowledge and are imperfectly inclined toward the good; however, what is lacking in their actions is compensated for by how they are acted upon. For they suffer what the eternal law dictates for them to the degree that they fail to do what is consonant with the eternal law. Hence in *De Libero Arbitrio* 1 Augustine says, "I believe that the just act under the eternal law." And in *De Catechizandis Rudibus* he says, "By means of His most fitting laws, God knew how to adorn the lower regions of His creation with the merited unhappiness of the souls who would desert Him."

Reply to objection 1: There are two possible ways to interpret this passage from the Apostle.

On the first interpretation, by 'is under the law' he means someone who unwillingly submits to the obligation imposed by the law as if it were a burden. Hence, the Gloss on the same passage says, "Someone who is 'under the law' abstains from evil deeds not because of his love for justice, but rather because of his fear of the punishment that the law threatens." Spiritual men are not under the law in this sense, since through their charity, which the Holy Spirit infuses into their hearts, they willingly fulfill the demands of the law.

On the other interpretation, the works of a man who is acted upon by the Holy Spirit are said to be the works of the Holy Spirit more than the works of the man himself. Hence, since, as was said above (a. 5), neither the Holy Spirit nor the Son is under the law, it follows that works of this sort, insofar as they belong to the Holy Spirit, are not under the law. And this is supported by what the Apostle says in 2 Corinthians 3:17 ("Where the Spirit of the Lord is, there is freedom").

Reply to objection 2: Prudence of the flesh cannot be subject to God's law as far as *acting* is concerned, since it inclines one to actions that are contrary to God's law. However, it is subject to God's law as far as *being acted upon* is concerned, since it merits the suffering of punishment in accord with the law of divine justice. Still, there is no man in whom prudence of the flesh dominates to such an extent that the whole good of his nature is corrupted. And so there remains in such a man an inclination to fulfill the demands of the eternal law. For it was established above (q. 85, a. 2) that sin does not destroy the whole good of nature.

Reply to objection 3: An entity is preserved in its end through the same thing through which it is moved toward its end. For instance, a heavy body is at rest in a lower place through its heaviness (*gravitas*), which is also that through which it is moved to that very place.

Accordingly, one should say that just as it is in accord with the eternal law that some men merit beatitude and some merit unhappiness, so it is through that same law that they are preserved in beatitude or in unhappiness. And in this sense both the blessed and the damned are subject to the eternal law.

QUESTION 94

The Natural Law

We next have to consider the natural law. And on this topic there are six questions: (1) What is the natural law? (2) Which precepts belong to the natural law? (3) Are all the acts of the virtues part of the natural law? (4) Is there a single natural law for everyone? (5) Is the natural law changeable? (6) Can the natural law be erased from the human mind (*possit a mente hominis deleri*)?

Article 1

Is the natural law a habit?

It seems that the natural law is a habit:

Objection 1: As the Philosopher says in *Ethics* 2, "There are three sorts of things in the soul: powers, habits, and passions." But as is clear from going through each of these one by one, the natural law is not one of the powers of the soul or one of the passions. Therefore, the natural law is a habit.

Objection 2: Basil says, "Conscience (*conscientia*) or synderesis (*synderesis*) is our intellect's law"—and by this he cannot mean anything other than the natural law. But as was established in the First Part (*ST* 1, q. 79, a. 12), synderesis is a certain habit. Therefore, the natural law is a habit.

Objection 3: As will be shown below (a. 6), the natural law remains within a man always. But a man's reason, which is what the law has to do with, is not always actually thinking about the natural law. Therefore, the natural law is a habit and not an act.

But contrary to this: In *De Bono Coniugali* Augustine says, "A habit is that by means of which something is done when there is need." But the natural law is not like this, since it exists even in children and in the damned, who cannot act through it. Therefore, the natural law is not a habit.

I respond: There are two senses in which something can be called a habit.

In the first sense, something is called a habit *properly and essentially*, and in this sense the natural law is not a habit. For it was explained above (q. 90, a. 1) that the natural law is something constituted by reason, in the same way that a proposition is a work of reason. But *what* someone does or makes is not the same as *that by means of which* he does it or makes it. For instance, it is by means of the habit of grammar that someone makes a coherent utterance. Therefore, since a habit is *that by means of which* one acts, no sort of law can be a habit properly and essentially.

In the second sense, *that which is had* by means of a habit can itself be called the habit—in the way that the Faith is that which is held by means of faith. And since the precepts of the natural law are such that even though at times they are actually being considered by reason, at other times they exist only habitually in reason, one can say in this sense that the natural law is a habit. In the same way, the indemonstrable principles in speculative matters are not the habit itself with respect to those principles; rather, they are principles with respect to which there is a habit.

Reply to objection 1: In this passage the Philosopher means to be looking for the genus of *virtue*, and since it is clear that a virtue is a principle of acts, he proposes only the sorts of things that serve as the principles of human acts, viz., powers, habits, and passions. However, besides these three, there are other sorts of things that exist in the soul. For instance, (a) certain kinds of acts exist in the soul, e.g., an act of willing exists in one who wills; (b) again, things that are known exist in the one who knows them; and (c) the natural properties of the soul exist in the soul, e.g., immortality and others of this sort.

Reply to objection 2: Synderesis is called our intellect's law because it is a habit containing the precepts of the natural law, which are first principles of human works.

Reply to objection 3: The conclusion of this argument is that the natural law is had in a habitual manner. This we concede.

Reply to argument for the contrary: By the very fact that something exists habitually in a man, it follows that he is sometimes unable to make use of it because of an impediment. For instance, a man who is sleeping cannot make use of his habit of knowing conclusions (*habitus scientiae*). In the same way, because he is not of the right age, a young child cannot make use of the habit of grasping first principles (*intellectus*); nor, again, can he make use of the natural law, which exists in him habitually.

Article 2

Does the natural law contain many precepts or just one precept?

It seems that the natural law contains just one precept and not many precepts:

Objection 1: As was explained above (q. 92, a. 2), law is contained under the genus *precept*. Therefore, if the natural law contained many precepts, it would follow that there are likewise many natural laws.

Objection 2: The natural law follows upon the nature of man. But human nature is one taken as a whole, even though it has multiple parts. Therefore, either (a) there is just one precept of the law of nature because of the oneness of the whole or (b) there are many precepts because of the multiplicity of the parts of human nature, in which case even what stems from the inclination of the concupiscible [part of the soul] will belong to the natural law.

Objection 3: As was explained above (q. 90, a. 1), law is something that belongs to reason. But there is just a single faculty of reason in a man. Therefore, the natural law contains just one precept.

But contrary to this: The precepts of the natural law play the same role in a man with respect to matters of action that first principles play with respect to matters of demonstration. But there are many indemonstrable first principles. Therefore, there are likewise many precepts of the natural law.

I respond: As was explained above (q. 91, a. 3), the precepts of the law of nature bear the same relation to practical reason that the first principles of demonstration bear to speculative reason. For in both cases they are principles that are known *per se* (*per se nota*).

Now there are two senses in which something is said to be known *per se*: (a) in its own right (*secundum se*) and (b) as regards us (*quoad nos*). Every proposition (*propositio*) said to be known *per se* in its own right is such that its predicate is part of the notion of its subject (*de ratione subiecti*); and yet it happens that such a proposition will not be known *per se* to someone who does not know the definition of the subject. For instance, the proposition 'A man is rational' is known *per se* given its own nature, since anyone who expresses *man* expresses *rational*; and yet this proposition is not known *per se* to someone who does not know the real definition (*quid sit*) of man. This is why, as Boethius points out in *De Hebdomadibus*, certain fundamental truths (*dignitates*) and propositions (*propositiones*) are known *per se* in general to everyone—and these are the ones whose terms are known to everyone, e.g., 'Every whole is greater than its part' and 'Things equal to one and the same thing are equal to each other'—whereas other propositions are known *per se* only to the wise, who understand what the terms of the proposition signify. For instance, to someone who understands that an angel is not a body it is known *per se* that an angel does not exist circumscriptively in a place;

however, this is not obvious to unsophisticated people, who do not grasp the point in question.

Now there is a certain ordering among those things that fall within everyone's apprehension. The first thing to fall within apprehension is *being*, a grasp of which is included in everything that anyone apprehends. So the first indemonstrable principle, founded upon the notions *being* and *non-being*, is 'One is not to affirm and deny [the same thing] at the same time'. And, as *Metaphysics* 4 says, all the other principles are founded upon this one.

Now just as *being* is the first thing to fall within apprehension absolutely speaking, so *good* is the first thing to fall within the apprehension of practical reason, which is ordered toward action. For every agent acts for the sake of an end, which has the character of a good. And so the first principle in practical reasoning is what is founded on the notion *good*, which is the notion (*quod fundatur supra rationem boni quae est*): *The good is what all things desire*. Therefore, the first precept of law is that good ought to be done and pursued and that evil ought to be avoided. And all the other precepts of the law of nature are founded upon this principle— so that, namely, all the things to be done or avoided that practical reason naturally apprehends as human goods are such that they belong to the precepts of the law of nature. For since what is good has the character of an end and what is bad has the character of the contrary of an end, it follows that all the things man has a natural inclination toward are such that (a) reason naturally apprehends them as goods and thus as things that ought to be pursued by action and (b) reason naturally apprehends their contraries as evils and thus things that ought to be avoided.

Therefore, there is an ordering of the precepts of the natural law that corresponds to the ordering of the natural inclinations.

First, man has an inclination toward the good with respect to the nature he shares in common with all substances, viz., insofar as every substance strives for the conservation of its own *esse* in accord with its own nature. And what belongs to the natural law in light of this inclination is everything through which man's life is conserved or through which what is contrary to the preservation of his life is thwarted.

Second, man has an inclination toward certain more specific [goods] with respect to the nature that he shares in common with the other animals. Accordingly, those things are said to belong to the natural law which nature teaches all the animals, i.e., the union of male and female, the education of offspring, etc.

Third, man has an inclination toward the good with respect to the rational nature that is proper to him; for instance, man has a natural inclination toward knowing the truth about God and toward living in society. Accordingly, those things that are related to this sort of inclination belong to the natural law, e.g., that a man avoid ignorance, that he not offend the others with whom he has to live in community, and other such things related to this inclination.

Reply to objection 1: Insofar as all these precepts of the law of nature are traced back to a single first principle, they have the character of a single natural law.

Reply to objection 2: All the inclinations of any of the parts of human nature, e.g., the concupiscible part and the irascible part, are relevant to the natural law insofar as they are regulated by reason, and, as has been explained, they are traced back to a single first precept. Accordingly, even though the precepts of the law of nature are many in themselves, they nonetheless share a single root.

Reply to objection 3: Even if reason is in itself one, it nonetheless orders all the things relating to men. Accordingly, the law of reason contains everything that can be regulated by reason.

Article 3

Do all the acts of the virtues belong to the law of nature?

It seems that not all the acts of the virtues belong to the law of nature:

Objection 1: As was explained above (q. 90, a. 2), it is part of the notion of law that it is ordered toward the common good. But as is especially clear in the case of acts of temperance, some acts of the virtues are ordered toward an individual's private good. Therefore, not all the acts of the virtues fall under the natural law.

Objection 2: All sins are opposed to some virtuous act or other. Therefore, if all the acts of the virtues belonged to the law of nature, then, as a result, all sins would seem to be contrary to nature. But this is said specifically [only] of certain sins.

Objection 3: All share in those things that are in accord with nature. But it is not the case that all share in acts of the virtues, since something that is virtuous for one person is vicious for another. Therefore, not all the acts of the virtues belong to the law of nature.

But contrary to this: In [*De Fide Orthodoxa*] 3 Damascene says,

"The virtues are natural." Therefore, virtuous acts likewise fall under the law of nature.

I respond: We can speak of virtuous acts in two ways: (a) first, insofar as they are virtuous and (b) second, insofar as they are acts of certain kinds considered in their own proper species.

Thus, if we are speaking of the acts of the virtues insofar as they are virtuous, then in this sense all the acts of the virtues belong to the law of nature. For it was explained above (a. 2) that everything toward which man is inclined in accord with his nature belongs to the law of nature. But every entity is naturally inclined toward action that is appropriate for it in light of its form, in the way that fire is naturally inclined to give warmth. Hence, since the rational soul is the proper form of man, every man has a natural inclination toward acting in accord with reason—which is just to act in accord with virtue. Hence, in this sense all the acts of the virtues belong to the natural law, since the faculty of reason proper to each man dictates by nature that he act virtuously.

By contrast, if we are speaking of virtuous acts in their own right, i.e., insofar as they are considered in their own proper species, then in this sense not all virtuous acts belong to the natural law. For many things done in accord with virtue are such that nature does not incline one toward them in the primary sense; rather, it is through reasoned inquiry that men have discovered these things to be, as it were, advantageous to living well.

Reply to objection 1: Temperance has to do with sensory desires for food and drink and sexual pleasure, all of which are ordered toward the common good of nature, just as other matters pertaining to the law are likewise ordered toward the common moral good.

Reply to objection 2: By 'nature of man' one can mean either (a) those things that are proper to man, and in this sense all sins, since they are contrary to reason, are likewise contrary to nature, as is clear from Damascene [in *De Fide Orthodoxa*] 2; or (b) those things that are common to man and the other animals, and in this sense certain specific sins are said to be contrary to nature. For instance, sexual intercourse between males is contrary to the sexual union between male and female, which is natural to all animals, and is in a special sense called a vice contrary to nature.

Reply to objection 3: This argument has to do with acts considered in their own right. For it happens in this way that, because of the diverse conditions men find themselves in, some acts are virtuous for some people, in the sense of being proportioned to and suitable for them, but are nonetheless vicious for others in the sense of not being proportioned to them.

Article 4

Is there a single law of nature for everyone?

It seems that it is not the case that there is a single law of nature for everyone:

Objection 1: *Decretals*, dist. 1, says, "Natural law (*ius naturale*) includes what is contained in the Law and what is contained in the Gospel." But this is not common to everyone, since as Romans 10:16 says, "Not everyone is obedient to the Gospel." Therefore, there is not a single natural law for everyone.

Objection 2: As *Ethics* 5 says, "Things that are in accord with the law are called just." But the same book says that nothing is just for everyone to such an extent that it is not different for some. Therefore, it is likewise not the case that the natural law is the same for everyone.

Objection 3: As was explained above (aa. 2–3), the law of nature has to do with what man is inclined toward in accord with his nature. But different men are naturally inclined toward different things; for instance, some are inclined toward a desire for pleasures, others toward a desire for honors, and others toward other things. Therefore, it is not the case that there is a single natural law for everyone.

But contrary to this: In *Etymologia* Isidore says, "The natural law (*ius naturale*) is common to all nations."

I respond: As was explained above (aa. 2–3), those things to which man is naturally inclined belong to the law of nature—and, among other things, it is proper to man that he be inclined to act in accord with reason.

Now as is clear from *Physics* 1, it belongs to reason to proceed from what is universal (*ex communibus*) to what is particular (*ad propria*). However, speculative reason and practical reason behave differently on this score. For since speculative reason deals principally with necessary things, which are such that it is impossible for them to be otherwise, truth is found without exception (*absque aliquo defectu*) in the particular conclusions in just the way it is found in the universal principles. By contrast, practical reason deals with contingent things, which include human actions, and so even if there is some sort of necessity in the universal principles, nonetheless, the further down one descends to particulars, the more exceptions there are. So, then, in speculative matters there is the same truth for everyone both in the principles and in the conclusions, even though the truth is known to everyone only in the principles, which are called common conceptions (*communes conceptiones*), and not in the conclusions. By contrast, in practical matters, there is the same practical truth or correctness (*rectitudo*) for everyone only with respect to the universal principles and not with respect to the particulars. Further, in the case of those for whom there is the same correctness in the particulars, it is not equally well known to all of them.

So, then, it is clear that *with respect to the universal principles of either speculative reason or practical reason*, there is the same truth or correctness for everyone and it is equally well known to everyone.

Again, *with respect to the particular conclusions of speculative reason*, there is the same truth for everyone, though it is not equally known to all of them. For instance, it is true for everyone that a triangle has three angles equal to two right angles, but this is not known to everyone.

However, *with respect to the particular conclusions of practical reason*, there is not the same truth, i.e., correctness, for everyone, and even in the case of those for whom it is the same, it is not equally well known to everyone. For instance, it is right and true for everyone that one ought to act in accord with reason, and from this principle it follows as a sort of particular conclusion that what has been entrusted to one for safe-keeping ought to be returned. To be sure, this is true in the greater number of cases (*ut in pluribus*). Yet, in a given case, to return what has been entrusted to you may be injurious and thus unreasonable (*irrationale*)—for instance, if someone were seeking to harm your country. And the further down one descends to particulars, the more often [the original rule] fails—as, for instance, when someone says that entrusted things ought to be returned with such-and-such precautions or in such-and-such a manner. For to the extent that more and more particular conditions are added, there are more ways in which [the original rule] can fail and thus be incorrect about returning or not returning what has been entrusted.

Therefore, one should claim that with respect to its first universal principles, the law of nature is the same for everyone both with respect to correctness and with respect to knowledge. On the other hand, with respect to various particular [rules], which are, as it were, the conclusions of those universal principles, the law of nature is the same for everyone in the greater number of cases (*ut in pluribus*) both with respect to correctness and with respect to knowledge, and yet there can be exceptions in a fewer number of cases (*ut in paucioribus*) both (a) with respect to *correctness*, and this because of certain impediments (just as the generable and corruptible natures are defective in a fewer number of cases because of impediments), and also (b) with respect to *knowledge*, and this because the faculty of reason has been perverted in some people by passion or by bad habits or by a bad natural condition. For instance, as Julius Caesar reports in *De Bello Gallico*, at one time among the Germans theft was not considered bad, even though it is clearly contrary to the law of nature.

Reply to objection 1: This passage should not be understood to mean that all the things contained in the Law and the Gospel belong to the law of nature. For many things set forth in the Law and the Gospel go beyond nature. Rather, the passage means that what belongs to the law of nature is found more fully in the Law and the Gospel.

This is why, after Gratian had claimed that the natural law is what is contained in the Law and the Gospel, he immediately added, by way of example, ". . . by which everyone is commanded to do to another what he wishes to be done to himself."

Reply to objection 2: This passage from the Philosopher should be understood to be talking about rules that are naturally just, not in the manner of universal principles, but rather in the manner of conclusions stemming from those principles. Such conclusions are correct in the greater number of cases and fail in a fewer number of cases (*quae ut in pluribus rectitudinem habent et ut in paucioribus deficiunt*).

Reply to objection 3: Just as man's reason rules and commands the other powers, so all the natural inclinations belonging to the other powers should be ordered in accord with reason. Hence, it is universally right for everyone that all the inclinations of men should be directed in accord with reason.

Article 5

Can the law of nature be changed?

It seems that the law of nature can be changed:

Objection 1: The Gloss on Ecclesiasticus 17:9 ("He gave them instructions, and the law of life") says, "He wanted the 'law of the letter' to be written in order to correct the natural law." But what is corrected is changed. Therefore, the natural law can be changed.

Objection 2: The killing of the innocent is contrary to the natural law, as are adultery and theft as well. But these have been changed by God, viz., (a) when God commanded Abraham to kill his innocent son, according to

Genesis 22:2; (b) when He commanded the Jews to steal the vases they had borrowed from the Egyptians, according to Exodus 12:35; and (c) when He commanded Hosea to take an adulterer as his wife, according to Hosea 1:2. Therefore, the natural law can be changed.

Objection 3: In *Etymologia* Isidore says, "The communal possession of all things and equal liberty belong to natural law." But we see that these have been changed through human laws. Therefore, it seems that the natural law is changeable.

But contrary to this: *Decretals*, dist. 5, says, "The natural law dates from the very beginnings of the rational creature. Neither does it change over time, but remains immutable."

I respond: There are two ways to understand what it is for the natural law to be changed.

First, it is changed by something's being added to it. In this sense nothing prevents the natural law from being changed. For many things useful to human life have been added to the natural law, both by the divine law and also by human laws.

Second, the natural law might be thought of as being changed by way of subtraction—so that, namely, something that was previously in accord with the natural law ceases to belong to the natural law. Given this sense of change, the law of nature is altogether unchangeable with respect to its first principles. On the other hand, with respect to its secondary precepts— which we have claimed to be, as it were, particular conclusions in the neighborhood of the first principles (*proprias conclusiones propinquas primis principiis*)—the natural law is not changed in such a way as to prevent the natural law from consistently being correct in the greater number of the particular cases (*quin ut in pluribus rectum sit semper quod lex naturalis habet*). However, as was explained above (a. 4), in a fewer number of cases it can be changed in some particular because of special causes that obstruct the observance of the secondary precepts.

Reply to objection 1: The written law is said to have been given in order to correct the law of nature, either because (a) what the natural law lacks was supplied by the written law, or because (b) the law of nature had in certain respects been corrupted in the hearts of some people to such an extent that they took what was naturally bad to be good—and this sort of corruption required correction.

Reply to objection 2: Everyone in general, whether innocent or guilty, dies a natural death, and according to 1 Kings 2:6 ("The Lord gives death and gives life"), natural death is imposed by God's power because of

Original Sin. And so by God's command death can be inflicted without any injustice on any man, guilty or innocent.

Similarly, adultery is sexual intercourse with someone else's wife, where it is by a divinely given law that she is sworn to that other man. Hence, for someone to be intimate with any woman by God's command is neither adultery nor fornication.

The same holds for theft, which is the taking of what belongs to another. For whatever someone takes at the command of God, who is the owner (*dominus*) of the universe, is such that he is not taking it against the owner's will—which is what theft is.

And not only is it the case that whatever is commanded by God in human affairs is by that very fact just, but also, as was explained in the first part (*ST* 1, q. 105, a. 6), whatever is done by God among natural things is in some sense natural.

Reply to objection 3: There are two ways in which something is said to belong to the natural law (*esse de iure naturali*).

First, something is said to belong to the natural law because nature inclines one toward it, e.g., that one should not harm another.

Second, something is said to belong to the natural law because nature has not induced the contrary. For instance, we could say that it belongs to the natural law that man is unclothed, since nature does not give him clothes, but instead human art invented them.

It is in the second sense that a communal possession of all goods and equal liberty for all are said to belong to the natural law—since, namely, servitude and the distinctions among possessions are induced not by nature but by men's reason because of their usefulness to human life. And so on this score the law of nature has not been changed except by addition.

Article 6

Can the natural law be wiped out of a man's heart?

It seems that the natural law can be wiped out of a man's heart (*possit aboleri a corde hominis*):

Objection 1: The Gloss on Romans 2:14 ("When the Gentiles, who do not have the Law, etc.") says, "The law of justice, which sin had erased, is written in the inner man who is made new through grace." But the law of justice is the same as the law of nature. Therefore, the law of nature can be erased (*potest deleri*).

Objection 2: The law of grace is more efficacious than the law of nature. But the law of grace is erased through sin. Therefore, *a fortiori*, the law of nature can be erased.

Objection 3: What is established by the law is proposed as being just. But there are many things established by men contrary to the law of nature. Therefore, the law of nature can be wiped out of the hearts of men.

But contrary to this: In *Confessiones* 2 Augustine says, "Your law was written in the hearts of men, and no sort of wickedness erases it." But the law written in the hearts of men is the natural law. Therefore, the natural law cannot be erased.

I respond: As was explained above (aa. 4–5), the natural law contains in the first place certain very general precepts that are known to everyone, but it also contains certain secondary, and more particular, precepts that are like conclusions lying in the neighborhood of the principles.

Thus, as far as the universal principles are concerned, the natural law cannot in any way be erased entirely from the hearts of men. However, it is erased with respect to particular actions insofar as reason is impeded from applying a universal principle to a particular action because of sensual desire or some other passion, as was explained above (q. 77, a. 2).

However, as far as the other, i.e., secondary, precepts are concerned, the natural law can be erased from the hearts of men, either (a) because of bad arguments, in the same way that errors occur in speculative matters with respect to necessary conclusions, or (b) because of depraved customs and corrupt habits—in the way that, as the Apostle points out in Romans 1:24ff., theft or even vices contrary to nature are not thought of as sins by some people.

Reply to objection 1: Sin erases the law of nature in particular cases, but not in general, except perhaps with respect to the secondary precepts of the law of nature in the way that has been explained.

Reply to objection 2: Even if grace is more efficacious than nature, nature nonetheless has more to do with man's essence (*essentialior est homini*) and is thus more permanent.

Reply to objection 3: This argument has to do with the secondary precepts of the law of nature. Some lawmakers have made statutes opposed to these precepts, and such statutes are wicked.

QUESTION 95

Human Law

We next have to consider human law: first, human law in itself (question 95); second, its force (question 96); and, third, its mutability (question 97).

On the first topic there are four questions: (1) Is human law useful? (2) What are its origins? (3) What are the characteristics of human law? (4) How is human law divided?

Article 1

Was it useful for laws to be made by men?

It seems not to have been useful for laws to be made by men:

Objection 1: As was explained above (q. 92, a. 1), the intention behind every law is that men should become good through it. But men are better led toward the good willingly through admonitions than by being coerced through laws. Therefore, it was unnecessary to make laws.

Objection 2: As the Philosopher says in *Ethics* 5, men have recourse to a judge as one who embodies 'living justice' (*justum animatum*). But living justice is better than the non-living justice contained in laws. Therefore, it would have been better to entrust the administration of justice to the decisions of judges rather than to issue laws over and beyond this.

Objection 3: As is clear from what was said above (q. 90, aa. 1–2), every law directs human acts. But since human acts comprise individual cases that are infinite in number, not everything that is relevant to directing human acts can be adequately taken into account except by some wise man who investigates the individual cases. Therefore, it would have been better for human acts to be directed by the decisions of wise men rather than by any law that might be made. Therefore, it was unnecessary to make human laws.

But contrary to this: In *Etymologia* Isidore says, "Laws have been made in order that human boldness might be held in check by fear of them, and in order that the innocent might be safe among the wicked, and in order that the ability of the wicked themselves to do harm might be curbed by their fear of punishment." But these things are especially necessary for the human race. Therefore, it was necessary to make human laws.

I respond: As is clear from what was said above (q. 63, a. 1 and q. 94, a. 3), man has a natural aptitude for virtue. It is through discipline, however, that he arrives at the *perfection* of virtue—just as we likewise see that it is man's industriousness that helps him acquire his necessities, e.g., food and clothing, with respect to which nature gives him certain initial resources, viz., his faculty of reason and his hands, but not full satisfaction—unlike the other animals, to whom nature has given adequate food and outer protection. But it is not easy for a man to be self-sufficient with respect to the discipline required for virtue. For perfecting a virtue is mainly a matter of restraining a man from inappropriate pleasures of the sort to which men are especially drawn—and, above all, young people, with whom discipline is more effective. And so men have to receive from others the sort of training through which virtue is acquired.

Now, to be sure, paternal discipline, which makes use of admonitions, is sufficient for those young people who are inclined toward acts of virtue by a good natural temperament, or by upbringing (*consuetudo*), or, better, by a gift of God. However, because there are some who are impudent and prone to the vices and who cannot be easily moved by words, it was necessary to restrain them from evil through force and fear, so that (a) ceasing to do evil, they might at least leave others to a peaceful life, and so that (b) in the end they might be led by this sort of habituation to the point of doing willingly what they were previously doing out of fear and so becoming virtuous.

Now the sort of discipline in question, which coerces by the fear of punishment, is the discipline of laws. Hence, it was for the sake of virtue and of peace among men that laws had to be established. For as the Philosopher says in *Politics* 1, "Just as man, if he is perfected in virtue, is the best of the animals, so, too, if he is cut off from the law and from justice, he is the worst of all animals." For unlike the other animals, man has the weapons of reason to satisfy his lustful desires and his taste for savage violence.

Reply to objection 1: Well-disposed men are best led to virtue by willingly heeded admonitions rather than by coercion, but ill-disposed men are not led to virtue unless they are coerced.

Reply to objection 2: As the Philosopher says in *Rhetoric* 1, "It is better for all things to be regulated by law than left to the decision of judges." There are three reasons for this:

First, a few wise men—which is all it takes to make good laws—are easier to find than a large number of wise men—which is what it would take to judge cases correctly one by one.

Second, lawmakers spend a long time considering what should be imposed by law, whereas judgments about individual cases are made quickly as the cases arise. Moreover, a man can more easily see what is right if he considers many instances than if he considers just a single instance.

Third, lawmakers make judgments that apply to all cases (*in universali*) and are future-oriented, whereas the men who render judgments are judging about present matters, concerning which they are affected by love or hate or some kind of excessive desire, and in this way their judgments become perverted.

Therefore, since there are not many cases of a judge's 'living justice', and since such justice can be skewed (*est flexibile*), it was necessary for the law to determine which judgments should be made in as many cases as possible and to leave very few cases to the decisions of men.

Reply to objection 3: As the Philosopher says in the same place, certain particular matters that cannot be included in a law—e.g., "those concerning what has or has not been done" and other things of this sort—"must be entrusted to judges."

Article 2

Does every humanly made law stem from the natural law?

It seems that not every humanly made law stems from the natural law (*a lege naturali derivetur*):

Objection 1: In *Ethics* 5 the Philosopher says, "What is legally just is such that at the beginning it did not matter whether it was done this way or some other way." But in things that arise from the natural law it does matter whether they are done this way or some other way. Therefore, not everything established by human laws stems from the law of nature.

Objection 2: As is clear both from Isidore in *Etymologia* and from the Philosopher in *Ethics* 5, positive law (*ius positivum*) is opposed to natural law (*ius naturale*). But as was explained above (q. 94, a. 4), what stems in the manner of a conclusion from the principles of the law of nature belongs to the law of nature. Therefore, what belongs to human law does not stem from the law of nature.

Objection 3: The law of nature is the same for everyone; for the Philosopher says in *Ethics* 5, "What is naturally just is such that it has the same force everywhere." Therefore, if human laws stemmed from the natural law, it would follow that these human laws are likewise the same for everyone. But this is clearly false.

Objection 4: A reason can be given for things that stem from the natural law. But as the Legal Expert points out, it is not the case that a reason can be given for everything that the elders (*maiores*) have established as law. Therefore, not every human law stems from the natural law.

But contrary to this: In his *Rhetorica* Tully says, "Fear and reverence sanctioned both what had come from nature and what had been approved by custom."

I respond: As Augustine says in *De Libero Arbitrio* 1, "A law that is not just does not seem to be a law at all." Hence, something has the force of law to the extent that it shares in justice.

Now in human affairs something is called just by virtue of its being right (*rectum*) according to the rule of reason. But as is clear from what was said above (q. 91, a. 2), the first rule of reason is the law of nature. Hence, every humanly made law has the character of law to the extent that it stems from the law of nature. On the other hand, if a humanly made law conflicts with the natural law, then it is no longer a law, but a corruption of law.

Note, however, that there are two possible modes in which things can stem from (*derivari*) the natural law: first, as *conclusions* from principles, and, second, (b) as *specifications* (*determinationes*) of what is general. The first mode is similar to the way in which demonstrative conclusions are produced from principles in the sciences. By contrast, in the second mode there is a similarity to the way in which general forms are narrowed down to something more specific in the arts—for instance, a craftsman must narrow down the general form *house* to this or that specific shape for a house.

Thus, some things stem from the universal principles of the law of nature in the manner of a *conclusion*; for instance, *One should not kill* can be derived as a conclusion from *One should not do evil to anyone*. On the other hand, some things are derived in the manner of a *specification*; for instance, the law of nature says *Let him who does evil be punished*, but it is a specification of the law of nature that an evildoer should be punished by *this specific* punishment.

Thus, both sorts of things are found posited in human law. However, what stems from the natural law in the first mode is not contained in human law in such a way that it is posited by that law alone; rather, it also has some of its force from the natural law. By contrast, what stems from the natural law in the second mode has its force from human law alone.

Reply to objection 1: In this passage the Philosopher is talking about what is posited by the law through a determination or specification of the precepts of the law of nature.

Reply to objection 2: This argument goes through for the case of those things that stem from the law of nature as conclusions.

Reply to objection 3: Because of the great variety in human affairs, the general principles of the law of nature cannot be applied in the same way to everyone. This is the source of the diversity of positive law for different people.

Reply to objection 4: This passage from the Legal Expert should be understood as applying to what is introduced by those in charge concerning particular specifications of the natural law. The judgment of men who are experienced and prudent bears the same relation to these specifications as it does to the principles—viz., that they directly see just which particular specifications are appropriate. Hence, the Philosopher says in *Ethics* 6 that in such matters "one should give no less respect to the indemonstrable pronouncements and opinions of experienced and older and prudent men than to demonstrations."

Article 3

Does Isidore appropriately describe
the characteristics of positive law?

It seems that Isidore does not appropriately describe the characteristics (*qualitatem*) of positive law when he says, "The law will be (a) morally upright (*honesta*), (b) just (*justa*), (c) possible according to nature, (d) in keeping with the customs of the country, (e) appropriate for the time and place, (f) necessary, (g) useful, (h) clear as well, lest it contain anything deceptive because of its obscurity, (i) written for no one's private advantage, but for the common advantage of the citizens."

Objection 1: He had previously explained the characteristics of law by listing [only] three conditions: "The law will be everything that builds upon reason, as long as it (a) agrees with religion, (b) contributes to discipline, and (c) promotes welfare (*salus*)." Therefore, it was unnecessary for him to multiply the conditions later on.

Objection 2: As Tully explains in *De Officiis*, justice (*iustitia*) is a part of moral uprightness (*honestas*). Therefore, once Isidore had said "morally upright," it was unnecessary to add "just."

Objection 3: According to Isidore, the written law is opposed to custom. Therefore, he should not have put "in keeping with the customs of the country" into the definition of law.

Objection 4: There are two types of necessary things. The first is what is necessary absolutely speaking, i.e., such that it is impossible for it to be otherwise; this type of necessary thing is not subject to human judgment and so this sort of necessity is irrelevant to human law. Something can also be necessary for the sake of an end, and this sort of necessity is the same as usefulness. Therefore, it is superfluous to posit both "necessary" and "useful."

But contrary to this is the authority of Isidore himself.

I respond: As *Physics* 2 makes clear, everything that exists for the sake of an end must be such that its form is proportioned to that end—in the way that the form of a saw is appropriate for cutting. In addition, everything that is rectified and measured must have a form proportioned to its rule and measure.

Now human law has both these features, since (a) it is something ordered toward an end and (b) it is a rule or measure that is itself ruled or measured by a higher measure—where, as is clear from what was said above (q. 93, a. 3), this higher measure is twofold, viz., divine law and the law of nature. Moreover, the end of human law is its usefulness for men, as the Legal Expert likewise points out.

And this is why, in giving the conditions for law, Isidore first lays down these three: that (a) law agrees with religion, viz., insofar as it is proportioned to the divine law, that (b) it contributes to discipline, insofar as it is proportioned to the law of nature, and that (c) it promotes welfare, insofar as it is proportioned to human usefulness. All the other characteristics that he posits later on are traced back to these three.

For the law's being morally upright is traced back to its being in agreement with religion.

And what he then adds—viz., "just, possible according to nature, in keeping with the customs of the country, appropriate for the time and place"—is added because it contributes to discipline. For human discipline is concerned in the first place with the order of reason, which is implied by his saying "just." Second, it has to do with the ability of the agents, since discipline should be appropriate for each one in accord with what is possible for him, likewise keeping in mind what is possible for nature (for the same discipline imposed on grown men should not be imposed on children), and in accord with human custom, since a man cannot live by himself in society and fail to defer to others. Third, as far as fitting circumstances are concerned, he says, "appropriate to the time and place."

Now what he then adds, viz., "necessary, useful, etc.," is traced back to the fact that law expedites human welfare, so that "necessity" refers to the removal of evils, "usefulness" to the pursuit of goods, and "clear" to the prevention of harm that could come from the law itself.

And since, as was explained above (q. 90, a. 2), law is ordered toward the common good, this point itself is made clear in the last part of the definition.

Reply to objection 1 and objection 2 and objection 3 and objection 4: The replies to the objections are clear from what has been said.

Article 4

Is Isidore's division of human laws appropriate?

It seems that Isidore proposes an inappropriate division of human statutes or human law:

Objection 1: Under human law (*ius*) he includes the law of nations (*ius gentium*), which, as he explains, is so-called because nearly all the nations make use of it. But as he himself says, the natural law is common to all nations. Therefore, the law of nations is contained under natural law rather than under positive human law.

Objection 2: Things that have the same force seem to differ from one another only materially and not formally. But statutes (*leges*), popular ordinances (*plebiscita*), senate decrees (*senatusconsulta*), etc., all seem to have the same force. Therefore, it seems that they differ from one another only materially. But a theory (*ars*) should not bother with this sort of distinction, since it could go on *ad infinitum*. Therefore, it is inappropriate to make this sort of division of human laws.

Objection 3: Just as a city has rulers and priests and soldiers, so too there are other roles men play as well. Therefore, it seems that just as one posits military law (*ius militare*) along with public law (*ius publicum*), which covers priests and magistrates, so too one should posit other types of law that correspond to other roles in the community.

Objection 4: What is incidental (*per accidens*) should be left out of consideration. But it is incidental to law that it is made by this or that man. Therefore, it is inappropriate to posit a division of human laws by reference to the names of lawmakers—as, for example, to call one sort of law Cornelian law and another sort Falcidian law, etc.

But contrary to this: The authority of Isidore is sufficient here.

I respond: Each thing is divisible *per se* on the basis of what is contained in its definition (*ratio*). For instance, *soul*, which is either *rational* or *non-rational*, is contained in the definition of *animal*, and so *animal* is divided properly and *per se* by *rational* and *non-rational*. By contrast, *animal* is not properly and *per se* divided by *white* and *black*, which lie completely outside of the definition of *animal*.

Now there are many elements in the definition of *human law*, and human law can be properly and *per se* divided in accordance with each of them.

First of all, as was explained above (a. 2), it is part of the definition of *human law* that human law stems from the law of nature. Accordingly, *positive law* (*ius positivum*) is divided into the law of nations (*ius gentium*) and civil law (*ius civile*), in keeping with the two modes, explained above (a. 2), in which something stems from the law of nature. For things that belong to the law of nations stem from the law of nature as *conclusions* from principles—e.g., justice in buying and selling, etc., in the absence of which men would be unable to live together with one another. This belongs to the natural law, since as *Politics* 1 shows, man is by nature a social animal. On the other hand, things that stem from the law of nature in the manner of particular *specifications* belong to civil law, according to which each community determines what is fitting for itself.

Second, it is part of the definition of *human law* that human law is ordered toward the common good of the community. Accordingly, human law can be divided by the diversity of roles played by those who work specifically for the common good—e.g., *priests*, who pray to God on behalf of the people; *rulers*, who govern the people; and *soldiers*, who fight for the safety of the people. And so special laws are adapted to these men as such.

Third, as was explained above (q. 90, a. 3), it is part of the definition of *human law* that human law is instituted by one who governs the civil community. Accordingly, human laws are divided by the diverse forms of civil government (*regimina*). One of these forms, according to the Philosopher in *Politics* 3, is the *kingdom* (*regnum*), viz., when the community is governed by one man, and, accordingly, this regime gives rise to the *Princely Constitutions*. Another form of government is *aristocracy*, i.e., rule by the best or by the party of the best (*optimates*), and, accordingly, this regime gives rise to the Counsels of the Wise (*Responsa Prudentum*) and also to the Senate Decrees (*Senatusconsulta*). The next form of government is *oligarchy*, i.e., rule by a few rich and powerful men, and, accordingly, this regime gives rise to the Praetorian Law (*Ius Praetorium*), which is also called the Law of Honor (*Ius Honararium*). Another form of government is government by the people, which goes by the name *democracy*, and, accordingly, this regime gives rise to Popular Ordinances (*plebiscita*). The last form of government is *tyranny*, which is altogether corrupt and hence does not give rise to any sort of law. There is also a mixed form of government—the best form—and, accordingly, this regime gives rise to a type of law which, as Isidore puts it, has been sanctioned by the elders along with the common people.

Fourth, it is part of the definition of *human law* that it directs human acts. Accordingly, laws are divided by the diverse acts about which laws are made. Sometimes these laws are named after their authors, e.g., the Julian law concerns acts of adultery, the Cornelian law concerns assassination, and so on. The laws are distinguished in this way not because of their authors, but because of the deeds they are concerned with.

Reply to objection 1: The law of nations is, to be sure, in some sense natural to man insofar as he is rational, since it stems from the natural law in the manner of a conclusion that is not very far removed from its principles. Hence, it was easy for men to agree to a law of this sort. However, the law of nations is nonetheless distinct from the natural law, especially from what is common to all animals.

Reply to objection 2 and objection 3 and objection 4: The replies to the other objections are clear from what has been said.

QUESTION 96

The Force of Human Law

We next have to consider the force (*potestas*) of human law. On this topic there are six questions: (1) Should human law be formulated in a general way? (2) Should human law restrain vices? (3) Should human law prescribe acts of all the virtues? (4) Does human law impose necessity on man with respect to his conscience? (5) Are all men subject to human law? (6) Is it permissible for those subject to the law to go beyond the letter (*praeter verba legis*) of the law in their actions?

Article 1

Should human law be made in a general way or for particular cases instead?

It seems that human law should not be made in a general way (*non debeat poni in communi*), but should instead be made for particular cases (*sed magis in particulari*):

Objection 1: In *Ethics* 5 the Philosopher says, "Legal justice consists in everything that is posited by law for individual cases, as well as decrees," which are likewise particular, since decrees are issued for particular actions. Therefore, law is made not only in a general way, but also for particular cases.

Objection 2: As was explained above (q. 90, aa. 1–2), the law directs human acts. But human acts are particulars. Therefore, human laws should not be made in a general way, but should be made for particular cases instead.

Objection 3: As was explained above (q. 90, aa. 1–2), law is a rule and measure of human acts. But as *Metaphysics* 10 puts it, a measure should be fixed with certitude (*certissima*). Therefore, since in human acts there is nothing general that is fixed to such an extent that it does not fail in some particular instances, it seems necessary for laws to be made for particular instances instead of being formulated in a general way.

But contrary to this: The Legal Expert says, "Laws have to be made for situations that come up very frequently, but laws are not made for situations that can come up perhaps only once."

I respond: If something exists for the sake of an end, then it must be proportioned to that end. Now the end of law is the common good, since, as Isidore says in *Etymologia*, "Law must be written for no one's private advantage, but for the common advantage of the citizens." But the common good is built up out of many things. And so the law must take into consideration a multiplicity of persons, actions, and times. For a civil community is composed of many persons, and its good is procured through a multiplicity of actions, and it is instituted not just to endure for a brief time, but to last for all time through a succession of citizens, as Augustine puts it in *De Civitate Dei* 12.

Reply to objection 1: In *Ethics* 5 the Philosopher posits three parts of legal justice, i.e., positive law.

Some laws are made in an absolutely general way, and these are the *general laws* (*leges communes*). It is with respect to laws of this sort that he says that what is legally just is such that at the beginning it does not matter whether it is this way or some other way, but that it does matter once the law is made—e.g., that captives are to be ransomed for such-and-such a mandated price.

On the other hand, there are certain laws that are general in one respect and particular in another respect. Laws of this sort are called *privileges* (*privilegia*)—private laws (*privatae leges*), as it were—since they have to do with particular persons; and yet they are such that their force extends to many actions. It is in this connection that he adds, ". . . everything that is posited by law for particular cases."

Again, certain things are called legal not because they are laws but because they involve the application of general laws to particular cases—for instance, *decrees* (*sententiae*), which are treated as laws. It is in this connection that he adds, "and also decrees."

Reply to objection 2: That which directs must direct a plurality of things. This is why in *Metaphysics* 10 the Philosopher says that everything belonging to a given genus is measured by some one thing that is first in that genus. For if there were as many rules and measures as there are things ruled and measured, then rules and measures would cease to be useful, since their usefulness consists in making it possible for many things to be understood on the basis of some one thing. Likewise, a law would not be useful if it did not extend beyond some one particular act. For as was explained above (q. 92, a. 2), it is the particular precepts of *prudent* men that are given for the purpose of directing *particular* acts, whereas a *law* is a *general* precept.

Reply to objection 3: As *Ethics* 1 says, we should not seek the same sort of certitude in all things. Hence, in contingent matters such as natural and human affairs, the certitude that something is true in most cases is sufficient, even if a few exceptions occur now and then.

Article 2

Should human law suppress all vices?

It seems that human law should suppress (*cohibere*) all vices:

Objection 1: In *Etymologia* Isidore says, "Laws have been made in order that boldness might be held in check by fear of them." But boldness would not be adequately held in check if not every evil were prohibited by the law. Therefore, human law should suppress every evil.

Objection 2: The lawmaker's intention is to make the citizens virtuous. But no one can be virtuous unless he is held back (*compescatur*) from all vices. Therefore, human law should suppress all vices.

Objection 3: As was explained above (q. 95, a. 2), human law stems from the natural law. But all vices are opposed to the law of nature. Therefore, human law should suppress all vices.

But contrary to this: *De Libero Arbitrio* 1 says, "It seems to me that the law written for ruling the people rightly permits those things and that God's providence punishes them." But God's providence does not punish anything except vices. Therefore, human law rightly permits certain vices by not suppressing them.

I respond: As has already been explained (q. 90, aa. 1–2), law is posited as a certain rule or measure of human acts. Now as *Metaphysics* 10 says, a measure must be homogenous with what it measures, since diverse things are measured by diverse measures. Hence, it must also be the case that laws are imposed on men according to their condition. For as Isidore says, "The law must be possible both according to nature and also according to the customs of the country."

Now the power or ability to act proceeds from an interior habit or disposition, and it is not the case that the same thing is possible both for someone who is virtuous and for someone who lacks the habit of the virtue, just as it is not the case that the same thing is possible both for a boy and for a grown man. It is for this reason that the law made for children is not the same as the law made for adults; for there are many things permitted to children that are punished by law or even vilified in adults. Similarly, there are many things permitted to men who are not perfected in virtue that would not be tolerable in virtuous men.

Now human law is made for the multitude of men, and the greater part of this multitude consists of men who are not perfected in virtue. And so not all the vices from which virtuous men abstain are prohibited by human law. Instead, the only vices prohibited are the more serious ones, which it is possible for the greater part of the multitude to abstain from—especially those vices which are harmful to others and without the prohibition of which human society could not be conserved. For instance, homicide and theft and other vices of this sort are prohibited by human law.

Reply to objection 1: 'Boldness' here has to do, it seems, with attacks against others. Hence, it mainly concerns those sins by which injury is inflicted on one's neighbors. As has been explained, these are the sins prohibited by human law.

Reply to objection 2: Human law has the intention of leading men to virtue, but of leading them gradually and not all at once. And so it does not immediately impose upon the multitude of imperfect men what is already characteristic of the virtuous, viz., that they abstain from every evil. Otherwise, those who are imperfect, unable to bear precepts of the sort in question, would erupt into worse evils—this according to Proverbs 30:33 ("He who violently blows his nose brings forth blood") and Matthew 9:17 ("If new wine [*read*: the precepts of the perfect life] is put into old wineskins (*read*: into imperfect men), then the wineskins burst and the wine runs out [*read*: the precepts are despised and out of contempt the men erupt into worse evils]").

Reply to objection 3: The natural law exists in us as a certain participation in the eternal law, but human law falls short of the eternal law. For in *De Libero Arbitrio* 1 Augustine says, "This law which is imposed to rule the civil communities allows and leaves unpunished many things that will be punished by God's providence. Nor is it the case that because this law does not do all things, one should disapprove of what it does do." Hence, human law likewise cannot prohibit everything that the law of nature prohibits.

Article 3

Does human law command the acts of all the virtues?

It seems that human law does not command the acts of all the virtues:

Objection 1: The acts of the vices are opposed to the acts of the virtues. But as has been explained (a. 2), human law does not prohibit all the vices. Therefore, human law does not command the acts of all the virtues.

Objection 2: An act of a virtue proceeds from that virtue. But virtue is the *end* of law, and so what *proceeds from* a virtue cannot fall under a precept of the law. Therefore, human law does not command the acts of all the virtues.

Objection 3: As has been explained (q. 90, a. 2), law is ordered toward the common good. But certain acts of the virtues are ordered not toward the common good, but instead toward [the agent's] private good. Therefore, the law does not command the acts of all the virtues.

But contrary to this: In *Ethics* 5 the Philosopher says, "The law commands the acts of the brave man and the acts of the temperate man and the acts of the mild-mannered man—and so on for the other virtues and vices, commanding the former and prohibiting the latter."

I respond: As is clear from what was said above (q. 54, a. 2), the species of virtue are distinguished by their objects. But all the objects of the virtues can be traced back either to the private good of an individual or to the common good of a multitude. For instance, one can execute acts of fortitude either for the sake of conserving the community or for the sake of preserving a friend's rights (*ius amici sui*).

Now as has been explained (q. 90, a. 2), law is ordered toward the common good. And so there is no virtue such that the law cannot command acts of that virtue. However, human law does not issue commands concerning all the acts of all the virtues; instead, it commands only those acts which can be ordered toward the common good either (a) *immediately*, as when certain acts are done directly because of the common good, or (b) *mediately*, as when the lawmaker commands certain acts pertaining to good discipline through which citizens are formed in such a way that they might conserve the good of justice and peace.

Reply to objection 1: Human law does not prohibit all vicious acts by an obligatory precept, just as it does not command all virtuous acts, either. Yet it prohibits certain acts of individual vices, just as it likewise commands certain acts of individual virtues.

Reply to objection 2: There are two ways in which an act is said to be an act of a virtue:

First, because the man *is doing something virtuous*. For instance, it is an act of justice to do something right and an act of fortitude to do something brave. In this sense the law commands some acts of the virtues.

Second, because the man is doing something virtuous *in the way that a virtuous man does it*. An act of this sort always proceeds from the virtue and never falls under a precept of the law, but is instead the end which the lawmaker intends to lead [the citizens] to.

Reply to objection 3: As has been explained, there is no virtue whose acts cannot be ordered toward the common good, either mediately or immediately.

Article 4

Does human law impose an obligation in conscience on a man?

It seems that human law does not impose an obligation in conscience on a man (*non imponat homini necessitatem in foro conscientiae*):

Objection 1: A lower authority (*potestas*) cannot impose a law on the judgment of a higher authority. But the authority of a man who makes human law is lower than God's authority. Therefore, human law cannot impose a law with respect to God's judgment, i.e., the judgment of conscience.

Objection 2: The judgment of conscience depends especially on God's commands. But sometimes God's commands are voided by human laws—this according to Matthew 15:6 ("You have made void the commandment of God on behalf of your traditions"). Therefore, human law does not impose an obligation in conscience on a man.

Objection 3: Human laws often inflict fraud and harm on men—this according to Isaiah 10:1–2 ("Woe to them who make wicked laws, and when they write, write injustice in order to oppress the poor in judgment, and do violence to the cause of the humble of my people"). But everyone is permitted to avoid oppression and violence. Therefore, human laws do not impose an obligation in conscience on a man.

But contrary to this: 1 Peter 2:19 says, "It is worthy of thanks if, because of his conscience, someone endure sorrows, suffering wrongfully."

I respond: Laws that are humanly made are either just or unjust.

If they are just, then they have their power to oblige in conscience from the eternal law, from which they stem—this according to Proverbs 8:15 ("By me kings reign, and lawgivers make just decrees"). Now laws are called just on the basis of (a) their *end*, viz., when they ordered toward the common good, and (b) their *author*, viz., when a law that is made does not exceed in its scope the power of the lawmaker, and (c) their *form*, viz., when they impose on those subject to them proportionately equal burdens in relation to the common good. For since a man is part of a multitude, each man is such that what he is and what he has belongs to the multitude, in the same way that any part is such that what it is belongs to the whole. This is why nature likewise inflicts a loss on a part in order to save the whole. Accordingly, laws of this sort, which impose proportionate burdens, are just, and they bind in conscience, and they are legal laws (*leges legales*).

On the other hand, there are two ways in which laws are unjust.

First, in counterpoint to what was said above, they are unjust when they are contrary to the *human* good either (a) because of their *end*, as when the lawmaker imposes burdens on his subjects that contribute not to the common welfare but to his own greed or glory, or (b) because of their *author*, as when someone makes laws that go beyond the authority entrusted to him, or (c) because of their *form*, as when burdens are distributed unequally over the multitude, even if those burdens are ordered toward the common good. Laws of this sort are outrages (*violentiae*) rather than laws, since, as Augustine puts it in *De Libero Arbitrio*, "What is not just does not seem to be a law." Hence, laws of this sort do not bind in conscience (*non obligant in foro conscientiae*)—except perhaps for the sake of preventing scandal or social unrest (*turbatio*), in which case a man should cede his right, in accord with Matthew 5:40–41 ("If someone forces you to go one mile, go with him another two . . . and if someone takes away your coat, give him your cloak as well").

The second way in which laws can be unjust is by being contrary to the *divine* good, as are tyrannical laws that induce men to idolatry or to doing anything else that is contrary to divine law. It is not permissible to obey such laws in any way at all, since as Acts 5:29 says, "We must obey God rather than men."

Reply to objection 1: As the Apostle says in Romans 13:1–2, "Every human authority is from God, and so whoever resists that authority (*read*: in the things that pertain to the scope of that authority) is resisting God's ordinance." And, accordingly, such a man is accused by his conscience (*efficitur reus quantum ad conscientiam*).

Reply to objection 2: This argument goes through in the case of human laws that are directed against a command of God's. The scope of the authority [of human law] does not extend this far. Hence, in such cases one must not obey the human law.

Reply to objection 3: This argument goes through in the case of a law that imposes an unjust burden on those subject to it. Again, the scope of the authority given by God does not extend this far, and so in such cases a man is not obligated to obey the law if he can resist it without giving scandal or causing some greater damage.

Article 5

Is everyone subject to human law?

It seems that not everyone is subject to human law:

Objection 1: The only ones subject to the law are those for whom the law is made. But in 1 Timothy 1:9 the Apostle says, "The law is not made for the just man." Therefore, the just are not subject to human law.

Objection 2: Pope Urban says (and one finds the same thing in *Decretals* 19, q. 2), "If someone is led by a private law, then he in no way needs to be bound by a public law." But all men who are sons of God are led by the private law of the Holy Spirit—this according to Romans 8:14 ("Those who are led by the Spirit of God are the sons of God"). Therefore, not every man is subject to human law.

Objection 3: The Legal Expert says, "The ruler is exempt from the law (*solutus a lege*)." But one who is exempt from the law is not subject to the law. Therefore, not everyone is subject to the law.

But contrary to this: In Romans 13:1 the Apostle says, "Let every soul be subject to the higher authorities." But one who is not subject to a law laid down by a given authority does not seem to be subject to that authority. Therefore, all men have to be subject to human law.

I respond: As is clear from what was said above (q. 90, aa. 1–3), law by its nature has two characteristics: first, it is a rule with respect to human acts; second, it has coercive force. It follows that there are two senses in which a man can be subject to the law.

In the first sense, he is subject to the law in the way that what is ruled is subject to what is doing the ruling. And everyone who is subject to an authority is in this sense subject to the law which that authority gives.

Now it can happen in two ways that someone is not subject to a given authority: (a) first, *because he is absolutely free of subjection to it*, and, hence, those who belong to one city or kingdom are not subject to the laws of the ruler of some other city or kingdom, just as they are not subject to his dominion; and (b) second, *insofar as he is ruled by a higher law.* For instance, someone subject to a proconsul should be ruled by his command—and yet not in those matters in which he receives a dispensation from the emperor. For with respect to those matters, since he is being directed by the command of someone higher, he is not bound by the command of someone lower. Accordingly, it is possible for someone who is subject to the law absolutely speaking not to be bound by the law in certain matters with respect to which he is under the rule of a higher law.

On the other hand, in the second sense, someone is said to be subject to the law in the way that what is coerced is subject to what is doing the coercing. In this sense it is only bad men, and not virtuous and just men, who are subject to the law. For what is coerced and violent is contrary to one's will. And the will of good men is consonant with the law, whereas the will of bad men disagrees with the law. Hence, in this respect only bad men, and not good men, are under the law.

Reply to objection 1: This argument goes through for the type of subjection that exists in the mode of coercion. For in this sense the law is not given for the just men, since, as the Apostle puts it in Romans 2:14–15, "they are a law unto themselves when they show the work of the law written in their hearts." Hence, the law does not exercise coercive power over them in the way it does over on the unjust.

Reply to objection 2: The law of the Holy Spirit is higher than any law that is humanly given. And so insofar as spiritual men are led by the law of the Holy Spirit, they are not subject to the law with respect to those things that are incompatible with the guidance of the Holy Spirit. However, part of the Holy Spirit's guidance is that spiritual men should be subject to human laws—this according to 1 Peter 2:13 ("Be subject to every human creature for the sake of God").

Reply to objection 3: The ruler is said to be exempt from the law as far as the law's *coercive force* is concerned, since no one properly coerces himself and the law has its coercive force only from the ruler's authority. Thus, the ruler is said to be exempt from the law in the sense that no one can bring a judgment of condemnation against him if he acts against the law. Hence, the Gloss on Psalm 50:6 ("Against you alone have I sinned") says, "There is no man who is the judge of the king's deeds."

However, as far as the *directive force* of the law is concerned, the ruler is subject to the law by his own will. Accordingly, *Extra, De Constitutionibus*, chapter beginning "Since everyone . . .", says, "If anyone establishes a law for another, then he himself should keep that same law."

And the authority of a wise man says, "Obey yourself the law that you have given." Again, our Lord rebukes those who "prescribe and do not do it" and who "impose grave burdens on others and do not themselves want to lift a finger to move them" (Matthew 23:3–4). Hence, as far as God's judgment is concerned, the ruler is not exempt from the directive force of the law, but instead should fulfill the law willingly and not under coercion.

In addition, the ruler is above the law in the sense that if it is expedient, he can change the law and give dispensations from it for given times and places.

Article 6

Is one who is subject to the law permitted to act outside the letter of the law?

It seems that one who is subject to the law is not permitted to act outside the letter of the law (*praeter verba legis agere*):

Objection 1: In *De Vera Religione* Augustine says, "In the case of temporal laws, even though men pass judgment on them before they institute them, still, once they have been instituted and confirmed, one is not permitted to pass judgment *on* them, but is permitted [only] to pass judgment *in accordance with* them." But if someone neglects the letter of the law, claiming that he is preserving the lawmaker's intention, then he seems to be passing judgment on the law. Therefore, one who is subject to the law is not permitted to neglect the letter of the law in order to preserve the lawmaker's intention.

Objection 2: Interpreting the laws is the role of the one who makes the laws. But it is not the role of the men who are subject to the law to make the laws. Therefore, it is not their role to interpret the lawmaker's intention; instead, they should always act in accord with the letter of the law.

Objection 3: Every wise man knows how to explain his own intention in words. But those who have made the laws should be considered wise, since in Proverbs 8:15 God's wisdom says, "By me kings reign, and lawgivers decree just things." Therefore, one should pass judgment about a lawmaker's intention only by reference to the letter of the law.

But contrary to this: In *De Trinitate* 4 Hilary says, "The meaning of what is said should be taken from the reasons for saying it, since the words should be subject to the things and not the things to the words." Therefore, one should pay more attention to the reasons that move the lawmaker than to the very words of the law.

I respond: As was explained above (a. 4), every law is ordered toward the common welfare of men, and this is how it gets its force and character as law; on the other hand, to the extent that it fails in this, it does not have the power to bind. Hence, the Legal Expert says, "Neither a reason in law nor kind fairness permits us to induce severity by means of a stricter interpretation, contrary to the welfare of men, of what had been beneficially introduced to be useful to them."

Now it often happens that even though the observance of a certain practice is useful for the common welfare in the greater number of cases, there are nonetheless some cases in which it is especially harmful. Therefore, since a lawmaker cannot foresee all the individual cases, he makes the law with an eye toward what happens in the greater number of cases, while directing his intention to the common advantage. Hence, if a case arises in which the observance of such a law is harmful to the common welfare, it should not be obeyed. For instance, if in a city under siege it is mandated by law that the city gates should remain closed, this is useful to the common welfare in the greater number of cases. However, if a situation arose in which the enemy were pursuing certain citizens who had important roles in preserving the city, then it would be extremely damaging to the city if the gates were not opened to them, and so in such a case the gates should be opened—in opposition to the letter of the law—in order to preserve the common welfare, which is what the lawgiver intends.

Notice, however, that if the observance of the letter of the law does not entail a sudden danger that has to be dealt with immediately, then not just anyone has the role of interpreting what is advantageous or disadvantageous; rather, this is the role only of the ruler, who has the authority to grant dispensations from the laws in light of cases of the sort in question. On the other hand, if there is a sudden danger that does not permit enough time to have recourse to someone in charge, then the necessity itself has a dispensation attached to it, since necessity is not subject to the law.

Reply to objection 1: Someone who acts outside the letter of the law in a case of necessity is not passing judgment on the law itself, but is rather passing judgment on a particular case, in which he sees that the letter of the law should not be obeyed.

Reply to objection 2: One who follows the lawmaker's intention is not interpreting the law absolutely speaking; rather, he is interpreting the law with respect to a case in which it is obvious, because of the evidentness of the harm, that the lawmaker had intended something else. For if there is a doubt, then he should either act in accord with the letter of the law or consult those in charge.

Reply to objection 3: No man has wisdom to such a degree that he is able to think of all the individual cases, and so no one can adequately express by his words what is in keeping with his intended end. Even if a lawmaker were able to take all the cases into consideration, he should not express them all—and this for the sake of avoiding confusion. Instead, he should issue a law in keeping with what happens in the greater number of cases.

QUESTION 97

Changes in Human Law

We next have to consider changes in human law. On this topic there are four questions: (1) Is human law changeable? (2) Should human law always be changed when something better comes along? (3) Is human law abolished by custom, and does custom acquire the force of law? (4) Should the practice of human law be changed by means of dispensations granted by the rulers?

Article 1

Should human law in any way be changed?

It seems that human law should not in any way be changed:

Objection 1: As was explained above (q. 95, a. 2), human law stems from the natural law. But the natural law persists unchanged. Therefore, human law should likewise remain unchanged.

Objection 2: As the Philosopher says in *Ethics* 5, a measure must be especially permanent. But as was explained above (q. 90, aa. 1–2), human law is a measure of human acts. Therefore, it should remain unchanged.

Objection 3: As was explained above (q. 95, a. 2), it is part of the nature of law that it is just and right. But what is once right is always right. Therefore, what is once the law should always be the law.

But contrary to this: In *De Libero Arbitrio* 1 Augustine says, "Even if a temporal law is just, it can nonetheless be justifiably modified as time goes on."

I respond: As was explained above (q. 91, a. 3), human law is a certain type of dictate of reason by which human acts are directed. Accordingly, there are two possible reasons why human law might justifiably be changed, one on the side of *reason* and the other on the side of the *men* whose acts are regulated by the law.

On the side of *reason*, it seems natural to human reason that it should gradually move from what is imperfect toward what is perfect. Hence, we see in the speculative sciences that those who first philosophized handed down what was imperfect and this was later made more perfect by their successors. The same thing holds true in the practical sciences. Those who first intended to discover something useful for the human community, unable to take everything into consideration on their own, instituted certain practices which were deficient in many ways and which their successors changed by instituting other practices that were less prone to fail with respect to the common welfare.

On the side of the *men* whose acts are regulated by the law, law can rightly be changed because of changes in the situations of men, for whom different things are expedient in different situations. In *De Libero Arbitrio* 1 Augustine presents an example: "If the people are mature and serious and diligently guard the common welfare, then it is right to adopt a law by which such people are permitted to appoint for themselves magistrates to administer the republic. However, if the same people, having been depraved little by little, hold a rigged election and entrust the government to dissolute and profligate men, then it is justifiable to deprive such people of the power of conferring public offices and to return to the judgment of a few good men."

Reply to objection 1: As was explained above (q. 91, a. 2), the natural law is a type of participation in the eternal law, and so it persists unchanged—a feature it has from the unchangeability and perfection of God's reason insofar as it institutes nature. By contrast, human reason is changeable and imperfect, and so its law is changeable.

Moreover, the natural law contains certain general precepts which always remain in force, whereas the law made by man contains certain particular precepts corresponding to the different situations that arise.

Reply to objection 2: A measure should be as permanent as possible. But among changeable entities there cannot be anything that persists altogether unchangeably. And so human law cannot be altogether unchangeable.

Reply to objection 3: Among corporeal things 'right' (*rectum*) is predicated absolutely, and so, as far as it itself is concerned, what is right always remains right. However, rightness (*rectitudo*) is predicated of the law in relation to the common welfare, which, as was explained above, is not such that one and the same thing is always proportioned to it. And so this sort of correctness changes.

Article 2

Should human law always be changed when something better comes along?

It seems that human law should always be changed when something better comes along:

Objection 1: Human laws, like other matters of art, have been arrived at by human reason. But in other matters of art, what was previously embraced is changed if something better comes along. Therefore, the same thing should be done in the case of human laws.

Objection 2: We can provide for the future by drawing on the past. But if human laws had not been changed in light of better discoveries that superceded them, then many anomalies would have followed, because old codes of law contain many elements of ignorance. Therefore, it seems that the laws should be changed as often as something better to institute comes along.

Objection 3: Human laws are established with respect to particular human acts. But the only way we reach complete cognition of particulars is through experience, which takes time, as *Ethics* 2 points out. Therefore, it seems that through the course of time something that is better to institute can come along.

But contrary to this: *Decretals*, dist. 12, says, "It is a ridiculous and wholly abominable disgrace for us to break off the traditions that we have received from our fathers."

I respond: As has been explained (a. 1), human law is justifiably changed to the extent that such a change in the law is a means of providing for the common welfare. However, the very changing of the law, taken just by itself, does a certain sort of damage to the common welfare. For custom (*consuetudo*) contributes to the observance of a great many laws, to the extent that whatever violates common custom—even if it is of little importance in its own right—is seen as rather serious. Hence, when a law is changed, the constraining force of the law is diminished to the extent that a given custom is nullified.

Therefore, human law should never be changed unless the damage done to the common welfare by the change is wholly compensated for in some other way. This happens either because (a) some very great and obvious advantage comes from the new statute, or because (b) there is some urgent necessity stemming from the fact that the established law either involves a manifest iniquity or is such that its observance is very harmful. Hence, the Legal Expert says, "In order to revoke a law that has been deemed just for a long time, there must be an obvious advantage in the new practices that are going to be instituted."

Reply to objection 1: Matters of art have their efficacy solely from reason, and so whenever a better reason comes along, what was previously embraced should be changed. By contrast, as the Philosopher points out in *Politics* 2, laws acquire an especially great force from custom. And so they are not to be changed so easily.

Reply to objection 2: This argument shows that laws should be changed, but not for the sake of just any sort of improvement. Instead, as has been explained, they should be changed for the sake of some great advantage or out of some urgent necessity.

Reply to objection 3: The same reply holds for the third objection.

Article 3

Can custom acquire the force of law or nullify a law?

It seems that custom (*consuetudo*) can neither acquire the force of law nor nullify a law:

Objection 1: As is clear from what was said above (q. 93, a. 3 and q. 95, a. 2), human law stems from the natural law and the divine law. But human custom cannot alter the law of nature or the divine law. Therefore, neither can it alter human law.

Objection 2: It is not the case that a good can come from many evils. But the one who first starts to act against the law acts badly. Therefore, it is not the case that something good will be produced by the multiplication of acts similar to that bad act. Now a law is a sort of good, since it is a rule of human acts. Therefore, a law cannot be nullified by custom in such a way that the custom itself acquires the force of law.

Objection 3: Making law is the function of public personages whose role it is to govern the community; hence, private persons cannot make law. But a custom increases in strength through the acts of private persons. Therefore, custom cannot acquire the force of a law by which some other law is nullified.

But contrary to this: In *Epistola ad Casulanum* Augustine says, "The customs of the people of God, as well as what has been instituted by the leaders, should be embraced as law. And like those who transgress divine laws, so too those who show contempt for ecclesiastical customs should be corrected."

I respond: Every sort of law proceeds from the lawmaker's reason and will—divine and natural law from God's rational will, and human law from the human will as regulated by reason. Now just as, in practical matters, a man's reason and will are made manifest by what he says, so too they are made manifest by what he does. For each man seems to choose as a good what he brings about by his action.

Now it is manifest that the law can be both explained and changed by human words, insofar as those words make manifest human reason's interior movement and conception. Hence, the law can also be explained and changed through acts which, especially when they are multiplied, engender customs; moreover, these acts can cause something that acquires the force of law, viz., because through repeated exterior acts the will's interior motion and reason's designs are effectively clarified. For when something is repeated many times, it seems to proceed from the deliberate judgment of reason. Accordingly, custom has the force of law, nullifies law, and serves to interpret law.

Reply to objection 1: As has been explained, natural law and divine law proceed from the divine will. Hence, they cannot be changed by any custom that proceeds from the human will; instead, they could be changed only by God's authority. And so no custom contrary to the divine law or natural law can acquire the force of law. For in the *Synonymes* Isidore says, "Let custom cede to authority; let law and reason subdue a depraved custom."

Reply to objection 2: As was explained above (q. 96, a. 6), human laws fail (*deficit*) in some cases, and so it is sometimes possible to act outside the law without the act's being bad, viz., in a case where the law fails. And when such cases are multiplied because of some change in the men, then it becomes clear through custom that the standing law is not advantageous—in just the way this would likewise become clear if a law were promulgated that was verbally contrary to the standing law.

However, if the reason for which the first law was advantageous still holds, then the law conquers the habit rather than the habit the law—unless, perhaps, the law seems disadvantageous precisely because it is not possible given the customs of the country, which was one of the conditions for law (cf. q. 95, a. 3). For it is difficult to abolish a custom of the people.

Reply to objection 3: The people among whom a custom is introduced can be in one of two conditions:

If it is a free people that can make laws for itself, then the consensus of the whole people to observe the practice that a custom makes manifest counts for more than the authority of the ruler, who does not have the power to make law except insofar as he stands in for the people. Hence, even if particular persons cannot make law, the whole people can nonetheless make law.

On the other hand, if the people does not have free power to make law for itself or to nullify a law made by someone in charge, then a custom that is widespread among such a people acquires the force of law to the extent that it is tolerated by those who have the role of imposing law on the people. For by this very toleration they seem to give their approval to what the custom has introduced.

Article 4

Can the rulers of the people give dispensations from human laws?

It seems that the rulers of the people cannot give dispensations from human laws:

Objection 1: As Isidore puts it, law is established "for the common welfare." But the common good should not be overridden in favor of any person's private advantage (*pro privato commodo alicuius personae*), since, as the Philosopher says in *Ethics* 1, "The good of the nation is more divine than the good of a single man." Therefore, it seems that no one should be given a dispensation to act against a general law.

Objection 2: Deuteronomy 1:17 gives this command to those who are placed in charge of others: "You shall hear the little as well as the great: neither shall you respect any man's person, because it is the judgment of God." But 'respecting persons' or favoritism (*acceptio personarum*) seems to consist in conceding to a given individual what is generally denied to everyone. Therefore, the rulers of the people cannot give dispensations of the sort in question, since this is contrary to God's command.

Objection 3: If human law is to be upright, then it must be consonant with the natural law and with divine law; otherwise, it would neither "agree with religion" nor "contribute to discipline"—which, as Isidore says, are required for law (cf. q. 95, a. 3). But no man can give a dispensation either from divine law or from the natural law. Therefore, neither can any man give a dispensation from human law.

But contrary to this: In 1 Corinthians 9:17 the Apostle says, ". . . a dispensation is committed to me."

I respond: 'Dispensation' (*dispensatio*) properly implies a measuring out of something common to individuals. Hence, the head of a family is called a 'dispenser' (*dispensator*) insofar as he distributes, in due weight and measure, the tasks and necessities of life to each member of the family.

So, then, every multitude is such that someone in it is called a dispenser by virtue of the fact that he determines how a general precept is to be implemented by each individual.

Now as is clear from what was said above (q. 96, a. 6), sometimes a precept that is appropriate for the multitude in the greater number of cases is not appropriate for this person or in this case, either because it would prevent something better or because it would lead to some evil. However, as was explained above (q. 96, a. 6), it would be dangerous to leave such matters to the judgment of each individual, except perhaps in the face of an evident and sudden threat. Thus, the one charged with ruling the people has the power to dispense from a human law that depends on his authority, with the result that when the law fails for given persons or cases, he may permit a precept of the law not to be obeyed. However, if he granted such permission just by his own will alone and without the sort of reason in question, then in granting such a dispensation he would be either unfaithful or imprudent—unfaithful if he did not intend the common good, and imprudent if he knew of no reason for the dispensation. This is why, in Luke 12:42, Our Lord says, "Who do you think is the faithful and prudent steward (*dispensator*), whom his lord sets over his family?"

Reply to objection 1: When someone is dispensed from obeying a general law, this should be done not with a prejudice against the common good, but rather with the intention of promoting the common good.

Reply to objection 2: There is no 'respecting of persons' (*acceptio personarum*) if it is not the case that persons who are equal are being treated as unequals. Hence, when a person's situation requires that, in accord with reason, something be observed in a special way in that situation, then it is not favoritism if some special favor is granted him.

Reply to objection 3: Insofar as the natural law contains general precepts that never fail, it cannot admit of dispensations.

On the other hand, with respect to those other precepts, which are like conclusions of the general precepts, men can sometimes give dispensations—for instance, a dispensation according to which a thing left in trust need not be returned to someone who has betrayed his country, or something of this sort.

However, every man is related to divine law in the way that a private person is related to a public law to which he is subject. Hence, just as in the case of human public law, the only one who can give dispensations is the one from whom the law has its authority or someone whom he has commissioned, so too in the case of the precepts of the divine law, which come from God, no one can give a dispensation except God or someone to whom He Himself has given a special commission.

QUESTION 98

The Old Law

We next have to consider the Old Law—first, the Law itself (question 98) and, second, its precepts (questions 99–105).

On the first topic there are six questions: (1) Was the Old Law good? (2) Was the Old Law from God? (3) Was the Old Law from God through the mediation of angels? (4) Was the Old Law given to everyone? (5) Did the Old Law oblige everyone? (6) Was the Old Law given at an appropriate time?

Article 1

Was the Old Law good?

It seems that the Old Law was not good:

Objection 1: Ezechiel 20:25 says, "I gave them precepts that were not good, and judgments in which they shall not live." But a type of law is called good only because of the goodness of the precepts it contains. Therefore, the Old Law was not good.

Objection 2: As Isidore points out, part of the goodness of a law consists in its promoting the common welfare (*communis salus*). But the Old Law did not bring salvation (*non fuit salutifera . . .*) and brought death and harm instead (*sed magis mortifera et novica*). For in Romans 7:8–10 the Apostle says, "Without the Law sin was dead. And I lived some time without the Law. But when the commandment came, sin revived, and I died." And in Romans 5:20 he says, "The Law entered in that sin might abound." Therefore, the Old Law was not good.

Objection 3: Part of the goodness of a law is that it is possible to observe it in a way that accords with both nature and human custom. But the Old Law lacked this characteristic; for in Acts 15:10 Peter says, "Why are you trying to impose on the necks of the disciples a yoke that neither our fathers nor we have been able to bear?" Therefore, it seems that the Old Law was not good.

But contrary to this: In Romans 7:12 the Apostle says, "And so the Law is indeed holy, and the commandment is holy and just and good."

I respond: There is no doubt that the Old Law was good. For just as a teaching (*doctrina*) is shown to be true by the fact that it is consonant with right reason, so too a law is shown to be good by the fact that it is consonant with reason. But the Old Law was consonant with reason. For as is clear from the commandment laid down in Exodus 20:15, "You shall not covet your neighbor's goods," the Old Law curbed concupiscence, which is opposed to reason. It likewise prohibited all the sins that are contrary to reason. Hence, it is clear that it was good. And in Romans 7:22 the Apostle's argument (*ratio*) is this: "I am delighted with the Law of God, according to the inward man"; and, again, "I consent to the Law, because it is good."

However, notice that, as Dionysius points out in *De Divinis Nominibus*, chap. 4, the good admits of different degrees. For some goods are perfect and some are imperfect. In the case of things that are ordered toward an end, perfect goodness consists in a thing's being such that it is sufficient *per se* to induce the end, whereas an imperfect good is such that it contributes something toward the acquisition of the end but is not sufficient to induce the end. For instance, a perfectly good medicine is one that cures a man, whereas an imperfect medicine is one that helps a man but is unable to cure him.

Now note that the end of human law is distinct from the end of divine law. For the end of human law is temporal peace within the political community (*temporalis tranquillitas civitatis*), and human law achieves this end by curbing exterior acts that involve evils capable of disturbing the peaceful state of the political community. By contrast, the end of divine law is to lead a man to the end of eternal happiness, and this end is impeded by any sin whatsoever—not just the exterior acts, but the interior acts as well. And so what suffices for the perfection of human law, viz., that it prohibit sins and mete out punishments, does not suffice for the perfection of divine law. Rather, divine law has to make a man totally fit for participation in eternal happiness.

Now this can be brought about only through the grace of the Holy Spirit, by which the charity that fulfills the law is diffused in our hearts. For as Romans 6:23 says, "The grace of God is eternal life." But the Old Law was unable to confer this grace, since this was reserved to Christ. For as John 1:17 says, "The law was given by Moses; grace and truth came by Jesus Christ." Hence, the Old Law is good, to be sure, but it is an imperfect good—this according to Hebrews 7:19 ("The Law brought nothing to perfection").

Reply to objection 1: The Lord is speaking here about the ceremonial precepts, which are called "not good" because they did not confer the grace through which men are washed of sin—even though precepts of this sort did show men to be sinners. That is why the verse expressly says, "and judgments in which they shall not live," i.e., judgments through which they cannot acquire the life of grace, "and I polluted them in their own gifts," i.e., I showed them to be polluted "when, because of their sins, they offered everything that opened the womb."

Reply to objection 2: The Law is said to have killed not as an *efficient cause* but as an *occasion*—and this because of its imperfection, viz., insofar as it did not confer the grace through which men would be able to fulfill what it commanded or to avoid what it forbade. And so this occasion was not given, but was instead taken by men. Hence, in the same place the Apostle says, "For sin, taking the occasion, seduced me through the commandment, seduced me, and by it killed me." It is for this same reason that he says, "The law entered in that sin might abound," where 'that' implies succession rather than causality—viz., insofar as men, taking the occasion from the Law, sinned more abundantly, both because their sin was more grave after it had been prohibited by the Law, and also because concupiscence increased, since we desire all the more what is forbidden to us.

Reply to objection 3: The yoke of the Law could not have been obeyed without the help of grace, which the Law did not give. For Romans 9:16 says, "So then it is not of him who wills, nor of him who runs"—i.e., to will and to run within God's precepts—"but of God who shows mercy." Hence, Psalm 118:32 says, "I have run the way of Your commandments, since You enlarged my heart"—i.e., through the gift of grace and of charity.

Article 2

Was the Old Law from God?

It seems that the Old Law was not from God:

Objection 1: Deuteronomy 32:4 says, "The works of God are perfect." But as was explained above (a. 1), the Old Law was imperfect. Therefore, the Old Law was not from God.

Objection 2: Ecclesiastes 3:14 says, "I have learned that all the works which God has made persevere forever." But the Old Law did not persevere forever; for in Hebrews 7:18 the Apostle says, "There is indeed a setting aside of the former commandment, because of its weakness and unprofitableness." Therefore, the Old Law was not from God.

Objection 3: It is a function of the lawmaker's wisdom to remove not only evils but the occasions of evil. But as was explained above (a. 1), the Old Law was an occasion of sin. Therefore, it was inappropriate that God—who, as Job 36:22 puts it, "is such that none is like Him among the lawmakers"—should hand down such a law.

Objection 4: 1 Timothy 2:4 says, "God wills all men to be saved." But as was explained above (a. 1), the Old Law did not suffice for the salvation of men. Therefore, it was inappropriate for God to make such a law. Therefore, the Old Law is not from God.

But contrary to this: In Matthew 15:6 our Lord, in speaking to the Jews, to whom the Old Law had been given, says, "You have made void the commandment of God because of your traditions." And just before this we find, "Honor your father and your mother," which is clearly contained in the Old Law (cf. Exodus 20:12 and Deuteronomy 5:16). Therefore, the Old Law is from God.

I respond: The Old Law was given by the good God, who is the Father of our Lord Jesus Christ. For the Old Law ordered men toward Christ in two ways.

First, it ordered men toward Christ by bearing witness to Christ. Hence, in the last chapter of Luke, verse 44, He Himself says, "All things had to be fulfilled which were written about me in the law of Moses and in the prophets and in the Psalms,." And in John 5:46 He says, "If you believed Moses, you would perhaps believe me also; for he wrote about me."

Second, the Old Law ordered men toward Christ in the manner of a disposition, since by drawing men back from idolatry, it enveloped them within the worship of the one God by whom the human race was to be saved through Christ. Hence, in Galatians 3:23 the Apostle says, "Before the faith came, we were guarded under the Law, enclosed for that faith which was to be revealed." But, clearly, the one who disposes things to the end is the same as the one who leads them to the end, and by 'the same' I mean either through himself (*per se*) or through those who are subject to him. For the devil would not have given a law by means of which men might be led to Christ, through whom he himself was going to be cast out—this according to Matthew 12:26 ("If Satan casts out Satan, then his kingdom is divided"). And so the Old Law was given by the same God by whom the salvation of men was effected through the grace of Christ.

Reply to objection 1: Nothing prevents a thing from being imperfect absolutely speaking and yet perfect with respect to a given time. For instance, a boy is not said to be perfect absolutely speaking, but is said to be perfect for his age (*secundum temporis conditionem*). So, too, precepts that are given to children are perfect for the condition of those to whom they are given, even if those precepts are not perfect absolutely speaking. The precepts of the Old Law were like this. Hence, in Galatians 3:24 the Apostle says, "The Law was our teacher (*paedagogus*) in Christ."

Reply to objection 2: The works of God that persevere forever are the ones which God made in such a way that they should persevere forever, and these are the ones that are perfect. By contrast, the Old Law was set aside at the time of the perfection of grace—not as something bad, but as something weak and unprofitable for that time. For as is added [in the cited passage], "The law did not bring anything to perfection." Hence, in Galatians 3:25 the Apostle says, "Now that faith has come, we are no longer under the teacher."

Reply to objection 3: As was explained above (q. 79, a. 4), God at times allows some men to fall into sin in order that they might thereby be made humble. So, too, He willed to a give a Law that men could not fulfill by their own power in order that men, in relying on themselves, might discover themselves to be sinners and, having been humbled, might have recourse to the assistance of grace.

Reply to objection 4: Even though the Old Law did not suffice for the salvation of man, there was nonetheless another sort of assistance which God offered to men along with the Law and by which they were able to be saved, viz., faith in the Mediator—a faith through which the ancient patriarchs were justified in the same way that we ourselves are justified. And so God did not remove Himself from men in the sense of not giving them the means to salvation.

Article 3

Was the Old Law given through the mediation of angels or was it given directly by God?

It seems that the Old Law was given directly (*immediate*) by God and not through the mediation of angels (*per angelos*):

Objection 1: *Angel* means *messenger*, and so the name 'angel' implies ministry and not dominion—this according to Psalm 102:20–21 ("Bless the Lord, all you His angels . . . His ministers [*ministri*]"). But the Old Law is said to have been given by the Lord; for Exodus 20:1 says, "The Lord spoke these words . . ." and later adds, "For I am the Lord your God." And this same manner of speaking is frequently repeated in Exodus and in the succeeding books of the Law. Therefore, the Law was given directly by God.

Objection 2: As John 1:17 says, "The Law was given by Moses." But Moses received it directly from God; for Exodus 33:11 says, "The Lord spoke to Moses face to face, as a man is wont to speak to his friend." Therefore, the Old Law was given directly by God.

Objection 3: As was explained above (q. 90, a. 3), it is the role of the ruler alone to make law. But God alone is the ruler of the salvation of souls, whereas the angels are "ministering spirits," as Hebrews 1:14 puts it. Therefore, since the Old Law was ordered toward the salvation of souls, it was inappropriate for it to be given through the mediation of angels.

But contrary to this: In Galatians 3:19 the Apostle says, "The Law was given through the angels at the hand of a Mediator." Again, in Acts 7:53 Stephen says, "You have received the Law under the direction of angels."

I respond: The Law was given by God through the mediation of angels. In addition to the general reason that Dionysius gives in *De Caelesti Hierarchia*, chap. 4, viz., that "it is appropriate for divine realities to be brought to men by the mediation of angels," there is a special reason why the Old Law had to be given through the mediation of angels.

For it was explained above (aa. 1–2) that the Old Law was imperfect and yet disposed men for the perfect salvation of the human race that was going to come about through Christ. But it is evident in the case of all ordered powers and crafts that the one who ranks higher performs the principal and perfect act by himself, whereas it is through the mediation of his helpers (*per suos ministros*) that he does the things that dispose [the patient] for the ultimate perfection. For instance, a ship-builder puts the ship together by himself, but he prepares the materials through the mediation of his assistant craftsmen.

So it was fitting that the perfect law of the New Covenant should be given directly by God Himself made man, but that the Old Law should be given to men through the mediation of God's ministers, viz., the angels. And it is in this way that the Apostle, at the beginning of Hebrews, establishes the preeminence of the New Law over the Old Law; for in the New

Testament God "has spoken to us in His own Son," whereas in the Old Testament "His word was given through the angels."

Reply to objection 1: As Gregory notes at the beginning of *Moralia*, "The angel who is described as having appeared to Moses is variously called 'the angel' and 'the Lord'. He is called 'the angel' by reason of the fact that he served by speaking exteriorly, whereas he is called 'the Lord' because, presiding interiorly, he administered the power of speaking." Hence, the angel was also, as it were, speaking in the person of the Lord.

Reply to objection 2: As Augustine points out in *Super Genesim ad Litteram* 12, Exodus 33:11 says, "The Lord spoke to Moses face to face," and a little later adds, "Show me Your glory." Therefore, Moses was sensing what he saw and desiring what he did not see. Therefore, he did not see the very essence of God, and in this sense he was not directly instructed by God.

Therefore, when Scripture says, "He spoke to him 'face to face,'" it is speaking in accord with the opinion of the people, who thought that Moses and God were speaking with their mouths, because God was speaking to him and appearing to him through creatures subject to Him, i.e., through the angel and through the cloud.

An alternative reply is that "seeing God's face" refers to a certain pre-eminent and intimate contemplation that falls short of the vision of God's essence.

Reply to objection 3: It is the role of the ruler alone to institute law by his own authority, but he sometimes promulgates an instituted law through others. And so God instituted the Law by His own authority, but He promulgated it through the angels.

Article 4

Was it fitting for the Old Law to have been given only to the Jewish people?

It seems that the Old Law should not have been given only to the Jewish people (*soli populo Iudaeorum*):

Objection 1: As has been explained (aa. 2–3), the Old Law disposed men to the salvation that was to come through Christ. But this salvation was going to take place in all the nations (*in omnibus gentibus*) and not just among the Jews—this according to Isaiah 49:6 ("It is a small thing that you should be my servant to raise up the tribes of Jacob and to convert the dregs of Israel. Behold, I have given you to be the light of the Gentiles, that you may be my salvation even to the farthest part of the earth"). Therefore, the Old Law should have been given to all the nations and not just to one people.

Objection 2: As Acts 10:34 says, "God is not a respecter of persons (*acceptor personarum*), but in every nation, he who fears Him and does works of justice is acceptable to Him." Therefore, He should not have opened the way of salvation more to one people than to the others.

Objection 3: As has been explained (a. 3), the Law was given through angels. But God has always granted the ministry of the angels to all the nations and not just to the Jews; for Ecclesiasticus 17:14 says, "Over every nation He set a ruler." He likewise gave temporal goods to all the nations— and God is less concerned with temporal goods than with spiritual goods. Therefore, He should likewise have given the Law to all the peoples.

But contrary to this: Romans 3:1–2 says, "What advantage then does the Jew have? Much, in every way. First, because the words of God were committed to them." And Psalm 147:20 says, "He has not done thus for any other nation, and He has not made known His judgments to them."

I respond: One reason that could be invoked for why the Law was given to the Jewish people rather than to the other peoples is that while the others had fallen into idolatry, the Jewish people alone remained steadfast in the worship of the one God. And so the other peoples were unworthy to receive the Law, lest what is holy should be given to the dogs (cf. Matthew 7:6).

However, this argument seems inappropriate. For the Jewish people fell into idolatry even after the Law had been given—which was a more grievous sin, as is clear from Exodus 32 and from Amos 5:25–26 ("Did you offer victims and sacrifices to me in the desert for forty years, O house of Israel? But you carried a tabernacle for your Moloch and the image of your idols, the star of your god, which you made for yourselves.") Again, Deuteronomy 9:6 says explicitly, "Know that it is not because of your acts of justice that the Lord your God gives you this excellent land for your possession; for you are an utterly stiff-necked people."

Instead, the correct reason is given in the preceding verse: ". . . in order that the Lord might fulfill His word, which He promised by an oath to your fathers, Abraham, Isaac, and Jacob." In Galatians 3:16 the Apostle shows which promise had been made to them, saying, "To Abraham were the promises made and to his seed. He does not say, 'and to your seeds', as of many, but 'and to your seed', as of one, who is the Christ." Therefore, God gave the Law and other special benefits to that people because of the promise He had made to their fathers that the Christ would be born of them. For it was fitting that the people from whom the Christ would be born should be enriched with a special sanctification—this according to Leviticus 19:2 ("You will be holy, because I am holy").

Again, it was not because of the merits of Abraham himself that such a promise was made to him; rather, it was because he was gratuitously elected and called (*ex gratuita electione et vocatio*). Hence, Isaiah 41:2 says, "Who has raised up the just one from the East, has called him to follow Him?"

So, then, it is clear that the patriarchs received the promise solely because of a gratuitous election, and that the people that descended from them received the Law—this according to Deuteronomy 4:36–37 ("You heard His words out of the midst of the fire, because He loved your fathers, and chose their seed after them").

However, if one were to ask again why He chose this people in order that the Christ might be born from them, then the response that Augustine gives in *Super Ioannem* is the right one: "Why did he choose this one and not that one? Do not look for an answer, if you do not want to be mistaken."

Reply to objection 1: Even though the future salvation through the Christ had been prepared for all the nations, it was still necessary for the Christ to be born from one people, who because of this had prerogatives in preference to the others. Accordingly, Romans 9:4–5 says, ". . . to whom [read: the Jews] belongs the adoption as of children of God, and the testament and the giving of the Law . . . to whom belong the fathers and from whom comes the Christ, according to the flesh."

Reply to objection 2: Respect for persons or favoritism (*acceptio personarum*) is possible in the case of things that are given because they are [in some sense] owed, but there is no question of favoritism in the case of things that are conferred gratuitously. For one is not playing favorites if out of generosity he gives something of his own to one person and not to another. By contrast, if he were responsible for dispensing communal goods (*si esset dispensator bonorum communium*) and did not distribute them equitably according to the merits of the relevant persons, then he would be playing favorites.

Now it is out of His graciousness (*ex sua gratia*) that God confers salvific benefits on the human race. Hence, there is no favoritism if He confers these benefits on some in preference to others. This is why Augustine says in *De Praedestinatione Sanctorum*: "All those whom God instructs are such that it is by His mercy (*misericordia*) that He instructs them; and those whom He does not instruct are such that it is by His justice (*iudicium*) that He does not instruct them." For this stems from the condemnation of the human race because of the sin of the first parent.

Reply to objection 3: The gifts of grace are taken away from man because of sin, but his natural gifts are not taken away. Among the latter is the ministry of the angels, which is required by (a) the very ordering of natures, so that the lowest beings should be governed by middle-level beings, as well as by (b) the corporeal gifts that God grants not only to men but also to beasts—this according to Psalm 35:7 ("Men and beasts You will preserve, O Lord").

Article 5

Were all men obliged to observe the Old Law?

It seems that all men were obliged (*obligarentur*) to observe the Old Law:

Objection 1: Anyone who is subject to a king must be subject to that king's law. But the Old Law was given by God, who is "the king of all the earth," as Psalm 46:8 puts it. Therefore, all the inhabitants of the earth were obliged (*tenebantur*) to observe the Law.

Objection 2: The Jews were unable to be saved unless they observed the Old Law; for Deuteronomy 27:26 says, "Cursed be he that abides not in the words of this Law, and fulfills them not in his works." Therefore, if other men were able to have been saved without observing the Old Law, then the Jews' situation would have been worse than that of other men.

Objection 3: Gentiles were admitted to the Judaic rites and to the observance of the Law; for Exodus 12:48 says, "If any stranger is willing to dwell among you, and to keep the Passover of the Lord, all his males shall first be circumcised, and then shall he celebrate it ritually, and he shall be like one that is born in the land." But it would not have made sense for the foreigners admitted by God's ordinance to observe the Law if they could have been saved without observing the Law. Therefore, no one was able to be saved unless he observed the Law.

But contrary to this: In *De Caelesti Hierarchia*, chap. 9, Dionysius says that many Gentiles were led to God by the angels. But it is clear that the Gentiles did not observe the Law. Therefore, some were able to be saved without observing the Law.

I respond: The Old Law made manifest the precepts of the law of nature and added certain precepts of its own.

Therefore, as regards the precepts of the law of nature that were contained in the Old Law, all men were obliged to observe the Old Law—not because these precepts belonged to the Old Law, but because they belonged to the law of nature.

However, as regards what the Old Law added to the law of nature, the only ones obliged to observe the Old Law were the Jewish people. The reason for this is that, as has been explained (a. 4), the Old Law was given to the Jewish people in order that they might acquire a certain privilege of holiness out of reverence for the Christ, who was to born of that people. But statutes established for the special sanctification of certain people oblige no one but them. For instance, clerics, who are set aside for divine ministry, have certain obligations that lay people do not have; similarly, religious are bound by their profession to certain works of perfection that seculars are not bound to. In the same way, the Jewish people had certain special obligations that other peoples did not have. Hence, Deuteronomy 18:13 says, "You shall be perfect and without stain before the Lord your God." It is for this reason that they made use of a type of profession, as is clear from Deuteronomy 26:3 ("I profess this day before the Lord your God . . .").

Reply to objection 1: If someone is subject to a king's rule, then he is obliged to observe the law that the king proposes for everyone in general. But if the king institutes certain laws to be observed by his closest ministers, then the others are not obliged to observe these laws.

Reply to objection 2: The more a man is conjoined to God, the better his situation becomes. And so to the extent that the Jewish people were bound more closely to the worship of God, they were better off than other peoples. Hence, Deuteronomy 4:8 asks, "What other nation is there so renowned that has ceremonies, and just judgments, and the whole of the Law?" Similarly, on this score clerics are in a better situation than lay people, and religious are in a better situation than seculars.

Reply to objection 3: Gentiles attained salvation more completely and more surely under the observances of the Old Law than under the natural law alone, and that is why they were admitted to these observances. So, too, even now lay people pass into the clerical state and seculars pass into the religious state, even though they can be saved without doing this.

Article 6

Was it appropriate for the Old Law to have been given at the time of Moses?

It seems that it was not appropriate for the Old Law to have been given at the time of Moses:

Objection 1: As was explained above (aa. 2–3), the Old Law disposed man for the salvation that was to come through the Christ. But man needed the remedy of this sort of salvation immediately after his sin. Therefore, the Old Law should have been given immediately after his sin.

Objection 2: The Old Law was given for the salvation of those from whom the Christ was going to be born. But as Genesis 12:7 says, the promise concerning "the seed, i.e., Christ" (cf. Galatians 3:16), was first made to Abraham. Therefore, the Law should have been given right away at the time of Abraham.

Objection 3: Just as Christ was not born of any descendants of Noah other than Abraham, to whom the promise was made, so too He was not born of any sons of Abraham other than David, to whom the promise was renewed—this according to 2 Kings 23:1 ("The man to whom it was appointed concerning the Christ of the God of Jacob said . . ."). Therefore, the Old Law should have been given after David, just as it was in fact given after Abraham.

But contrary to this: In Galatians 3:19 the Apostle says, "The Law was set because of transgressions, until the seed should come to whom He made the promise, being ordained by angels in the hand of a Mediator"— i.e., "being given in an orderly way," as the Gloss puts it. Therefore, it was fitting for the Old Law to have been handed down in that particular temporal order.

I respond: It was utterly appropriate for the Old Law to have been given at the time of Moses. We can cite two reasons for this, given that there are two kinds of men on whom any law, whatever it might be, is imposed. For some of those on whom a law is imposed are stubborn and proud, and these men are restrained and subdued by the law; and a law is also imposed on those who are good, and these men, instructed by the law, are aided in fulfilling what they intend.

Therefore, it was fitting for the Old Law to be given at a time appropriate for conquering men's pride. Man is proud with respect to two things, viz., knowledge and power. He is proud with respect to knowledge in the sense of thinking that natural reason can suffice for his salvation. So in order that man's pride on this score might be conquered, he was left to the guidance of his own reason without the support of a written law, and man was able to learn that he suffered from deficiencies of reason—and he learned this from experience, in virtue of the fact that by the time of Abraham men had fallen into idolatry and into the most shameful vices. And so it was necessary for the written Law to be given after that time as a remedy for human ignorance; for as Romans 3:20 says, "The knowledge of sin comes through the Law."

But after man had been instructed through the Law, his pride was conquered in his weakness (*infirmitas*), when he was unable to fulfill the Law which he now knew. And so, as the Apostle concludes in Romans 8:3–4, "What the Law, weakened by the flesh, was powerless to do, this God has done by sending his own Son . . . so that the righteous decree of the law might be fulfilled in us."

On the other hand, as far as the good men are concerned, the Law was given to assist them. This was especially necessary for the people at a time when the Law had begun to be obscured because of the excesses of their sins. However, assistance of this sort had to be given in a certain order, so that they might be led by the hand through what was imperfect to perfection. And so the Old Law had to be given in the time between the law of nature and the law of grace.

Reply to objection 1: It was not fitting for the Old Law to be given immediately after the sin of the first man, both because man, confident in his own power of reason, did not yet recognize his need for the Law, and also because the dictates of the law of nature had not yet been obscured by habitual sinning.

Reply to objection 2: The Law should be given only to a people, since, as was explained above (q. 96, a. 1), a law is a communal precept (*praeceptum commune*). And so certain of God's familial and, as it were, domestic precepts were given to men at the time of Abraham. But afterwards, when Abraham's posterity had multiplied to such an extent as to constitute a people and had been liberated from slavery, the Law could appropriately be given. For as the Philosopher says in *Politics* 3, slaves are not part of a people or political community, and it is to a people or political community that law is appropriately given.

Reply to objection 3: Since it was necessary for the Law to be given to a certain people, the Law was received not only by those individuals from whom Christ was born but by the whole people marked with the seal of circumcision, which was the sign of the promise made to Abraham and believed in by him, as the Apostle puts it in Romans 4:11. And so the Law had to be given to this people, now already gathered together, even before David.

QUESTION 99

The Precepts of the Old Law

We next have to consider the precepts of the Old Law—first, the distinction among the precepts (question 99) and, second, each of the distinct types of precepts (questions 100–105).

On the first topic there are six questions: (1) Does the Old Law contain many precepts or just one precept? (2) Does the Old Law contain any moral precepts? (3) Does the Old Law contain ceremonial precepts in addition to the moral precepts? (4) Does the Old Law contain judicial precepts in addition to the moral and ceremonial precepts? (5) Does the Old Law contain any type of precept besides these three? (6) How did the Old Law induce the observance of these precepts?

Article 1

Does the Old Law contain just one precept ?

It seems that the Old Law contains only one precept (*praeceptum*):

Objection 1: As was established above (q. 92, a. 2), a law is nothing other than a precept. But the Old Law is a single law. Therefore, it contains only one precept.

Objection 2: In Romans 13:9 the Apostle says, "If there is any other commandment, it is comprised in this word: 'You shall love your neighbor as yourself'." But this is a single commandment (*mandatum*). Therefore, the Old Law contains only one commandment.

Objection 3: Matthew 7:12 says, "All things whatsoever you would that men should do to you, do you also to them; for this is the Law and the prophets." But the whole of the Old Law is contained in the Law and the prophets. Therefore, the whole of the Old Law contains just one precept.

But contrary to this: In Ephesians 2:15 the Apostle says, ". . . making void the Law of commandments contained in decrees." And he is talking about the Old Law, as is clear from the Gloss on this same passage. Therefore, the Old Law contains many commandments within itself.

I respond: Since a precept of the law is obligatory, it concerns something that ought to be done. But the fact that something ought to be done stems from its being necessary for some end. Hence, it is clearly part of the notion of a precept that it implies an ordering to an end, insofar as what is commanded is necessary or expedient for that end.

Now it is possible for a single end to be such that many things are necessary or expedient for it. Accordingly, precepts can be given with respect to different things insofar as they are ordered to a single end. Hence, one should claim that (a) all the precepts of the Old Law are one insofar as they are ordered to a single end, and yet that (b) they are many because of the diversity of the things that are ordered to that end.

Reply to objection 1: The Old Law is called a single law because it is ordered to a single end, and yet it contains diverse precepts because of the distinction among the things that are ordered to that end. Similarly, the craft of building is a single craft because of the oneness of its end, since it aims at building a house; and yet it contains diverse precepts because of the diversity of the acts that are ordered to this end.

Reply to objection 2: As the Apostle says in 1 Timothy 1:5, "The goal of the precept is charity." For every law aims at establishing the friendship either of men with one another or of man with God. And so the whole of the Law is fulfilled in the single commandment, "You shall love your neighbor as yourself," taken as the goal of all the commandments. For the love of God is also included in the love of neighbor when the neighbor is loved because of God. Hence, the Apostle used this one precept in place of the two precepts which have to do with the love of God and the love of neighbor and about which our Lord says in Matthew 22:40, "On these two commandments depend the whole Law and the prophets."

Reply to objection 3: As *Ethics* 9 puts it, "The friendly acts directed toward another proceed from the friendly acts that a man directs toward himself," viz., as long as the man is related to the other in the same way that he is related to himself. And so when it says, "All things whatsoever you would that men should do to you, do you also to them," a certain rule for the love of neighbor, implicitly contained in "You shall love your neighbor as yourself," is being explicated. Hence, it is a sort of explication of that commandment.

Article 2

Does the Old Law contain moral precepts?

It seems that the Old Law does not contain any moral precepts:

Objection 1: As was established above (q. 91, aa. 4–5), the Old Law is distinct from the law of nature. But moral precepts belong to the law of nature. Therefore, they do not belong to the Old Law.

Objection 2: Divine law was supposed to assist men in cases where human reason is deficient; this is clear with those things pertaining to the Faith that lie beyond human reason. But man's reason seems to be sufficient for moral precepts. Therefore, moral precepts are not part of the Old Law, which is a type of divine law.

Objection 3: The Old Law is called "the letter that kills," as is clear from 2 Corinthians 3:6. But moral precepts give life and do not kill—this according to Psalm 118:93 ("I will never forget Your precepts (*iustificationes*), because in them You give me life.") Therefore, no moral precepts belong to the Old Law.

But contrary to this: Ecclesiasticus 17:9 says, "He gave them discipline and the law of life for an inheritance." But 'discipline' (*disciplina*) pertains to morals, since the Gloss on Hebrews 12:11 ("Every chastisement [*disciplina*] . . .") says, "Discipline involves the learning of morals through difficulties." Therefore, the Law given by God contained moral precepts.

I respond: As is clear from Exodus 20:13 and 15 ("You shall not kill. . . . You shall not steal"), the Old Law contained certain moral precepts. And this makes sense. For just as the main intention of human law is to establish the friendship of men with one another, so too the intention of divine law is mainly to establish man's friendship with God. Now since, according to Ecclesiasticus 13:19 ("Every beast loves its like"), likeness is a reason for love, it is impossible for there to be friendship between man and God, who is absolutely good, unless men are made good. Hence, Leviticus 19:2 says, "You will be holy, for I am holy." But the goodness of a man is virtue, which makes the one who has it good. And so precepts of the Old Law had by all means to be given concerning the acts of the virtues. And these are the moral precepts of the Law.

Reply to objection 1: The Old Law is distinguished from the law of nature not in the sense of being altogether different from it, but in the sense of adding something to it. For just as grace presupposes nature, so too divine law must presuppose the natural law.

Reply to objection 2: It was appropriate for divine law to provide for man not only in those matters for which reason is insufficient, but also in those matters concerning which man's reason can be impeded. Now as far as the moral precepts are concerned, man's reason cannot be mistaken about the universal principle in the case of the most general precepts of the law of nature, but it can nonetheless, because of habitual sinning, be blinded with respect to particular actions. On the other hand, there are many whose reason goes awry with respect to those other moral precepts that are like conclusions deduced from the most general precepts of the law of nature, with the result that many people are such that their reason judges as permissible things that are evil in themselves (*mala secundum se*). Hence, man had to be given assistance, through the authority of divine law, against both kinds of error.

Similarly, in order to prevent the error of human reason that was occurring with many people, the things proposed to us for acceptance by faith (*credenda*) include not only some that reason cannot attain to, e.g., that God is three, but also some that right reason can attain to, e.g., that there is one God.

Reply to objection 3: As Augustine shows in *De Spiritu et Littera*, the letter of the law can be an occasion of 'killing' even in the case of the moral precepts, viz., insofar as it commands what is good without offering the assistance of grace to fulfill what it commands.

Article 3

Does the Old Law contain ceremonial precepts in addition to the moral precepts?

It seems that the Old Law does not contain ceremonial precepts in addition to the moral precepts:

Objection 1: Every law that is given to men directs human acts. But as was explained above (q. 1, a. 3), human acts are called moral acts. Therefore, it seems that the Old Law given to men should have contained only moral precepts.

Objection 2: Precepts called 'ceremonial' seem to pertain to divine worship. But divine worship is an act of one of the virtues, viz., the virtue of religion, which, as Tully says in *Rhetorica*, "offers worship and ceremony to the divine nature." Therefore, since, as has been explained (a. 2), the moral precepts are concerned with the acts of the virtues, it seems that the ceremonial precepts should not be distinguished from the moral precepts.

Objection 3: The precepts that seem to be ceremonial are those which signify something in a figurative way. But as Augustine says in *De*

Doctrina Christiana 2, "Among men it is words that have attained preeminence in signifying." Therefore, there was no need for the Law to contain ceremonial precepts concerned with certain figurative actions.

But contrary to this: Deuteronomy 4:13–14 says, "Ten words He wrote in two tables of stone, and He commanded me at that time that I should teach you the ceremonies and judgments which you shall do." But the ten percepts of the Law are moral precepts. Therefore, besides the moral precepts there are also distinct ceremonial precepts.

I respond: As has been explained (a. 2), divine law is instituted mainly to order men toward God, whereas human law is instituted mainly to order men toward one another.

So human laws have concerned themselves with divine worship only in relation to the common good of men, and for this reason they have also concocted many things about divine matters insofar as this seemed expedient to them for the shaping of human morals; this is clear in the rites of the Gentiles.

By contrast, divine law ordered men toward one another insofar as this was consonant with their being ordered toward God—which is what divine law was mainly concerned with. Now man is ordered toward God not only through interior mental acts, i.e., acts of faith, hope, and love (*credere, sperare et amare*), but also through the exterior acts by which man professes his submission (*servitudo*) to God. And these acts are said to pertain to the worship of God.

According to some, this worship is called 'ceremony' (*caeremonia*) from the *munia*, i.e., gifts, of Ceres (*Caeres*), who was called the goddess of fruits, because they first offered oblations to God from their fruits. An alternative explanation is that, as Valerius Maximus claims, the name 'ceremony' was introduced to signify divine worship among the Latins because of a certain town near Rome called 'Caere'; for when Rome was captured by the Gauls, the sacred artifacts of the Romans were taken there and reverently preserved. So, then, the precepts in the Law that are concerned with the worship of God are specifically called *ceremonial* precepts.

Reply to objection 1: Human acts also extend to divine worship, and so the Old Law given to men contains precepts concerning these acts as well.

Reply to objection 2: As was explained above (q. 91, a. 3), the precepts of the law of nature are general and stand in need of specification. They are specified both by human law and by divine law. And just as the specifications that are made by human law are themselves said to belong not to the law of nature but to positive law instead, so too the specifications of the precepts of the law of nature that are made by divine law are distinguished from the moral precepts that belong to the law of nature.

Therefore, since *worshipping God* is an act of virtue, it has to do with a *moral* precept; however, the *specification* of this precept—viz., that God should be worshiped with such-and-such sacrifices and such-and-such gifts—belongs to the *ceremonial* precepts. And it is in this way that the ceremonial precepts are distinguished from the moral precepts.

Reply to objection 3: In *De Caelesti Hierarchia*, chap. 1 Dionysius says that divine realities cannot be made manifest to men except under certain sensible likenesses. But these likenesses move the soul more when they are not only expressed in words but also proffered to the senses. And so divine realities are handed down in Scripture not only through likenesses expressed in words, but also through likenesses of things that are proposed to sight—and this is what the ceremonial precepts are concerned with.

Article 4

Does the Old Law contain judicial precepts in addition to the moral and ceremonial precepts?

It seems that the Old Law does not contain any judicial precepts in addition to the moral and ceremonial precepts:

Objection 1: In *Contra Faustum* Augustine says that in the Old Law "there are precepts that have to do with living life and precepts that have to do with signifying life." But the precepts that have to do with living life are the moral precepts, whereas the precepts that have to do with signifying life are the ceremonial precepts. Therefore, one should not posit distinct judicial precepts in the law over and beyond these two types of precepts.

Objection 2: The Gloss on Psalm 118:102 ("I have not turned from your judgments") says, "That is, I have not turned from what you have set up as a rule for living." But a rule for living pertains to the moral precepts. Therefore, the judicial precepts should not be distinguished from the moral precepts.

Objection 3: Judgment seems to be an act of justice—this according to Psalm 93:15 ("Until justice is turned into judgment"). But acts of justice, like acts of the other virtues, have to do with the moral precepts. Therefore, the moral precepts include the judicial precepts within themselves and so should not be distinguished from them.

But contrary to this: Deuteronomy 6:1 says, "These are the precepts and ceremonies and judgments." But 'precepts' refers antonomastically to the moral precepts. Therefore, in addition to the moral and ceremonial precepts there are also judicial precepts.

I respond: As has been explained (a. 2), it is the function of divine law to order men to one another and to God. Both of these functions belong in a general way to the dictates of the law of nature, which the moral precepts are concerned with, but both must be specified by divine law or human law. For in speculative matters as well as in practical matters (*tam in speculativis quam in activis*) the naturally known principles are general. Therefore, just as the specification of the general precept regarding divine worship is accomplished through the ceremonial precepts, so too the specification of the general precept of justice that must be observed among men is specified through the judicial precepts.

Accordingly, one must posit three types of precepts in the Old Law, viz., (a) the *moral* precepts, which have to do with the dictates of the law of nature, (b) the *ceremonial* precepts, which are specifications of divine worship, and (c) the *judicial* precepts, which are specifications of the justice that is to be observed among men. Hence, in Romans 7:12, after having claimed that "the law is holy," the Apostle adds, "The commandment is just and holy and good" (*iustum et sanctum et bonum*)—'just' with respect to the judicial precepts, 'holy' with respect to the ceremonial precepts (for 'holy' means what has been dedicated to God), and 'good', i.e., 'noble' (*honestum*), with respect to the moral precepts.

Reply to objection 1: Both the moral precepts and the judicial precepts have to do with directing human life. And they are both contained under one of the disjuncts Augustine posits, viz., under 'precepts that have to do with living life'.

Reply to objection 2: 'Judgment' signifies the execution of justice, which consists in the application of reason in a determinate way to particular actions. Hence, the judicial precepts share something in common with the moral precepts, viz., being derived from reason, and something in common with the ceremonial precepts, viz., being specifications of general precepts. And this is why the judicial and moral precepts are sometimes included together under 'judgments', as in Deuteronomy 5:1 ("Hear, O Israel, the ceremonies and judgments . . ."), while at other times it is the judicial and ceremonial precepts that are included together under 'judg-ments', as in Leviticus 18:4, "You shall do my judgments, and shall observe my precepts"—where 'precepts' refers to the moral precepts and 'judgments' refers to the judicial and ceremonial precepts.

Reply to objection 3: An act of justice, taken in general, pertains to the moral precepts, whereas the specification of that act as a particular per-tains to the judicial precepts.

Article 5

Are there any precepts contained in the Old Law in addition to the moral, ceremonial, and judicial precepts?

It seems that there are precepts contained in the Old Law in addition to the moral, ceremonial, and judicial precepts:

Objection 1: The judicial precepts have to do with the act of justice, which is between man and man, whereas the ceremonial precepts have to do with the act of religion, by which God is worshipped. But as was explained above (q. 60, a. 5), there are many other virtues besides these two, e.g., temperance, fortitude, generosity, and lots of others. Therefore, the Old Law contains many other precepts in addition to those mentioned above.

Objection 2: Deuteronomy 11:1 says, "Love the Lord your God and observe His precepts and ceremonies, His judgments and mandates." But as has been explained (a. 4), 'precepts' (*praecepta*) refers here to the moral precepts. Therefore, besides the moral, judicial, and ceremonial precepts, there are still other precepts contained in the Law, and these are called 'mandates' (*mandata*).

Objection 3: Deuteronomy 6:17 says, "Keep the precepts of the Lord your God, and the testimonies and ceremonies which I have commanded you." Therefore, in addition to all the other precepts mentioned above, there are also testimonies (*testimonia*) contained in the Law.

Objection 4: Psalm 118:93 says, "I will never forget Your justifica-tions (*iustificationes*)." Therefore, the precepts of the Old Law include not only the moral, ceremonial, and judicial precepts, but justifications as well.

But contrary to this: Deuteronomy 6:1 says: "Here are the precepts, and ceremonies, and judgments which the Lord your God commanded you." And these three are set forth at the beginning of the Law. Therefore, all the precepts of the Law are included in them.

I respond: Certain things are posited in the Law as precepts, whereas others are posited as ordered toward the fulfillment of the precepts. The precepts concern things that are to be done. For the fulfillment of these precepts man has two inducements, viz., (a) the authority of the one commanding and (b) the advantage associated with the fulfillment, i.e., the acquisition of some useful, pleasurable, or noble good, or the avoidance of some contrary evil.

Therefore, certain things had to be proposed in the Old Law which would indicate the authority of God commanding, e.g., Deuteronomy 6:4 ("Hear, O Israel, the Lord God your God is one") and Genesis 1:1 ("In the beginning God created the heaven and the earth"). These are called *testimonies* (*testimonia*).

Again, certain things had to be proposed as rewards for those who observed the law and punishments for those who transgressed it, as is clear from Deuteronomy 28:1 ("If you will listen to the voice of the Lord your God, He will make you higher than all the nations . . ."). And these are called *justifications* (*iustificationes*), insofar as God justly punishes some or rewards others.

Now things that are to be done fall under a precept only insofar as they have something of the character of what is owed. But there are two kinds of debts, one having to do with the rule of reason and the other having to do with the rule of a specifying law—just as the Philosopher in *Ethics* 5 distinguishes two modes of the just, viz., the morally just and the legally just.

There are two kinds of moral debts. For reason dictates that a thing is to be done either (a) as something necessary, without which the order of virtue cannot exist, or (b) as something useful for preserving the order of virtue in a better way. Accordingly, certain things pertaining to what is moral are either precisely commanded or precisely forbidden in the Law— e.g., "You shall not kill" and "You shall not steal." And these are called *precepts* (*praecepta*) in the proper sense. On the other hand, certain things are commanded or forbidden not as precisely owed, but for the sake of what is better. And these can be called *mandates* (*mandata*), since they contain a certain inducement and persuasiveness—e.g., Exodus 22:26 ("If you take a garment from your neighbor in pledge, you should return it to him before sunset") and others of this sort. This is why Jerome says that there is justice in the precepts and charity in the mandates.

Now debts arising from a specification of law have to do with the judicial precepts in human matters and with the ceremonial precepts in divine matters—although those having to do with punishments and rewards can also be called testimonies, insofar as they are declarations of divine justice. On the other hand, all the precepts of the Law can be called justifications, insofar as they are executions of legal justice.

In addition, there is an alternative way to distinguish mandates from precepts, viz., what are called precepts are such that God issues them through Himself, whereas mandates are such that He gives them through others, as the name 'mandate' seems to suggest.

From all of this it is clear that all the precepts of the Law are included among the moral, ceremonial, and judicial precepts, whereas the other things do not have the character of precepts, but instead, as has been explained, are ordered toward the observance of the precepts.

Reply to objection 1: Justice alone, among the other virtues, implies the notion of what is owed. And so the moral is specifiable by law to the extent that it pertains to justice, a certain part of which is religion, as Tully says. Hence, legal justice cannot include anything except the ceremonial precepts and judicial precepts.

Reply to objection 2 and objection 3 and objection 4: The replies to the other objections are clear from what has been said.

Article 6

Was it right for the Old Law to have induced the observance of its precepts by temporal promises and threats?

It seems that it was not right for the Old Law to have induced observance of its precepts by temporal promises and threats:

Objection 1: The intention behind divine law is that men should submit to God through fear and love; hence, Deuteronomy 10:12 says, "And now, Israel, what does the Lord your God require of you, but that you fear the Lord your God, and walk in His ways, and love Him?" But a passionate desire (*cupiditas*) for temporal things leads one away from God; for in *83 Quaestiones* Augustine says, "Passionate desire is poison with respect to charity." Therefore, temporal promises and threats seem to be contrary to the lawmaker's intention—and this renders a law worthy of condemnation, as is clear from the Philosopher in *Politics* 2.

Objection 2: Divine law is more excellent than human law. But we see that among the sciences, a given science is higher to the extent that it proceeds by means of higher middle terms. Therefore, since human law tries to induce men by temporal threats and promises, it was not right for divine law to proceed in this way; instead, it should have proceeded by means of something loftier.

Objection 3: What happens indifferently to good men and bad men cannot be the reward for justice or the punishment for sin. But as Ecclesiastes 9:2 says, "All things equally happen to the just and to the wicked, to the good and to the evil, to the clean and to the unclean, to him that offers victims of sacrifice and to him that despises sacrifices." Therefore, temporal goods or evils are not appropriately used as the rewards or punishments attached to the commandments of divine law.

But contrary to this: Isaiah 1:19–20 says, "If you are willing and listen to me, you shall eat the good things of the land. But if you are unwilling and provoke me to anger, the sword shall devour you."

I respond: Just as in the speculative sciences men are induced to assent to the conclusions by means of syllogistic middle terms, so too in the case of all laws men are induced to observe the precepts by means of punishments and rewards. Now we see in the case of the speculative sciences that the middle terms are proposed to the hearer in a way corresponding to his condition. Hence, in the sciences one must proceed in an orderly fashion so that learning might begin with things that are better known. So, too, one who wishes to induce a man to the observance of the precepts must begin to move him by appealing to things he has an affection for; for instance, children are enticed into doing things by childish treats.

Now it was explained above (q. 98, aa. 1–3) that the Old Law disposed men for the Christ in the way that something imperfect disposes one for something perfect. Hence, the Old Law was given to a people still imperfect in comparison with the perfection that was to come through the Christ, and so, as is clear from Galatians 3:24, this people was comparable to a child who is under the tutelage of a teacher. Now man's perfection consists in his adhering to spiritual things while holding temporal things in contempt, as is clear from what the Apostle says in Philippians 3:13 and 15 ("Forgetting the things that are behind and stretching forth myself to those that are before. . . . Let us therefore, as many as are perfect, be thus minded.") And the mark of imperfect men is that they desire temporal things and yet in relation to God, whereas the mark of corrupt men is that they set up temporal goods as their end. Hence, it was fitting that it should be through temporal things, which imperfect men had an affection for, that the Old Law led men to God.

Reply to objection 1: The passionate desire by which a man sets up temporal goods as his end is poison with respect to charity. But the pursuit of temporal goods that a man desires in relation to God is a sort of path that leads the imperfect to love God—this according to Psalm 48:19 ("He will praise You when You are good to him.")

Reply to objection 2: Human law induces men by temporal rewards or punishments that are to be delivered by men, whereas divine law induces men by rewards or punishments that are to be given by God. And it is in this way that divine law proceeds through more lofty middle terms.

Reply to objection 3: As is clear to one who reflects on the stories in the Old Testament, the general situation of the people under the Law was always prosperous as long as they observed the law, and as soon as they turned away from the precepts of the Law, they fell into many adversities. But some particular people, even while observing the justice of the Laws, fell into adversities, either because (a) they had already become spiritual, so that through this adversity they were drawn even further away from an affection for temporal things and their virtue was proved, or because (b) while fulfilling the exterior works of the Law, they had fixed their hearts wholly on temporal things and had separated their hearts from God—this according to Isaiah 29:13 ("This people honors me with their lips, but their heart is far from me").

QUESTION 100

The Moral Precepts of the Old Law

We next have to consider each of the types of precept in the Old Law—first, the moral precepts (question 100); second, the ceremonial precepts (questions 101–103); and third, the judicial precepts (questions 104–105).

On the first topic there are twelve questions: (1) Do all the moral precepts of the Old Law belong to the law of nature? (2) Do the moral precepts of the Old Law have to do with the acts of all the virtues? (3) Are all the moral precepts of the Old Law traced back to the ten precepts of the Decalogue? (4) What about the way in which the precepts of the Decalogue are distinguished? (5) What about the number of precepts? (6) What about their order? (7) What about the way in which they are set down? (8) Is it possible to be dispensed from the precepts of the Decalogue? (9) Does the mode of practicing a virtue fall under a precept? (10) Does the mode of charity fall under a precept? (11) How are the other moral precepts distinguished? (12) Do the moral precepts of the Old Law give justification [before God]?

Article 1

Do all the moral precepts of the Old Law belong to the law of nature?

It seems that not all the moral precepts [of the Old Law] belong to the law of nature:

Objection 1: Ecclesiasticus 17:9 says, "He gave them teaching, and the law of life for an inheritance." But teaching (*doctrina*) is distinct from the law of nature, since the law of nature is not taught, but is instead had by natural instinct (*ex naturali instinctu*). Therefore, not all the moral precepts [of the Old Law] belong to the law of nature.

Objection 2: Divine law is more perfect than human law. But human law adds some things pertaining to good morals to what belongs to the law of nature; this is clear from the fact that the law of nature is the same for everyone, whereas diverse moral practices have been instituted among diverse peoples. Therefore, *a fortiori*, it was fitting for divine law to add some things pertaining to good morals over and beyond the law of nature.

Objection 3: Just as reason induces men to good morals, so too does faith; hence, Galatians 5:6 says, "Faith works through love" (*per dilectionem*). But faith is not included in the law of nature, since what belongs to the Faith lies beyond natural reason. Therefore, not all the moral precepts of divine law belong to the law of nature.

But contrary to this: In Romans 2:14 the Apostle says, "The Gentiles, who have not the Law, do by nature those things that are of the Law." This has to be understood as referring to things that have to do with good morals. Therefore, all the moral precepts of the Law belong to the law of nature.

I respond: The moral precepts—as opposed to the ceremonial and judicial precepts—concern things that in their own right (*secundum se*) have to do with good morals.

Now since human morals are set apart by their relation to reason, which is the proper principle of human acts, morals are called good when they are consonant with reason and bad when they are at variance with reason. And just as every judgment of speculative reason stems from the natural cognition of first principles, so too, as was explained above (q. 94, a. 2), every judgment of practical reason stems from naturally known principles on the basis of which one can proceed to make judgments in various ways about various matters.

For instance, among human acts there are some so clear that they can immediately, with very little consideration, be approved of or disapproved of on the basis of these general first principles.

By contrast, there are others such that judging them requires an extensive consideration of various circumstances that only the wise, and not just anyone, can carefully investigate—in the way that the role of investigating the particular conclusions of the sciences falls only to the philosophers and not to just anyone.

Lastly, there are some acts such that in order for a man to pass judgment on them, he needs to be assisted by divine teaching. This is the case with the things that have to be taken on faith (*credenda*).

So, then, it is clear that since (a) the moral precepts concern matters that belong to good morals, and (b) these good morals are consonant with reason, and (c) every one of human reason's judgments stems in some way or other from natural reason, it must be the case that all the moral precepts belong to the law of nature—though in different ways.

For some precepts are such that every man's natural reason judges immediately and *per se* that such-and-such should be done or should not be done, e.g., "Honor your father and your mother," "You shall not kill," and "You shall not steal" (Exodus 20:12–15). Precepts of this sort belong to the law of nature absolutely speaking.

But other precepts are such that it is the wise who, after a more subtle investigation by reason, judge that they should be observed. And these precepts belong to the law of nature, but in such a way that they require the sort of teaching by which the young are instructed by the wise—e.g., "Stand up in the presence of a hoary head, and honor the elderly person" (Leviticus 19:32), and others of this sort.

Finally, there are other precepts such that in order to make a judgment about them, human reason needs divine instruction, through which we learn about divine things, e.g., "You shall not make for yourself a graven image, nor any likeness . . . nor shall you take the name of your God in vain" (Exodus 20:4,7).

Reply to objection 1 and objection 2 and objection 3: The replies to the objections are clear from has been said.

Article 2

Do the moral precepts of the Law have to do with all the acts of the virtues?

It seems that the precepts of the Law do not have to do with all the acts of the virtues:

Objection 1: The observance of the precepts of the Old Law is called 'justification'—this according to Psalm 118:8 ("I will keep Your justifications"). But a justification is an execution of justice. Therefore, the moral precepts have to do only with acts of justice.

Objection 2: Whatever falls under a precept has the character of something owed (*debitum*). But the character of what is owed belongs not to the other virtues but only to justice, whose proper act is to render to each person what is owed to him. Therefore, the moral precepts of the Law have to do only with acts of justice and not with acts of the other virtues.

Objection 3: As Isidore says, every law is made for the common good. But as the Philosopher points out in *Ethics* 5, among the virtues it is only justice that has to do with the common good. Therefore, the moral precepts have to do only with acts of justice.

But contrary to this: Ambrose says, "Sin is a transgression of divine law and disobedience against the heavenly commandments." But all the acts of the virtues are such that sins are opposed to them. Therefore, divine law has to give directives about the acts of all the virtues.

I respond: Since, as has been established (q. 90, a. 2), the precepts of the Law are ordered toward the common good, the precepts of the Law must be distinguished in a way corresponding to the different types of communities. Hence, in his *Politics* the Philosopher teaches that in a city ruled by a king it is necessary to establish laws different from those established in a city ruled by the people or by certain people who are in charge of the city.

Now the type of community to which human law is ordered is different from that toward which divine law is ordered. For human law is ordered toward the civil community (*ad communitatem civilem*), which is a community of men with respect to each other. Now men are ordered toward one another through the exterior acts by which men share a common life (*communicant*) with one another, and it is a common life of this sort that is relevant to the nature of justice, which properly directs the human community. And so human law proposes precepts having to do only with acts of justice; and, as is clear from the Philosopher in *Ethics* 5, if human law commands acts of the other virtues, this is so only to the extent that those acts take on the character of justice.

By contrast, the community directed by divine law is the community of men with God, whether in the present life or in the future life. And so divine law sets forth precepts having to do with all the things through which men are well-ordered toward their common life with God (*ad communicationem cum Deo*). Now man is joined to God by his reason (*ratio*), or mind (*mens*), in which the image of God resides. And so divine law sets forth precepts having to do with all the things through which man's reason is well-ordered. But this ordering occurs through the acts of all the virtues; for the intellectual virtues render acts of reason well-ordered in themselves, whereas the moral virtues render the acts of reason well-ordered with respect to interior passions and exterior operations. And so it is clearly fitting for divine law to set forth precepts having to do with the acts of all the virtues—yet in such a way that those acts without which the order of virtue (i.e., the order of reason) cannot be maintained fall under the obligation of a *precept*, whereas others that have to do with the flourishing of perfect virtue (*bene esse virtutis perfectae*) fall under the admonition of a *counsel*.

Reply to objection 1: The fulfillment of the commandments of the Law, even of those commandments having to do with the acts of the other virtues, has the character of justification insofar as it is just that man should obey God—or, alternatively, insofar as it is just that everything having to do with man should be subject to reason.

Reply to objection 2: Justice, properly speaking, has to do with what one man owes to another (*debitum unius hominis ad alium*), whereas with all the other virtues there is a 'debt' (*debitum*) that the lower powers owe to reason. And corresponding to the notion of this latter sort of debt, the Philosopher in *Ethics* 5 speaks of a sort of metaphorical justice.

Reply to objection 3: The reply to the third objection is clear from what has been said about the different kinds of community.

Article 3

Are all the moral precepts of the Old Law traced back to the ten precepts of the Decalogue?

It seems that not all the moral precepts of the Old Law are traced back to (*reducantur*) the ten precepts of the Decalogue:

Objection 1: As Matthew 22:37,39 puts it, the first and principal precepts of the Law are "You shall love the Lord your God" and "You shall love your neighbor." But these two precepts are not contained in the precepts of the Decalogue. Therefore, not all the moral precepts are contained in the precepts of the Decalogue.

Objection 2: The moral precepts are not traced back to the ceremonial precepts, but rather vice versa. But among the precepts of the Decalogue there is one ceremonial precept, viz., "Remember to keep holy the Sabbath day" (Exodus 20:8). Therefore, the moral precepts are not traced back to all the precepts of the Decalogue.

Objection 3: The moral precepts have to do with all the acts of the virtues. But only precepts having to do with acts of justice are found among the precepts of the Decalogue—as is clear from running through them one by one. Therefore, the precepts of the Decalogue do not contain all the moral precepts.

But contrary to this: The Gloss on Matthew 5:11 ("Blessed are you when they shall revile you . . .") says, "After Moses had proposed the ten precepts, he afterwards explained them through their parts (*per partes*)." Therefore, all the precepts of the Law are, as it were, parts of the precepts of the Decalogue.

I respond: The precepts of the Decalogue differ from the other precepts of the Law in the fact that the precepts of the Decalogue are such that God Himself (*Deus per seipsum*) is said to have presented them to the people, whereas He presented the other precepts to the people through Moses. Therefore, the precepts belonging to the Decalogue are those that man has knowledge of from God Himself. But these precepts include (a) the ones that can be known immediately, with very little reflection, on the basis of first general principles and, again, (b) the ones that are known immediately on the basis of divinely infused faith.

Therefore, there are two kinds of precepts that are not counted among the precepts of the Decalogue, viz., (a) precepts which are first general principles and which do not need to be made known (*editio*) in any way other than by being written in natural reason as something known *per se*, e.g., 'A man should not do evil to anyone' and others of this sort, and, again, (b) precepts that are found to be consonant with reason through the diligent inquiry of the wise, since these precepts come to the people from God through the teaching of the wise. Still, both of these sorts of precepts are contained in the precepts of the Decalogue, though in different ways. For the ones that are first general principles are contained in the precepts of the Decalogue in the way that principles are contained in their proximate conclusions, whereas, conversely, the ones that are known through the wise are contained in the precepts of the Decalogue in the way that conclusions are contained in their principles.

Reply to objection 1: The two precepts in question are first general precepts of the law of nature, and they are known *per se* to human reason, either by nature or by faith. And so all the precepts of the Decalogue are traced back to these two precepts in the way that conclusions are traced back to their general principles.

Reply to objection 2: The precept about the observance of the Sabbath is a moral precept in a certain respect, viz., insofar as it commands man to free up some time (*aliquo tempore vacet*) for divine matters—this according to Psalm 45:11 ("Be still (*vacate*) and see that I am God"). It is in this sense that it is counted among the precepts of the Decalogue.

However, it is not a moral precept as far as the exact specification of the time is concerned (*quantum ad taxationem temporis*), since in this respect it is a ceremonial precept.

Reply to objection 3: The character of something's being owed (*ratio debiti*) is less noticeable (*magis latens*) in the case of the other virtues than it is in the case of justice. And so the precepts having to do with the other

virtues are not as well known to the people as the precepts about the acts
of justice are. It is for this reason that acts of justice fall specifically under
the precepts of the Decalogue, which are the first elements of the Law.

Article 4

Are the precepts of the Decalogue
correctly distinguished from one another?

It seems that the precepts of the Decalogue are not correctly distinguished from one another [in Exodus 20 and Deuteronomy 5:7–22]:

Objection 1: Worship (*latria*) is a virtue different from faith (*fides*),
and the precepts are given with respect to acts of the virtues. But what it
says at the beginning of the Decalogue, viz., "You shall not have strange
gods before me," has to do with faith, whereas what is then added, viz.,
"You shall not make graven images," has to do with worship. Therefore, as
Augustine says, these are two precepts and not just one.

Objection 2: The affirmative precepts contained in the Law, e.g.,
"Honor your father and your mother," are distinct from the negative precepts, e.g., "You shall not kill." But "I am the Lord your God" is affirmative, whereas what is added, "You shall not have strange gods before me,"
is negative. Therefore, as Augustine claims, they are two precepts and are
not contained under a single precept.

Objection 3: In Romans 7:7 the Apostle says, "I would not have
known concupiscence if the Law had not said, 'You shall not covet'." So it
seems that the precept "You shall not covet" is a single precept. Therefore,
it should not be split into two precepts.

But contrary to this is the authority of Augustine in *Glossa super
Exodum*, where he says that there are three precepts having to do with God
and seven having to do with our neighbor.

I respond: The precepts of the Decalogue are divided up in different
ways by different authors.

For example, Hesychius, in commenting on Leviticus 26:26 (". . . so
that ten women are baking bread in one oven"), says that the observance of
the Sabbath does not belong to the ten precepts, because it is not the case
that the letter of this precept must be observed for all times. Yet he distinguishes four precepts that have to do with God:

(a) The first is: "I am the Lord your God."

(b) The second is: "You shall not have strange gods before me." (In like manner, Jerome also distinguishes these two in commenting on Hosea 10:10 [". . . because of their two iniquities"].)

(c) The third precept, he claims, is: "You shall not make graven images for yourselves."

(d) The fourth is: "You shall not take the name of the Lord your God in vain."

On the other hand, he claims that there are six precepts that have to do with our neighbor:

(a) The first is: "Honor your father and your mother."

(b) The second is: "You shall not kill."

(c) The third is: "You shall not commit adultery."

(d) The fourth is: "You shall not steal."

(e) The fifth is: "You shall not bear false witness."

(d) The sixth is: "You shall not covet."

First of all, however, it seems wrong for the precept having to do with the observance of the Sabbath to be placed among the precepts of the Decalogue if it has nothing at all to do with the Decalogue.

Second, since Matthew 6:24 says, "No man can serve two masters," it would seem that "I am the Lord your God" and "You shall not have strange gods" have the same import (*eiusdem rationis esse*) and fall under the same precept. This is why Origen, who also distinguishes four precepts ordered toward God, takes these two as one precept, while positing (a) "You shall not make graven images" as the second precept, (b) "You shall not take the name of the Lord your God in vain" as the third precept, and (c) "Remember to keep holy the Sabbath" as the fourth precept. The other six precepts he posits in the same way that Hesychius does.

However, since making graven images or likenesses is prohibited only insofar as they are not worshiped as gods (for as Exodus 25:18–20 says, God commanded that an image of the Seraphim be made for the tabernacle itself), Augustine more correctly places "You shall not have strange gods" and "You shall not make graven images" under a single precept.

Similarly, coveting (*concupiscentia*) another's wife for sexual intercourse has to do with concupiscence of the flesh (*concupiscentia carnis*), whereas coveting other things that are desired as possessions has to do with concupiscence of the eyes (*concupiscentia oculorum*). Hence, Augustine posits two precepts here, one against coveting another's goods and one against coveting another's wife. And so Augustine posits three precepts in relation to God and seven in relation to one's neighbor. And this is better.

Reply to objection 1: Worship is nothing other than a certain declaration (*protestatio*) of faith, and so it is not the case that one precept should be given about worship and another about faith. Instead, a precept should be given about worship rather than about faith, since the precept of faith (*praeceptum fidei*) is presupposed by the Decalogue in the same way that the precept of love (*praeceptum dilectionis*) is. For just as the first general precepts of the law of nature are known *per se* to anyone who has natural reason and so do not need to be promulgated, so too the precept that one ought to believe in God (*credere in Deum*) is a first precept and is known *per se* to anyone who has faith. For as Hebrews 11:6 says, "He who comes to God must believe that He exists." And so this precept needs no promulgation other than the infusion of faith.

Reply to objection 2: The affirmative precepts are distinct from the negative precepts when the one is not included in the other. For instance, the precept that no man should be killed is not included in the precept about honoring one's parents, or vice versa.

By contrast, when the affirmative precept is included in the negative one, or vice versa, then it is not the case that there are different precepts about the matter in question. For instance, the precept "You shall not steal" is not a different precept from "Take care of another's property" or "Return another's property to him." And for the same reason, the precept about believing in God and the precept about not believing in strange gods are not diverse precepts.

Reply to objection 3: All types of coveting (*concupiscentia*) share a general definition, and this is why the Apostle speaks in the singular about the commandment concerning coveting. Yet the reason why Augustine distinguishes different precepts about not coveting is that the types of coveting differ from one another in species. For as the Philosopher says in *Ethics* 10, the types of desire (*concupiscentia*) differ from one another in species according to the differences among the actions or among the things desired.

Article 5

Is there an appropriate number of precepts in the Decalogue?

It seems that there is an inappropriate number of precepts in the Decalogue:

Objection 1: As Ambrose says, "Sin is a transgression of divine law and disobedience against the heavenly commandments." But sins are distinguished from one another by whether a man sins against God, against his neighbor, or against himself. Therefore, since among the precepts of the Decalogue there are none that order a man toward himself, but only ones that order him toward God and toward his neighbor, it seems that there is an insufficient number of precepts in the Decalogue.

Objection 2: Just as the observance of the Sabbath had to do with the worship of God, so also did the observance of the other solemn feasts (*solemnitates*) and the immolation of sacrifices. But among the precepts of the Decalogue there is a single precept having to do with the observance of the Sabbath. Therefore, there should also be some precepts having to do with the other solemn feasts and with the rite of sacrifices.

Objection 3: Just as one can sin against God by perjuring himself, so too he can sin against God by blasphemy or by various deceptions that are opposed to divine teaching. But there is a single precept forbidding perjury, when it says, "You shall not take the name of the Lord your God in vain." Therefore, the sins of blasphemy and false teaching should be prohibited by some precept of the Decalogue.

Objection 4: Just as a man has a natural love for his parents, so too he has a natural love for his children; indeed, the commandment of charity extends to all one's neighbors. But the precepts of the Decalogue are ordered toward charity—this according to 1 Timothy 1:5, "The end of the commandment is charity." Therefore, just as there is a precept having to do with one's parents, so also there should have been precepts having to do with one's children and other neighbors.

Objection 5: In every genus of sin it is possible to sin with one's heart and to sin with one's deeds. But within certain genera of sin, viz., in the case of theft and adultery, sinning by deed is prohibited in one place—viz., when it says, "You shall not commit adultery" and "You shall not steal"—and sinning with the heart is prohibited in a separate place—viz., when it says, "You shall not covet your neighbor's goods" and "You shall not covet your neighbor's wife." Therefore, the same thing should have been done with the sin of homicide and the sin of false witness.

Objection 6: Just as a sin can stem from a disorder of the concupiscible appetite, so too a sin can stem from a disorder of the irascible appetite. But there are certain precepts prohibiting disordered desire, when it says, "Do not covet . . ." Therefore, the Decalogue should also have contained some precepts prohibiting a disordered irascible appetite. Therefore, it does not seem that there is an appropriate number of precepts in the Decalogue.

But contrary to this: Deuteronomy 4:13 says, "He showed you His covenant, which He commanded you to do, and the ten words that He wrote in the two tables of stone."

I respond: As was explained above (a. 2), just as the precepts of human law order a man toward the human community, so the precepts of divine law order a man toward a sort of community or republic of men under God. Now in order for someone to live a good life in a community, two things are required. The first is that he behave well toward the one who presides over the community, and the second is that the man behave well toward the others who are his companions and co-participants in the community. Therefore, divine law must first lay down some precepts ordering a man toward God and, second, it must lay down other precepts ordering a man toward those others who are living together with him as his neighbors under God.

Now there are three things a man owes to the ruler of his community: (a) fidelity, (b) reverence, and (c) service (*famulatus*). Fidelity to one's lord consists in not conferring on someone else the honor of preeminence; and on this score there is the first precept, when it says, "You shall not have strange gods." Reverence to one's lord requires that nothing injurious be done to him; and on this score there is the second precept, i.e., "You shall not take the name of the Lord your God in vain." Service is owed to a lord in repayment for the benefits his subjects receive from him; and here the relevant precept is the third, which has to do with the sanctification of the Sabbath in remembrance of the creation of things.

On the other hand, someone behaves well toward his neighbor both in a specific way and in a general way:

He behaves well in a specific way to the extent that he renders what he owes to those he is indebted to. And on this score there is the precept that has to do with honoring one's parents.

He behaves well in a general way, i.e., with respect to everyone, in that he inflicts no harm on anyone either by his deeds or with his mouth or with his heart.

As for deeds, in some cases harm is inflicted on one's neighbor in his very person, i.e., with respect to his existence as a person; and this is prohibited when it says, "You shall not kill." Again, in some cases the harm is inflicted in a person joined to him in the propagation of offspring; and this is prohibited when it says, "You shall not commit adultery." And in some cases the harm is inflicted in his possessions, which are ordered both to him and to those conjoined to him, and this is prohibited by saying, "You shall not steal."

On the other hand, harm caused with the mouth is prohibited when it says, "You shall not bear false witness against your neighbor."

And harm caused with the heart is prohibited when it says, "You shall not covet."

Moreover, the three precepts ordered toward God could also be distinguished in accord with the specific differences *by deed*, *with the mouth*, and *with the heart*. The first of these three precepts has to do with deeds, and thus it says there, "You shall not make graven images." The second precept has to do with the mouth, and thus it says, "You shall not take the name of your God in vain." The third precept has to do with the heart, since in the sanctification of the Sabbath, insofar as this is a moral precept, the stillness of the heart is directed toward God.

Alternatively, according to Augustine, through the first precept we revere the unity of the First Principle, through the second precept we revere God's truth, and through the third precept we revere His goodness, by which we are sanctified and in which, as our end, we come to rest.

Reply to objection 1: There are two possible replies to this objection.

First, the precepts of the Decalogue are traced back to the precept of love. Now a precept had to be given to man concerning the love of God and neighbor, since in this regard the natural law had been obscured because of sin. By contrast, this was not the case with respect to the love of self, because (a) in this regard the natural law was still alive—or, alternatively, because (b) the love of self is also included in the love of God and neighbor, since it is in ordering himself to God that a man has genuine love for himself. And this is why the precepts of the Decalogue contains only precepts having to do one's neighbor and with God.

The second possible reply is that the precepts of the Decalogue are the ones that the people received directly from God. Hence, Deuteronomy 10:4 says, "He wrote in the tables, according as He had written before, the ten words, which the Lord spoke to you." Thus, the precepts of the Decalogue had to be such that they could be immediately understood by the people. Now a precept has the character of something that is owed, and the fact that a man necessarily owes something to God or to his neighbor is easily grasped by a man—and especially by a man of faith (*fidelis*). However, it is not so readily apparent that a man is necessarily owed something in those matters that pertain to himself and not to another. For at first glance it seems that everyone is free in matters that pertain to himself. And so the precepts that prohibit a man's disorders with respect to himself come to the people later on through the instruction of the wise. This is why they do not belong to the Decalogue.

Reply to objection 2: All the solemn feasts of the Old Testament were instituted in commemoration of some divine favor, either a past favor remembered or a future favor prefigured; and, likewise, it was for this reason that all the sacrifices were offered. Now among all of God's favors, the first and foremost is the favor of creation, which is commemorated in the sanctification of the Sabbath. Hence, Exodus 20:11 gives the following as the reason for this precept: "For in six days God made heaven and earth, etc." Moreover, among all the future favors that had to be prefigured, the principal and final one was rest in the mind of God, either in the present life through grace or in the future life through glory. This was likewise prefigured by the Sabbath observance. Hence, Isaiah 58:13 says, "If you turn away your foot from the Sabbath, from doing your own will in My holy day, and call the Sabbath delightful, and the holy of the Lord glorious . . . ." For these are the favors that are first and foremost in the minds of men, especially men of faith.

By contrast, the other solemn feasts are celebrated because of certain particular favors that were temporally transitory. Take, for instance, the celebration of the Passover because of the favor of the past liberation from Egypt and because of the future passion of Christ. These events have passed in time, leading us into the rest of the spiritual Sabbath. That is why, among the precepts of the Decalogue, mention was made only of the Sabbath, while all the other solemn feasts and sacrifices were left out.

Reply to objection 3: As the Apostle says in Hebrews 6:16, "Men swear by one greater than themselves, and an oath for confirmation is the end of all their controversy." And so since oaths are common to everyone, the prohibition of disordered oaths is specifically made in a precept of the Decalogue.

By contrast, the sin of false teaching is relevant only to a few people, and hence it did not have to be mentioned among the precepts of the Decalogue. (Still, according to one interpretation, the precept "You shall not take the name of your God in vain" does prohibit false teaching; for instance, there is a Gloss that expounds it as follows: "You shall not claim that Christ is a creature.")

Reply to objection 4: Natural reason directly dictates to a man that he should not inflict injury on anyone, and so the precept prohibiting harm extends to everyone. However, natural reason does not directly dictate that a man should do something for another's benefit, except in the case of someone to whom the man is indebted. Now the debt a child owes to his father is so obvious that it cannot be denied by any sort of evasion. For the father is a principle of generation and of *esse* and, afterwards, of upbringing and teaching. And this is why it does not fall under a precept of the Decalogue that support or obedience should be given to anyone other than one's parents.

On the other hand, parents do not seem to be indebted to their children because of any favors received from them; rather, just the opposite is the case. Likewise, as the Philosopher puts it in *Ethics* 8, a child is a part of his father, and fathers love their children as a part of themselves. Hence, the reason why there are no precepts in the Decalogue with regard to love of one's children is the same as the reason why there are likewise no precepts that order a man toward himself.

Reply to objection 5: The pleasure of adultery and the usefulness of riches are desirable for their own sake, insofar as they have the character of a pleasurable good or a useful good. For this reason, what had to be prohibited in their case was not just the deed, but the desire (*concupiscentia*) as well.

By contrast, homicide (*homicidium*) and falsehood are horrific in their own right; for we naturally love our neighbor and love the truth, and they are not desired for the sake of anything else. And so as far as the sins of homicide and false witness were concerned, it was unnecessary to prohibit the sin of the heart, but necessary only to prohibit the deed.

Reply to objection 6: As was explained above (q. 25, a. 1), all of the irascible passions stem from the concupiscible passions. And so in the precepts of the Decalogue, which are, as it were, the first elements of the Law, mention had to be made only of the concupiscible passions and not of the irascible passions.

Article 6

Are the precepts of the Decalogue correctly ordered?

It seems that the precepts of the Decalogue (see Exodus 20 and Deuteronomy 5:7–22) are not correctly ordered:

Objection 1: Love of neighbor seems to be prior to love of God, since our neighbor is better known to us than God is—this according to 1 John 4:20 ("If one does not love his brother whom he sees, how can he love God whom he sees not?"). But the first three precepts have to do with love of God, whereas the other seven have to do with love of neighbor. Therefore, the precepts of the Decalogue are incorrectly ordered.

Objection 2: Acts of the virtues are commanded by the affirmative precepts, whereas acts of the vices are prohibited by the negative precepts. But according to Boethius in his commentary on the *Categories*, the vices must first be rooted out before the virtues are planted. Therefore, among the precepts having to do with our neighbor, the negative precepts, rather than the affirmative precepts, should have come first.

Objection 3: The precepts of the Law are given with respect to human acts. But the act of the heart comes before the act of the mouth or the exterior deed. Therefore, it is incorrect for the precepts to be ordered in such a way that the ones having to do with not coveting, which pertain to the heart, come last.

But contrary to this: In Romans 13:1 the Apostle says, "The things that are from God are orderly (*ordinata*)." But as has been explained (a. 3), the precepts of the Decalogue are directly from God. Therefore, they are in the correct order.

I respond: As has been explained (a. 5, ad 1), the precepts of the Decalogue are given with respect to those things that the human mind grasps immediately and quickly. But it is clear that something is better grasped by reason to the extent that its contrary has a greater and more serious (*gravius*) opposition to reason.

Now it is clear that since reason's ordering takes its inception from the end, it is maximally opposed to reason that a man should find himself disordered with respect to his end. But the end of human life and society is God. And so man had to be ordered by the precepts of the Decalogue in the first place toward God, since the contrary of this is the most serious of all contraries—just as in an army, which is ordered toward the general as an end, the soldier first of all submits himself to the general, the contrary of this being the most serious of all, whereas, second, he is coordinated with the other soldiers.

Now among the steps by which we are ordered toward God, the first is that a man faithfully submit himself to God and that he have no commerce (*habens nullam participationem*) with God's rivals. The second step is that he exhibit reverence for Him, whereas the third is that he offer Him his service. In an army, it is a greater sin if a soldier, acting unfaithfully, makes a pact with the enemy than if he does something disrespectful to the general, and the latter is more serious than if he is found deficient in some matter of obedience (*obsequium*).

On the other hand, among the precepts ordering one toward his neighbor, it is clear that it is more repugnant to reason, and a graver sin, if a man does not observe the due ordering to those persons whom he is more indebted to. And so among the precepts that order one toward his neighbor, the first to be posited is the precept having to do with one's parents. Among the other precepts there is likewise an ordering that corresponds to the gravity of the sins. For it is more grave, and more repugnant to reason, to sin by a deed than to sin with one's mouth, and it is more grave to sin with one's mouth than in one's heart. Furthermore, among the sins that involve deeds, homicide, by which an already existing man's life is taken, is graver than adultery, which undermines certitude about the offspring who are to be born (*per quod impeditur certitudo prolis nasciturae*); and adultery is graver than theft, which has to do with external goods.

Reply to objection 1: Even though our neighbor is better known to us than God according to the way of the senses, love of God is nonetheless the reason for love of neighbor. This will be explained below (*ST* 2–2, q. 25, a. 1). And so the precepts ordering one toward God had to be placed ahead of the others.

Reply to objection 2: Just as God is the universal principle of *esse* for all things, so too the father is a sort of principle of *esse* for his child (*principium quoddam essendi filio*). And so it is appropriate that after the precepts having to do with God, there should be a precept having to do with one's parents.

Now the argument [contained in objection 2] goes through when the affirmative and negative precepts in question have to do with the same genus of action—although even then the argument does not have complete efficacy. For even if, in the order of execution, vices must be uprooted before virtues are planted—this according to Psalm 33:15 ("Turn away from evil and do good") and Isaiah 1:16–17 ("Cease to act perversely, learn to act well")—still, virtue is cognitively prior to sin, since, as *De Anima* 1 says, it is through what is straight that one comes to know what is crooked. As Romans 3:20 puts it, "By the Law is knowledge of sin."

According to this line of reasoning, it was right for the affirmative precept to have come first. Still, this is not the reason for the ordering [we have]; rather, the reason is the one set forth [at the beginning of this reply]. For in the precepts having to do with God, which are on the first tablet, the

affirmative precept comes last, since transgressing it produces a less grievous sin (*inducit minorem reatum*).

Reply to objection 3: Even if the sin of the heart is prior in execution,
nonetheless, the prohibition of it comes later conceptually (*in ratione*).

Article 7

Are the precepts of the Decalogue set down in an appropriate way?

It seems that the precepts of the Decalogue are not set down (*tradan-
tur*) in an appropriate way:

Objection 1: The affirmative precepts order one toward acts of the
virtues, whereas the negative precepts draw one back from acts of the
vices. But with respect to any subject matter whatsoever, there are virtues
and vices opposed to one another. Therefore, in any subject matter about
which a precept of the Decalogue gives direction, there should have been
both an affirmative precept and a negative precept. Therefore, it is inappropriate for there to be affirmative precepts for some subject matters and
negative precepts for others.

Objection 2: Isidore says that every law is based on reason. But all the
precepts of the Decalogue belong to divine law. Therefore, a reason should
have been given for each of the precepts, and not just for the first and third.

Objection 3: Through the observance of the precepts one merits
rewards from God. But God's promises have to do with the rewards
attached to the precepts. Therefore, a promise should have been made in
each of the precepts, and not just in the first and the fourth.

Objection 4: The Old Law is called the 'law of fear', because it was
through threats of punishment that it induced men to observe the precepts.
But all the precepts of the Decalogue belong to the Old Law. Therefore, a
threat of punishment should have been made in each of the precepts, and
not just in the first and the second.

Objection 5: All the precepts of God should be retained in memory;
for Proverbs 3:3 says, "Write them on the tablets of your heart." Therefore,
it was inappropriate for a mention of memory to be made in just the third
precept. And so it seems that the precepts of the Decalogue were inappropriately set down.

But contrary to this: Wisdom 11:21 says, "You have ordered all
things in measure, and number, and weight." Therefore, *a fortiori*, He has
preserved an appropriate mode of setting down the precepts of His law.

I respond: The highest wisdom is contained in the precepts of divine law; hence, Deuteronomy 4:6 says, "This is your wisdom, and understanding in the sight of the nations." But it is the role of wisdom to dispose all things in a fitting manner and order. And so it ought to be clear that the precepts of the Law have been set down in an appropriate way.

Reply to objection 1: The negation of one of two opposites always follows from the affirmation of the other, but it is not always the case that the affirmation of one of two opposites follows from the negation of the other. For instance, 'If something is white, then it is not black' is valid, but 'If something is not black, then it is white' is not valid. For the negation extends to more things than the affirmation does. Hence, it is likewise the case that 'One should not do harm', which is a negative precept, extends to more persons (*personas*) as a primary dictate of reason than does 'One ought to give obedience (or benefits) to someone'.

However, it is a dictate of reason in the first instance that one ought to give obedience (or benefits) to those from whom he has received benefits, as long as he has not yet repaid them. But, as *Ethics* 8 says, there are two beings in return for whose benefits no one can make sufficient repayment, viz., God and his father. And this is why there are only two affirmative precepts, one having to do with honoring one's parents and the other having to do with the celebration of the Sabbath in commemoration of God's favors.

Reply to objection 2: The precepts that are purely moral have an obvious reason behind them, and so there was no need for a reason to be added to them.

However, some precepts are such that either a ceremonial precept or the specification of a moral precept is added to them. For instance, in the first precept there is the addition of "You shall not make graven images," and in the third precept the day of the Sabbath is specified. And this is why a reason had to be given in these two cases.

Reply to objection 3: Men order their acts for the most part toward some sort of usefulness. And so the promise of a reward had to be attached to those precepts from which no usefulness seemed to follow or by which some sort of usefulness was impeded. Now since parents are already in their receding years, no usefulness is expected from them. And so a promise is attached to the precept about honoring one's parents. The same holds for the precept that prohibits idolatry. For this precept seems to impede the apparent usefulness which men believe they can attain by entering into a pact with the demons.

Reply to objection 4: As *Ethics* 10 says, punishments are especially necessary for those who are prone to evil. And so a threat of punishment is added only to those precepts in which there was a tendency toward evil.

Now men were prone to idolatry because of the general practice of the Gentiles. Similarly, there were also men prone to perjury because of the frequency of oaths. This is why a threat is attached to the first two precepts.

Reply to objection 5: The precept about the Sabbath is posited as a commemoration of a past favor, and this is why it contains a specific mention of memory.

An alternative reply is that the precept about the Sabbath has adjoined to it a specification that does not belong to the law of nature, and that is why this precept requires a special admonition.

Article 8

Can dispensations be granted from the precepts of the Decalogue?

It seems that there can be dispensations from the precepts of the Decalogue:

Objection 1: The precepts of the Decalogue belong to the natural law, and as the Philosopher says in *Ethics* 5, what is naturally just fails in some cases and is mutable, just as human nature is. But as was explained above (q. 96, a. 6 and q. 97, a. 4), the failure of the law in some particular cases is the reason for granting a dispensation. Therefore, a dispensation can be granted from the precepts of the Decalogue.

Objection 2: God is related to divinely given law in the same way that man is related to human law. But man is able to grant dispensations from those precepts of the law that are man-made. Therefore, since the precepts of the Decalogue were established by God, it seems that God is able to grant dispensations from them. But prelates function on earth in the place of God; for in 2 Corinthians 2:10 the Apostle says, "If I have pardoned anything, for your sakes have I done it in the person of Christ." Therefore, prelates, too, can grant dispensations from the precepts of the Decalogue.

Objection 3: The prohibition of homicide is included among the precepts of the Decalogue. But it seems that men grant dispensations from this precept, e.g., when, in accord with the precepts of human law, certain men, viz., evildoers and enemies, are lawfully killed. Therefore, dispensations can be granted from the precepts of the Decalogue.

Objection 4: The observance of the Sabbath is included among the precepts of the Decalogue. But a dispensation was granted from this precept; for 1 Maccabees 2:41 says, "And they determined in that day, saying, 'Whoever shall come up against us to fight on the Sabbath day, we will fight against him'." Therefore, dispensations can be granted from the precepts of the Decalogue.

But contrary to this: In Isaiah 24:5 certain people are rebuked because "they have changed the Law, they have broken the everlasting covenant"—which must, it seems, refer especially to the precepts of the Decalogue. Therefore, the precepts of the Decalogue cannot be altered by a dispensation.

I respond: As was explained above (q. 96, a. 6 and q. 97, a. 4), a dispensation should be granted from a precept when some particular case occurs in which the observance of the letter of the law is contrary to the lawmaker's intention. Now the intention of every lawmaker is ordered first and principally toward the common good and, second, toward the order of justice and virtue, in accord with which the common good is attained and preserved.

Therefore, if there are any precepts which embody the very conservation of the common good or the very order of justice and virtue, then precepts of this sort preserve the lawmaker's intention and so are such that dispensations cannot be granted from them. For instance, if a community were to establish the precept 'No one may destroy the republic or betray the city-state to the enemy', or the precept 'No one may do anything in an evil or unjust way', then there could not be dispensations from precepts of this sort.

By contrast, if there were other precepts which were ordered to the [primary] precepts and which specified certain particular modes for them, then a dispensation could be granted from such precepts to the extent that their being overridden (*per omissionem huiusmodi praeceptorum*) in certain cases would not be prejudicial to the primary precepts that embody the lawmaker's intention. For instance, if, in order to save the republic, it were decreed in a city that certain men should take turns keeping guard over the city when it is under siege, then some men could be dispensed from this precept for the sake of some greater advantage.

Now the precepts of the Decalogue embody the intention of the lawmaker, viz., God. For the precepts of the first tablet, which are ordered toward God, embody the very ordering toward the common and final good, which is God. On the other hand, the precepts of the second tablet embody the very order of justice to be observed among men, so that, namely, nothing undue is done to anyone and what is due is rendered to each one; for the precepts of the Decalogue should be understood according to this rationale. And so there cannot be any dispensations at all from the precepts of the Decalogue.

Reply to objection 1: The Philosopher is not speaking here of the naturally just, which embodies the very order of justice; for the precept 'Justice is to be preserved' never fails. Rather, he is speaking about specific modes of observing justice, and in some cases these modes fail.

Reply to objection 2: As the Apostle says in 2 Timothy 2:13, "God remains faithful; He cannot deny Himself." But He would be denying Himself if He destroyed the very order of His justice, since He is Justice Itself. And so God cannot grant a dispensation that would permit a man either (a) to behave in a disordered way toward God or (b) not to submit to the order of His justice, even in those matters in which men are ordered toward one another.

Reply to objection 3: The killing of a man is prohibited in the Decalogue insofar as it has the character of something undue; for this is the sense in which a precept embodies the very nature of justice.

Now human law cannot permit that a man should be killed both lawfully and in an undue way. But it is not undue for an evildoer, or for the enemies of the republic, to be killed. Hence, this is not contrary to the precept of the dialogue; nor is such a killing (*occisio*) a homicide (*homicidium*)—which is what the precept prohibits, as Augustine says in *De Libero Arbitrio* 1. Similarly, if what belongs to someone is taken from him, then if it is due that he should lose it, this is not theft or robbery, which is what the precept of the Decalogue prohibits.

And so when, by God's command, the children of Israel took the spoils from the Egyptians (Exodus 12:35), this was not theft, since these spoils were owed to them by God's decree. Similarly, when Abraham consented to kill his son (Genesis 22), he did not consent to homicide, since by the command of God, who is the Lord of life and death, it had been made due that his son should be killed. For it is God who inflicts the punishment of death on all men, both the just and the unjust, because of the sin of our first parent; and if a man executes this sentence by God's authority, then he will not be committing homicide (*non erit homicida*), just as God does not commit homicide. Similarly, when Hosea takes to himself a "wife of fornications," i.e., an adulterous woman (Hosea 1), he is not an adulterer or a fornicator; for he took a woman who belonged to him according to the command of God, the author of the institution of matrimony.

So, then, the precepts of the Decalogue are immutable with respect to the character of justice that they embody. However, regarding the specification of the precepts as applied to singular acts—that is, as regards whether this or that act is or is not homicide or theft or adultery—there is indeed mutability, sometimes by God's authority alone, viz., in those things that have been instituted by God alone (e.g., matrimony and other things of this sort), and sometimes also by human authority, as in those matters that have been entrusted to the jurisdiction of men. With respect to those matters, but not with respect to all matters, men act in the place of God.

Reply to objection 4: The thought expressed here was more of an interpretation of the precept than a dispensation. For someone who does what is necessary for human welfare is not thought of as violating the Sabbath, as the Lord shows in Matthew 12:1–15.

Article 9

Does the mode of virtue fall under a precept of the Law?

It seems that the mode of virtue falls under a precept of the Law:

Objection 1: The mode of virtue involves one's doing just things in a just way, and courageous things in a courageous way, and so on for the other virtues. But Deuteronomy 16:20 commands, "You shall do justly that which is just." Therefore, the mode of virtue falls under a precept.

Objection 2: It is what the lawmaker intends that principally (*maxime*) falls under a precept. But as *Ethics* 2 says, the lawmaker's intention is mainly to make men virtuous, and virtuous men are those who act in a virtuous manner. Therefore, the mode of virtue falls under a precept.

Objection 3: The mode of virtue, properly speaking, seems to involve one's acting willingly (*voluntarie*) and with delight (*delectabiliter*). But this falls under a precept of divine law. For Psalm 99:2 says, "Serve the Lord in gladness," and 2 Corinthians 9:7 says, ". . . not with sadness or out of necessity; for God loves a cheerful giver," and the Gloss on this second passage says, "Whatever good you do, do it with cheerfulness, and then you will do well; but if you do it with sadness, though it comes from you, you are not doing it." Therefore, the mode of virtue falls under a precept of the Law.

But contrary to this: As is clear from the Philosopher in *Ethics* 2 and 5, no one can act in the way a virtuous man acts unless he has the habit of the virtue. But anyone who transgresses a precept of the Law merits punishment. Therefore, it would follow that one who does not have the habit of a virtue is such that whatever he does merits punishment. But this is contrary to the intention of the Law, which intends to lead man to virtue by making him accustomed to good works. Therefore, it is not the case that the mode of virtue falls under a precept.

I respond: As was explained above (q. 90, a. 3), a precept of the law has coercive force. Therefore, what directly falls under a precept of the law is that toward which the law coerces one. But as *Ethics* 10 says, the law's coercive force comes from the fear of punishment, since what properly falls under a precept of the law is such that the law's punishment is inflicted in light of it.

Now divine law and human law go about instituting punishments in different ways. For the law's punishment is inflicted only for those things over which the lawmaker exercises judgment, since the law punishes in light of this judgment. But man, who makes human law, is able to pass judgment only about exterior acts, since, as 1 Kings 16:7 puts it, "Men see things that appear to be the case." By contrast, only God, who makes divine law, can judge the interior movements of wills—this according to Psalm 7:10 ("The searcher of hearts and affections [*corda et renes*] is God"). Accordingly, then, one should claim that there is one respect in which the mode of virtue is relevant to both human law and divine law, and a second respect in which it is relevant to divine law but not human law, and a third respect in which it is relevant to neither divine law nor human law.

Now according to the Philosopher in *Ethics* 2, the mode of virtue consists of three elements:

The first is that the agent acts *knowingly* (*sciens*). This falls under the judgment of both divine law and human law. For what someone does in ignorance, he does *per accidens*. Hence, as far as punishment and pardon are concerned, some matters are judged by reference to ignorance—and this according to both divine law and human law.

The second is that the agent acts *willingly* (*volens*), i.e., "by choosing [the act] and choosing it for its own sake." This involves two interior movements, viz., an act of willing (*voluntas*) and an act of intending (*intentio*), which were explained above (q. 8 and q. 12). Only divine law, and not human law, passes judgment on these two acts. For human law does not punish someone who wills to kill and yet does not kill, whereas divine law does punish him—this according to Matthew 5:22 ("Whoever is angry with his brother shall be in danger of the judgment").

The third element is that the agent *has, and acts from, a firm and unchangeable character* (*ut firme et immobiliter habeat et operetur*). This firmness properly involves a habit, so that he is acting from a rooted habit (*ex habitu radicato*). As far as this element is concerned, the mode of virtue does not fall under a precept of either divine law or human law. For even if someone who gives the honor due to his parents does not have the habit of piety, he is not punished by man or by God as a transgressor of the precept.

Reply to objection 1: In the performance of an act of justice, the mode that falls under the precept is not that something be done from the habit of justice, but that it be done according to the order of uprightness (*secundum ordinem iuris*).

Reply to objection 2: The lawmaker's intention involves two things. The first is what he intends to lead his subjects toward by means of the precepts of the law, and this is *virtue*. The second is what he intends to make his precept about, and this is what leads or disposes them toward virtue, viz., *acts of virtue*. For the end of the precept is not the same as what the precept is about—just as, in other matters, the end is not the same as what is ordered toward the end.

Reply to objection 3: Performing an act of a virtue without sadness (*sine tristitia*) does fall under a precept of divine law, since anyone who acts with sadness is acting reluctantly (*non volens*).

On the other hand, acting with delight (*delectabiliter*)—whether with joy (*cum laetitia*) or with cheerfulness (*cum hilaritate*)—falls under a precept in one sense, viz., to the extent that the delight follows from the love of God and neighbor, which itself falls under a precept. For love is a cause of delight. However, there is a sense in which acting with delight does not fall under a precept, since, as *Ethics* 2 says, "Delight in the act is a sign of a habit that has already been generated." For an act can be delightful either because of its end or because of the agreeableness of its habit.

Article 10

Does the mode of charity fall under a precept of divine law?

It seems that the mode of charity falls under a precept of divine law:

Objection 1: Matthew 19:17 says, "If you wish to enter into life, keep the commandments," and from this it is apparent that the observance of the commandments is sufficient for entering into life. But good works are not sufficient for entering into life unless they are done out of charity; for 1 Corinthians 13:3 says, "If I should distribute all my goods to feed the poor, and if I should deliver my body to be burned, but have not charity, it profits me nothing." Therefore, the mode of charity is contained in a precept.

Objection 2: The mode of charity properly concerns doing all things for the sake of God. But this falls under a precept; for in 1 Corinthians 10:31 the Apostle says, "Do everything for the glory of God." Therefore, the mode of charity falls under a precept.

Objection 3: If the mode of charity does not fall under a precept, then someone can fulfill the precepts of the law without having charity. But what can be done without charity can be done without grace, which is always joined to charity. Therefore, someone can fulfill the precepts of the Law without grace. But as is clear from Augustine in *De Haeresibus*, this is the error of Pelagius. Therefore, the mode of charity is contained in a precept.

But contrary to this: Whoever does not observe a precept commits a mortal sin. Therefore, if the mode of charity fell under a precept, it would follow that if someone did something without acting out of charity, he would commit a mortal sin. But anyone who does not have charity is such that he acts without acting out of charity. Therefore, it follows that anyone who does not have charity commits a mortal sin in every act that he does, no matter how good it is. But this is absurd.

I respond: There have been contrary opinions on this matter.

Some have claimed that, absolutely speaking, the mode of charity falls under a precept. Nor is it impossible for someone lacking charity to observe this precept, since he can dispose himself to having charity infused in him by God. Moreover, it is not the case that whenever someone lacking charity does something good, he commits a mortal sin. For the precept 'Act out of charity' is an affirmative precept and imposes an obligation not for all times, but only for those times at which someone has charity.

By contrast, others have claimed that the mode of charity does not fall under a precept in any way at all.

Both sides have asserted the truth in a certain respect. For there are two possible ways to think of the act of charity:

In the first way, one is thinking of it as a certain act in its own right (*quidam actus per se*). And in this sense it falls under the precept of the Law that is proposed specifically about this act, viz., "You shall love the Lord your God, and you shall love your neighbor." And on this score, the first opinion has asserted the truth, since it is not impossible to observe this precept, which has to do with the act of charity. For a man can dispose himself to have charity, and then, when he has it, he can make use of it.

In a second way, the act of charity can be thought of insofar as it is a mode of the acts of the other virtues, i.e., insofar as the acts of the other virtues are ordered to charity, which is, as 1 Timothy 1:5 says, the end of the precept. For as was explained above (q. 12, a. 1), the intending of an end is a sort of formal mode of an act ordered to that end. And in this sense, what the second opinion asserted is true, viz., that the mode of charity does not fall under a precept. That is to say, the precept "Honor your father, etc." includes only honoring one's father and not honoring one's father out of charity. Hence, even if someone who is honoring his father does not have charity, he is not transgressing this precept—and this is so even if he is transgressing the precept that has to do with the act of charity and so merits punishment because of this transgression.

Reply to objection 1: Our Lord did not say, "If you wish to enter into life, keep one commandment." Rather, He said, "Keep all the commandments"—among which is the commandment about love of God and neighbor.

Reply to objection 2: The commandment of charity includes loving God with one's whole heart, which involves referring all things to God. And so a man cannot fulfill the precept of charity without referring all things to God. So, then, one who honors his parents is obligated to honor them out of charity, but this obligation comes from the force of the precept "You shall love the Lord your God with your whole heart" and not from the force of the precept "Honor your parents." Moreover, since these two affirmative precepts do not impose an obligation for all times, they can impose obligations for diverse times. And so it is possible for someone to fulfill the precept about honoring one's parents at a time when the precept concerning the omission of the mode of charity is not being transgressed.

Reply to objection 3: A man cannot observe all the precepts of the Law unless he fulfills the precept of charity, which cannot be done without grace. And so what Pelagius claimed is impossible, viz., that a man fulfills the Law without grace.

Article 11

Is it correct to mark out moral precepts of the Law in addition to the Decalogue?

It seems incorrect to mark out (*distinguere*) moral precepts of the Law other than the Decalogue:

Objection 1: As our Lord says in Matthew 22:40, "On these two precepts [of charity] depends the whole Law and the prophets." But these two precepts are explicated by the ten precepts of the Decalogue. Therefore, it is unnecessary for there to be other moral precepts.

Objection 2: As has been explained (q. 99, a. 3), the moral precepts are distinct from the judicial and ceremonial precepts. But specifications of the general moral precepts are contained in the judicial and ceremonial precepts, whereas, as has been explained (a. 3), the general moral precepts themselves are contained in the ten precepts of the Decalogue—or are at least presupposed by the Decalogue. Therefore, it is inappropriate for other moral precepts to be handed down in addition to the Decalogue.

Objection 3: As was explained above (a. 2), the moral precepts are about the acts of all the virtues. Therefore, just as, in addition to the Decalogue, the Law contains moral precepts that deal with worship, generosity, mercy, and chastity, so too there should be precepts dealing with the other virtues, e.g., fortitude, sobriety, and others of this sort. But such precepts are not to be found. Therefore, it is inappropriate for other moral precepts that go beyond the Decalogue to be marked out in the Law.

But contrary to this: Psalm 18:8 says, "The law of the Lord is pure, converting souls." But there are other moral precepts, in addition to the Decalogue, through which a man is preserved without the stain of sin and through which his soul is converted. Therefore, it was the Law's function to hand down other moral precepts as well.

I respond: As is clear from what was said above (q. 99, aa. 3–4), the judicial and ceremonial precepts have force solely by virtue of their being instituted, since before they were instituted, there was no apparent difference between things being done one way or another. By contrast, the moral precepts would have had efficacy on the basis of the dictates of natural reason even if they had never been codified in the Law.

Now there are three levels (*gradus*) of moral precept:

(a) Some moral precepts are absolutely certain and so evident that they do not need to be made known publicly (*editione non indigent*). For as was explained above (a. 3), the commandments about love of God and neighbor and others of this sort are, as it were, the ends of the precepts (*fines praeceptorum*) and so such that no one can make a mistaken judgment of reason about them.

(b) Other moral precepts are more specific (*determinata*) and such that anyone, even an ordinary man, can grasp the reason behind them easily and immediately. However, since human judgment about these precepts can be perverted in a fewer number of cases, precepts of this sort need to be made known publicly (*indigent editione*). These precepts are the precepts of the Decalogue.

(c) Still other moral precepts are such that the reason behind them is not evident to everyone; instead, it is evident only to the wise. These precepts are the ones that were added to the Decalogue and given to the people by God through the mediation of Moses and Aaron.

Now since things that are evident are the basis for knowing things that are not evident, these other moral precepts that were added to the Decalogue are traced back to the precepts of the Decalogue in the sense that they are a sort of addition to them.

For instance, the first precept of the Decalogue prohibits the worship of strange gods, and to this are added other precepts that prohibit things that are ordered toward the worship of idols—as, e.g., in Deuteronomy 18:10–11: "Do not let there be found among you anyone that shall purify his son or daughter by making them to pass through the fire. . . . Neither let there be any evil magician or enchanter, or anyone who consults prophetic spirits, or fortune-tellers, or who seeks truth from the dead."

The second precept of the Decalogue prohibits perjury, and to this are added the prohibition of blasphemy in Leviticus 24:15 and the prohibition of false teaching in Deuteronomy 13.

To the third precept are added all the ceremonial precepts.

To the fourth precept, the one about honoring one's parents, is added a precept about honoring the elderly—this according to Leviticus 19:32 ("Stand up in the presence of a hoary head, and honor the elderly person")—and, more generally, all the precepts that induce one to show respect for one's betters or to give benefits to one's equals or inferiors.

To the fifth precept, which prohibits homicide, are added the prohibition of hatred or any sort of injury (*violatio*) against one's neighbor, as in Leviticus 19:16 ("You shall not stand against the blood of your neighbor"), and the prohibition of hatred of one's brother, as in Leviticus 19:17 ("You shall not hate your brother in your heart").

To the sixth precept, which prohibits adultery, is added the prohibition against prostitution (*meretricium*)—this according to Deuteronomy 23:17 ("There shall be no prostitutes among the daughters of Israel, nor fornicators among the sons of Israel"). Again, also added is the prohibition of the vice against nature—this according to Leviticus 28:22–23 ("You shall not have sex with a male. . . . You shall not copulate with any beast").

To the seventh precept, which prohibits theft (*furtum*), are added the precept prohibiting usury (*usura*)—this according to Deuteronomy 23:19 ("You shall not lend your brother money to usury")—and the prohibition of fraud (*fraus*)—this according to Deuteronomy 25:13 ("You shall not have diverse weights in your bag")—and, more generally, everything having to do with the prohibition of cheating (*calumnia*) and plundering (*rapina*).

To the eighth precept, which prohibits false witness, are added the prohibition of false judgment—this according to Exodus 23:2 ("You shall not acquiesce in judgment to the opinion of the majority, so as to stray from the truth")—and the prohibition against lying, which is added in the same place ("You shall avoid lying"), and the prohibition against detraction— this according to Leviticus 19:16 ("You shall not be a detractor (*criminator*) or a whisperer among the people").

However, no other precepts are added to the last two precepts of the Decalogue, since these precepts prohibit all evil desires in general.

Reply to objection 1: The precepts of the Decalogue are ordered toward the love of God and neighbor with the evident rationale of what is owed (*secundum manifestam rationem debiti*) to God and to neighbor. By contrast, the ordering of the other precepts toward the love of God and neighbor has a more hidden reason behind it.

Reply to objection 2: The ceremonial and judicial precepts specify the precepts of the Decalogue by instituting something and not, as with the additional moral precepts, by the force of a natural inclination (*ex vi naturalis instinctus*).

Reply to objection 3: As was explained above (q. 90, a. 2), the precepts of law are ordered toward the common good. And it is because the virtues that order us toward other people are directly relevant to the common good—and, likewise, chastity, insofar as the act of generation subserves the common good—that both the precepts of the Decalogue and the additional precepts are given directly about these virtues.

By contrast, as far as the act of fortitude is concerned, the relevant precept has to be proposed by leaders giving exhortations in a war undertaken for the common good—as is clear from Deuteronomy 20:3, where the priest is commanded [to say], "Do not be afraid! Do not yield!"

Similarly, the prohibition of the act of gluttony is entrusted to paternal warnings, since gluttony is contrary to the good of the household (*bonum domesticum*). Hence, Deuteronomy 21:20 says in the personage of the parents, "He hates listening to our admonitions; he is idle with his reveling and debauchery and socializing."

Article 12

Did the moral precepts of the Old Law give justification [before God]?

It seems that the moral precepts of the Old Law gave justification [before God] (*iustificatio*):

Objection 1: In Romans 2:13 the Apostle says, "For it is not the hearers of the Law who are justified before God; rather, it is the doers of the Law who shall be justified." But the ones who are called doers of the Law are those who fulfill the precepts of the Law. Therefore, when the precepts of the Law were fulfilled, they gave justification.

Objection 2: Leviticus 18:5 says, "Abide by my laws and judgments; the man who fulfills them will have life in them." But a man's spiritual life comes through justice. Therefore, when the precepts of the Law were fulfilled, they gave justification.

Objection 3: Divine law is more efficacious than human law. But human law gives justification, since there is a kind of justice in the fulfillment of the precepts of the law. Therefore, the precepts of the Law gave justification.

But contrary to this: In 2 Corinthians 3:6 the Apostle says, "The letter kills . . ." According to Augustine in *De Spiritu et Littera*, the Apostle is referring here even to the moral precepts. Therefore, the moral precepts did not give justification.

I respond: Just as 'healthy' is said first and primarily of that which has health, whereas it said secondarily of that which is a sign of health or of that which preserves health, so too 'justification' is said first and primarily of the very effecting of justice, whereas 'justification' can be said secondarily—and, as it were, improperly—of a sign of justice or of a disposition toward justice.

There are two ways in which the precepts of the Law clearly gave justification, viz., (a) insofar as they disposed men toward the justifying grace of Christ and (b) insofar as they also signified that grace. For as Augustine says in *Contra Faustum*, "Even the life of that people was prophetic and a figure of Christ."

However, if we are talking about justification properly speaking, then note that 'justice' can be understood either as it exists in a habit or as it exists in an act, and so 'justification' is predicated in two ways: (a) first, insofar as a man becomes just by acquiring the habit of justice and (b) second, insofar as he performs the works of justice, in which case justification is nothing other than the execution of justice.

Now as is clear from what was said above (q. 63, a. 4), justice, like the other virtues, can be understood either as acquired justice or as infused justice. Acquired justice is caused by actions. By contrast, infused justice is caused by God Himself through His grace; and this is the true justice about which we are now talking and in light of which someone is said to be just before God—this according to Romans 4:2 ("If Abraham was justified by the works of the Law, then he has glory, but not before God"). Therefore, this sort of justice could not have been caused by the moral precepts, which have to do with human actions. Accordingly, the moral precepts could not have given justification by effecting justice.

On the other hand, if 'justification' is understood as the execution of justice, then all the precepts of the Law gave justification, though in different ways.

For the ceremonial precepts contained justice in its own right in a general way (*justitia secundum se in generali*) insofar as they had to do with the worship of God. However, they did not contain justice in its own right in a specific way, but were just solely because of the determination of divine law. And so these precepts are said to have given justification only because of the devotion and obedience of those who observed them.

By contrast, the moral and judicial precepts contained what was just in its own right, either in a general way or in a specific way. The moral precepts contained what is just in itself by *general justice,* which, as *Ethics* 5 explains, involves "every virtue," whereas the judicial precepts involved *special justice*, which has to do with the contractual interchanges (*contractus*) of human life that take place among men in their dealings with one another.

Reply to objection 1: The Apostle is using 'justification' here to refer to the execution of justice.

Reply to objection 2: A man who observes the precepts of the Law is said "to have life in them" in the sense that he does not incur the punishment of death that the law inflicts on those who transgress it. This is the Apostle's meaning in Galatians 3:12.

Reply to objection 3: The precepts of human law give justification by means of acquired justice, which we are not discussing at present; rather, we are talking only about that justice which is justice before God.

The Ceremonial Precepts of the Old Law in Themselves

We next have to consider the ceremonial precepts. First, we have to consider them in themselves (question 101); second, we have to consider the reasons for them (question 102); and, third, we have to consider their duration (question 103).

On the first topic there are four questions: (1) What is the reason for the ceremonial precepts? (2) Are the ceremonial precepts figurative (*figuralia*)? (3) Was it right for there to have been a multiplicity of ceremonial precepts? (4) How are the ceremonial precepts distinguished from one another?

Article 1

Does the reason for the ceremonial precepts lie in their having to do with the worship of God?

It seems that the reason for the ceremonial precepts does not lie in their having to do with the worship of God:

Objection 1: As is clear from Leviticus 11, precepts about abstaining from certain foods are given to the Jews in the Old Law; and as is clear from Leviticus 19:19 ("You shall not wear a garment that is woven from two [kinds of thread]") and, again, from the command given at Numbers 15:38 ("Tell them to make to themselves fringes in the corners of their garments"), there are also precepts about avoiding certain kinds of clothing. But precepts of this sort are not moral precepts, since they do not remain in the New Law; nor are they judicial precepts, since they do not have to do with making judgments among men. Therefore, they are ceremonial precepts. But they seem to have nothing to do with the worship of God. Therefore, it is not the case that the reason for the ceremonial precepts is that they have to do with the worship of God.

Objection 2: Some claim that the ceremonial precepts are the ones having to do with the solemn feasts (*solemnitates*), and that the name 'ceremonial' is taken from the word for wax candles (*cerei*), which are lit on the feast days. But there are many other things besides the solemn feasts that have to do with the worship of God. Therefore, it does not seem that the reason why these precepts are called 'ceremonial' is that they have to do with the worship of God.

Objection 3: According to some, the precepts in question are called 'ceremonial' because they are norms or rules for salvation (*regulae salutis*), where 'χαîρε' in Greek is the same as the Latin '*salve*'. But all the precepts of the Law—and not just those having to do with the worship of God—are rules for salvation. Therefore, it is not the case that the only precepts called 'ceremonial' are those that have to do with the worship of God.

Objection 4: Rabbi Moses claims that the precepts called 'ceremonial' are such that the reason behind them is not obvious. But many things that have to do with the worship of God have an obvious reason behind them, e.g., the observance of the Sabbath, the celebration of the Passover (*Phase*), and the celebration of the Feast of Tabernacles (*Secopegia*). Therefore, it is not the case that the ceremonial precepts are the ones that have to do with the worship of God.

But contrary to this: Exodus 18:19–20 says, "Be present to the people in those things that pertain to God . . . to show the people the ceremonies and the rite of worship."

I respond: As was explained above (q. 99, a. 4), the ceremonial precepts specify the moral precepts with respect to God, whereas the judicial precepts specify the moral precepts with respect to one's neighbor. But man is ordered to God through the worship that is owed to Him, and so the precepts that have to do with the worship of God are properly called 'ceremonial precepts'.

Moreover, the explanation of the name 'ceremonial' was given above (q. 99, a. 3) when the ceremonial precepts were distinguished from the other precepts.

Reply to objection 1: Sacrifices and other such things that seem to be immediately ordered to God are not the only things having to do with the worship of God. In addition, those who worship God have to be duly prepared for worshiping Him—just as, in other subject matters, whatever serves as a preparation for the end falls under the science that deals with the end.

Now precepts of the sort that are given in the Law about the clothing and food of those who worship God, along with other such things, have to do with the preparation of the ministers themselves, in order that they might be fit for worshipping God—in just the way that some of those who minister to a king engage in special observances. Hence, these precepts are likewise contained among the ceremonial precepts.

Reply to objection 2: This explanation of the name 'ceremonial' does not seem very plausible, especially in light of the fact that there is little in the Law about wax candles being lit on the solemn feasts; instead, as is clear from Leviticus 24:2, even the lamps of the Candlestick itself were prepared with olive oil.

Still, one could claim that on the solemn feasts everything that had to do with the worship of God was observed more carefully and that, accordingly, all the ceremonial precepts are included in the observance of the solemn feasts.

Reply to objection 3: This explanation of the name 'ceremonial' does not seem very plausible, either. For the name 'ceremony' (*ceremonia*) comes from the Latin rather than the Greek.

Still, one could claim that since man's salvation (*salus*) is from God, it is the precepts that order man toward God which seem to be the rules of salvation, and that it is for this reason that the precepts pertaining to the worship of God are called ceremonial.

Reply to objection 4: This explanation of the nature of the ceremonial precepts is in a certain sense plausible—not that these precepts are called 'ceremonial' because the reason behind them is not obvious, but rather that this is a certain consequence of their being ceremonial. For, as will be explained below (a. 2), the precepts having to do with the worship of God must necessarily be figurative, and so in this regard the reason behind them is not very obvious.

Article 2

Are the ceremonial precepts figurative?

It seems that the ceremonial precepts are not figurative (*figurativa*):

Objection 1: As Augustine says in *De Doctrina Christiana* 4, every teacher (*doctor*) has the responsibility of speaking in such a way that he can be easily understood—and this seems especially necessary in the giving of law, since the precepts of the law are being proposed to ordinary people (*populus*). Hence, as Isidore puts it, law ought to be evident. Therefore, if the ceremonial precepts were given as figures of something else, then Moses, in not explaining what they were figures of, seems to have handed down precepts of this kind in the wrong way.

Objection 2: What is done in the worship of God ought to have the highest integrity (*maxime debent habere honestatem*). But performing certain actions in order to represent other actions seems theatrical or poetical; for in the theater it used to be that certain actions of others were represented by the things enacted there. Therefore, it seems that actions of this sort ought not to be performed in the worship of God. But as has been explained, (a. 1), the ceremonial precepts are ordered toward the worship of God. Therefore, the ceremonial precepts ought not to be figurative (*figuralia*).

Objection 3: In *Enchiridion* Augustine says, "God is especially worshiped by faith, hope, and charity." But the precepts given about faith, hope, and charity are not figurative. Therefore, the ceremonial precepts should not be figurative.

Objection 4: In John 4:24 our Lord says, "God is a spirit, and those who adore Him must adore Him in spirit and in truth." But a figure is not the truth itself—in fact, *figure* and *truth* are divided off from one another as contraries. Therefore, the ceremonial precepts, which have to do with the worship of God, should not be figurative.

But contrary to this: In Colossians 2:16–17 the Apostle says, "Let no man therefore judge you in meat or in drink or with respect to a feast day or a new moon or the Sabbaths, which are a shadow of things to come."

I respond: As has already been explained (a. 1), the precepts called 'ceremonial' are the ones that are ordered toward the worship of God. Now there are two types of worship of God, interior and exterior. For since man is composed of body and soul, both must be applied to the worship of God—so that, namely, the soul worships with interior worship and the body worships with exterior worship. This is why Psalm 83:3 says, "My heart and my flesh have rejoiced in the living God." And just as the body is ordered toward God through the soul, so too exterior worship is ordered toward interior worship.

Now interior worship consists in the soul's being joined to God through understanding and affection (*per intellectum et affectum*). And so insofar as there are different modes in which the understanding and affection of the worshiper of God are correctly joined to God, there are correspondingly different ways in which a man's exterior acts are applied to worshiping God.

For instance, in the state of future beatitude the human intellect will see the divine Truth in itself, and so exterior worship will consist not in any sort of figures but solely in the praise of God that proceeds from interior cognition and affection—this according to Isaiah 51:3 ("Joy and gladness shall be found therein, thanksgiving, and the voice of praise").

On the other hand, in the state of the present life, we are unable to see the divine Truth in itself; instead, as Dionysius puts it in *De Caelesti Hierarchia*, chap. 1, the ray of divine truth must illumine us under certain sensible figures—though in diverse ways corresponding to the diverse states of human cognition.

For instance, as the Apostle says in Hebrews 9:8, in the Old Law it was not the case either that the divine truth was evident in itself or even that the way to attain it was made known. And so it was necessary for exterior worship under the Old Law not only to prefigure the future truth that is going to be made manifest in heaven, but also to prefigure Christ, who is the Way leading men to that truth in heaven.

By contrast, in the state of the New Law this Way has already been revealed. Hence, the Way does not have to be prefigured as something future, but instead has to be brought to mind as something past or present—and the only thing that needs to be prefigured is the truth of the glory that has not yet been revealed.

And so it is that the Apostle says in Hebrews 10:1, "The Law has the shadow of the good things to come, not the very image of the things." For a shadow is something less than an image, and so 'image' has to do with the New Law and 'shadow' with the Old Law.

Reply to objection 1: What is divine must be revealed to men only in a way corresponding to their capacity for understanding; otherwise, there would be an occasion for their downfall, since they might scorn what they cannot understand. And thus it was more advantageous for the divine mysteries to be handed down to an unsophisticated people under the veil of figures, so that they might have at least an implicit cognition of the mysteries as long as they used the figures to honor God.

Reply to objection 2: Just as poetical things fail to be understood by human reason because of the imperfect nature of the truth contained in them, so human reason cannot perfectly understand divine things because of their excess of truth. And so in both cases what is needed is a representation by means of sensible figures.

Reply to objection 3: In this passage Augustine is talking about interior worship. Still, as has been explained, exterior worship must be ordered toward interior worship.

Reply to objection 4: The same reply holds for the fourth objection, since it is through Christ that men are introduced more fully to the spiritual worship of God.

Article 3

Was it right for there to be a multiplicity of ceremonial precepts?

It seems that it was not right for there to be a multiplicity of ceremonial precepts:

Objection 1: Things that are ordered toward an end should be proportioned to that end. But as has been explained (aa. 1–2), the ceremonial precepts are ordered toward the worship of God and toward being a figure of Christ. But as 1 Corinthians 8:6 says, "There is but one God, from whom are all things . . . and one Lord Jesus Christ, through whom are all things." Therefore, the ceremonial precepts should not have been multiplied.

Objection 2: The multitude of ceremonial precepts was an occasion of sin (*occasio transgressionis*)—this according to Peter in Acts 15:10 ("Why do you tempt God by putting a yoke upon the necks of the disciples which neither our fathers nor we have been able to bear?") But the transgression of divine precepts is contrary to human salvation. Therefore, since, as Isidore says, every law should be consistent with human salvation, it seems that a multiplicity of ceremonial precepts should not have been given.

Objection 3: As has been explained (a. 2), the ceremonial precepts have to do with the exterior and corporeal worship of God. But the law ought to have put less emphasis on (*diminuere*) this sort of corporeal worship, since it was ordered toward Christ, who taught men to worship God "in spirit and in truth," as John 4:23–24 says. Therefore, it was not right for a multiplicity of ceremonial precepts to be given.

But contrary to this: Hosea 8:12 says, "I shall write within them my many laws." And Job 11:6 says, ". . . that He might show you the secrets of wisdom, and that His law is manifold."

I respond: As was explained above (q. 96, a. 1), every law is given to a particular people, and every people contains two kinds of men. Some men are prone to evil, and they have to be coerced by the precepts of the law, as was noted above (q. 95, a. 1); other men have an inclination toward the good—either by nature or by habit (or, better, by grace)—and they have to be instructed by the precepts of the law and moved to become better.

It was with respect to both kinds of men that it was advantageous for the ceremonial precepts to be multiplied in the Old Law.

For among this people there were some prone to idolatry, and so they had to be recalled from idolatrous worship to the worship of God by means of the ceremonial precepts. And since there were many ways in which men devoted themselves to idolatry, a multiplicity of contrary precepts had to be instituted in order to repress each of those ways. Again, a multiplicity of precepts had to be imposed on such men, so that burdened, as it were, by things that had to do with the worship of God, they would not have the free time to devote themselves to idolatry.

On the other hand, as far as those who were inclined toward the good are concerned, the multiplication of ceremonial precepts was likewise necessary, both because in this way their minds were recalled to God in diverse ways and more assiduously, and also because the mystery of Christ, which was prefigured through these ceremonial precepts, brought a multiplicity of benefits to the world, and there were many things to consider about this mystery that needed to be prefigured through diverse ceremonial precepts.

Reply to objection 1: When what is ordered to an end is sufficient for attaining that end, then a single such thing is sufficient for a single end. For instance, if a single medicine is efficacious, then it is sometimes sufficient for inducing health, and in such a case there is no need for the medicines to be multiplied.

On the other hand, if there is a lack of power or perfection on the part of what is ordered to the end, then it has to be multiplied, in the way that many remedies are applied to someone who is sick when a single remedy is not sufficient to cure him.

Now the ceremonies of the Old Law were weak and imperfect both in representing the mystery of Christ, which is surpassing, and in subjecting the minds of men to God. Hence, in Hebrews 7:18–19 the Apostle says, "There is indeed a setting aside of the former commandment, because of the weakness and unprofitableness thereof. For the law brought nothing to perfection." And that is why ceremonies of this sort had to be multiplied.

Reply to objection 2: A wise lawgiver permits lesser sins in order that greater sins might be avoided. And so in order that the sin of idolatry might be avoided, along with the sin of pride, which would be nurtured in the hearts of the Jews if they were to fulfill all the precepts of the Law, God did not refrain from handing down a multiplicity of ceremonial precepts simply because the Jews might easily take this as an occasion for sinning.

Reply to objection 3: In many ways the Old Law put less emphasis on corporeal worship. It was for this reason that the Law decreed that sacrifices were not to be offered in every place or by just anyone. And it established a multiplicity of precepts of this sort in order to put less emphasis on exterior worship, as Rabbi Moses of Egypt likewise points out. Yet it was necessary not to attenuate the corporeal worship of God to such an extent that men would fall into the worship of demons.

Article 4

Are the ceremonies of the Old Law correctly divided into sacrifices, sacred things, sacraments, and observances?

It seems that the ceremonies of the Old Law are not correctly divided into sacrifices (*sacrificia*), sacred things (*sacra*), sacraments (*sacramenta*), and observances (*observantiae*):

Objection 1: The ceremonies of the Old Law prefigured Christ. But this was done solely through the sacrifices, which prefigured the sacrifice by which Christ offered Himself, in the words of Ephesians 5:2, "as an oblation and a sacrifice to God." Therefore, only the sacrifices were ceremonial.

Objection 2: The Old Law was ordered toward the New Law. But in the New Law the sacrifice is itself the Sacrament of the Altar. Therefore, in the Old Law sacrifices should not have been distinguished from sacraments.

Objection 3: A thing called 'sacred' is one that has been dedicated to God, in the sense in which a tabernacle and its vessels were said to be 'made sacred' (*sacrificari*). But as has been explained (a. 1), all the ceremonial precepts were ordered toward the worship of God. Therefore, all the ceremonial precepts were sacred things. Therefore, it is incorrect for just one part of the ceremonial precepts to be named 'sacred things'.

Objection 4: Observances (*observantiae*) are so-called from 'observing' (*ab observando*). But all the precepts of the Law were supposed to be observed; for Deuteronomy 8:11 says, "Take heed, and beware lest at any time you forget the Lord your God, and neglect His commandments and judgments and ceremonies." Therefore, observances should not be posited as just one part of the ceremonies.

Objection 5: The solemn feasts (*solemnitates*) are counted among the ceremonies, since they are a foreshadowing of what is to come, as is clear from Colossians 2:16–17; the same holds for oblations (*oblationes*) and gifts (*munera*), as is clear from the Apostle in Hebrews 9:9. But none of these seems to be contained under any of the above divisions. Therefore, the division of the ceremonies set forth above is incorrect.

But contrary to this: In the Old Law each of the divisions set forth above is called a ceremony. For *sacrifices* are called ceremonies in Numbers 15:24 ("The multitude shall offer a calf . . . and the sacrifices and libations thereof, as the ceremonies require"). Again, Leviticus 7:35 says of the *sacrament* of Orders, "This is the anointing of Aaron and his sons in the ceremonies." Likewise, Exodus 38:21 says of the *sacred things*, "These are the instruments of the tabernacle of the testimony . . . in the ceremonies of the Levites." And 3 Kings 9:6 says of the *observances*, "If you . . . shall turn away from following me and will not observe my . . . ceremonies which I have set before you . . ."

I respond: As was explained above (a. 1), the ceremonial precepts are ordered toward the worship of God. In this worship we can consider (a) the worship itself, (b) the worshipers, and (c) the instruments of worship.

The worship itself consists specifically in the *sacrifices* that are offered in reverence for God.

The instruments of worship are the *sacred things*, e.g., the tabernacle, the vessels, and other things of this sort.

As for the worshipers, there are two things to consider:

The first is their being ordained for divine worship (*institutio ad cultum divinum*), which takes place through a consecration of the people or of the ministers; and this is what the *sacraments* have to do with.

The second is their unique way of life (*singularis conversatio*), through which they are distinguished from those who do not worship God; and this is what the *observances* concerning food, clothing, and other such things have to do with.

Reply to objection 1: Sacrifices had to be offered in certain places by certain men, and all of this pertains to the worship of God. Hence, just as the immolated Christ is signified through their sacrifices, so too the sacraments and sacred things of the New Law were prefigured through their sacraments and sacred things. What's more, the way of life of the people of the New Law was prefigured through their observances. And all these things have to do with Christ.

Reply to objection 2: The sacrifice of the New Law, i.e., the Eucharist, contains Christ Himself, who is the author of sanctification; for as Hebrews 13:12 says, "He sanctified the people by His own blood." And that is why this sacrifice is also a sacrament.

By contrast, the sacrifices of the Old Law did not contain Christ but instead prefigured Him, and so they are not called sacraments. Instead, in order to signify this separately, there were certain sacraments in the Old

Law that were figures of the future consecration—even though it was also the case that sacrifices were adjoined to some of the consecrations.

Reply to objection 3: The sacrifices and sacraments were also 'sacred things'. However, there were certain things which were called 'sacred' because they had been dedicated to the worship of God and yet which were neither sacrifices nor sacraments. And so these things retained for themselves the general name 'sacred things'.

Reply to objection 4: Those things that had to do with the way of life of the people worshiping God retained for themselves the general name 'observances' insofar as they did not fall under the previously mentioned divisions. For instance, they were not called 'sacred things', since they did not have an immediate relation to the worship of God in the way that the tabernacle and its vessels did. Instead, they were ceremonial through a certain entailment, viz., insofar as they had to do with the fitness of the people worshiping God.

Reply to objection 5: Just as sacrifices were offered in a determinate place, so too they were offered at determinate times. Hence, the solemn feasts seem to be numbered among the sacred things.

On the other hand, oblations and gifts are counted with the sacrifices, since they were offered to God. Thus in Hebrews 5:1 the Apostle says, "Every high priest taken from among men is ordained for men in things that pertain to God, that he might offer up gifts and sacrifices."

QUESTION 102

The Reasons for the Ceremonial Precepts

We next have to consider the reasons (*causae*) for the ceremonial precepts. On this topic there are six questions: (1) Are there reasons for the ceremonial precepts? (2) Do the ceremonial precepts have literal reasons or just figurative reasons? (3) What are the reasons for the sacrifices? (4) What are the reasons for the sacred things? (5) What are the reasons for the sacraments? (6) What are the reasons for the observances?

Article 1

Are there reasons for the ceremonial precepts?

It seems that there are no reasons for the ceremonial precepts (*non habeant causam*):

Objection 1: The Gloss on Ephesians 2:15 (". . . making void the Law of the commandments by the decrees") says, "That is, making the Law void with respect to bodily observances, by means of the decrees, i.e., by means of the Gospel precepts, which are based on reasons (*ex ratione*)." But if the observances of the Old Law had been based on reasons, then there would not have been no point to making them void by means of the reasoned decrees (*per rationabilia decreta*) of the New Law. Therefore, there were no reasons for the ceremonial observances of the Old Law.

Objection 2: The Old Law is the successor of the law of nature. But as Augustine says in *Super Genesim ad Litteram* 8 about the prohibition regarding the tree of life, the law of nature contained a precept that had no reason behind it except to test man's obedience. Therefore, in the Old Law some precepts likewise had to be given by which man's obedience would be tested and which had no intrinsic reason behind them (*de se nullam rationem haberent*).

Objection 3: A man's deeds are called moral insofar as they proceed from reason. Therefore, if there were reasons for the ceremonial precepts, then the ceremonial precepts would not differ from the moral precepts. Therefore, it seems that the ceremonial precepts have no causes, since the reason for a precept is taken from some cause.

But contrary to this: Psalm 18:9 says, "The precept of the Lord is clear, enlightening the eye." But the ceremonial precepts are God's precepts. Therefore, they are clear. But they would not be clear unless they had a reasoned cause (*nisi haberent rationabilem causam*). Therefore, the ceremonial precepts have a reasoned cause.

I respond: Since, according to the Philosopher in *Metaphysics* 1, "one who is wise has the role of giving order," what proceeds from God's wisdom must be well-ordered, as the Apostle says in Romans 13:1.

Now for things to be well-ordered, there are two requirements:

The first is that they be ordered toward a fitting end, since the end is the principle of all order in things to be done. For if things occur by chance without tending toward an end (*praeter intentionem finis*), or if they are done playfully and not in earnest, we say that they are unordered (*inordinata*).

Second, what is ordered toward an end must be proportioned to the end. From this it follows that the reasons for things that are ordered toward an end are themselves taken from the end—in the way that, as *Physics* 2 points out, the reason for the configuration of a saw is taken from the act of cutting.

Now it is clear that the ceremonial precepts, like all the other precepts of the Law, were instituted by God's wisdom; hence, Deuteronomy 4:6 says, "This is your wisdom and your understanding in the sight of the nations." Thus, one must assert that the ceremonial precepts are ordered toward an end and that their reasoned causes can be gathered (*assignari*) from that end.

Reply to objection 1: The observances of the Old Law can be described as being 'without reason' (*sine ratione*) in the sense that the deeds themselves did not have an explanation (*ratio*) in terms of their own nature—for instance, that a garment should not be made from wool and linen. However, they were able to be reasoned observances because of their relation to something else, viz., either because they were a figure of something or because they prevented something.

By contrast, the decrees of the New Law, which consist principally in having faith in God and in loving God, take their reason from the very nature of the act.

Reply to objection 2: The prohibition regarding the tree of the knowledge of good and evil was not made because the tree was evil by its nature; instead, this prohibition had a reason that was taken from its relation to something else, viz., insofar as it was a figure of something. In the same way, the ceremonial precepts of the Old Law have their reason in their relation to something else.

Reply to objection 3: It is by their very nature that moral precepts such as 'You shall not kill' and 'You shall not steal' have reasoned causes. By contrast, as has been explained, the ceremonial precepts have their reasoned causes from their relation to something else.

Article 2

Do the ceremonial precepts have literal reasons or only figurative reasons?

It seems that the ceremonial precepts have only figurative reasons (*causa figuralis*) and not literal reasons (*causa litteralis*):

Objection 1: The main ceremonial precepts were circumcision and the immolation of the Paschal lamb. But each of these had only a figurative reason, since each was given as a sign. For Genesis 17:11 says, "You shall circumcise the flesh of your foreskin, that it may be a sign of the covenant between me and you." And regarding the celebration of the Passover, Exodus 13:9 says, "It shall be as a sign in your hand, and as a memorial before your eyes." Therefore, *a fortiori*, the other ceremonial precepts have only figurative reasons.

Objection 2: An effect is proportioned to its cause. But as was explained above (q. 101, a. 2), all the ceremonial precepts are figurative. Therefore, they have only a figurative reason.

Objection 3: If something is of itself indifferent with respect to its being done this way or that way, then it does not seem to have a literal reason. But there are some ceremonial precepts that do not seem to determine whether things should be done this way or that way—for instance, with respect to the number of animals that are to be offered or with respect to other particular circumstances of this sort. Therefore, the [ceremonial] precepts of the Old Law do not have literal reasons.

But contrary to this: Just as the ceremonial precepts were figures of Christ, so too was the history (*historia*) of the Old Testament; for 1 Corinthians 10:11 says, "All these things happened to them in figure." But in the historical events of the Old Testament there is, besides a mystical or figurative meaning (*intellectus mysticus seu figuralem*), a literal meaning as well. Therefore, the ceremonial precepts likewise had literal reasons in addition to their figurative reasons.

I respond: As was explained above (a. 1), the reason behind what is ordered toward an end must be taken from that end. Now the ceremonial precepts have two ends, since they were ordered (a) toward the worship of God for that time and (b) toward being figures of Christ—in the same way that, as Jerome points out in his commentary on Hosea, the words of the prophets were related to the present time in such a way that they were spoken to prefigure the future as well.

So, then, there are two ways to think of the reasons for the ceremonial precepts of the Old Law.

In the first way, the reasons are derived from the worship of God that was to be observed for that time. These are the *literal* reasons, which have to do (a) with preventing idolatrous worship, or (b) with commemorating certain favors bestowed by God, or (c) with intimating God's excellence, or (d) with making clear the mental disposition required for that time in those who were worshiping God.

In the second way, the reasons are derived from the fact that the precepts are ordered toward being figures of Christ. And in this way the precepts have *figurative* and *mystical* reasons—whether these reasons are taken (a) from Christ Himself and the Church (and this pertains to the *allegorical sense*), or (b) from the practice of the Christian people (and this pertains to the *moral sense*), or (c) from the state of future glory insofar as we are led to it by Christ (and this pertains to the *anagogical sense*).

Reply to objection 1: Just as the interpretation of a metaphorical locution in Scripture is literal, given that the words were used in order to signify metaphorically, so too the signification of those ceremonies of the Law that commemorate God's favors and have been instituted because of those favors does not go beyond the order of literal reasons. Hence, the fact that the reason for the celebration of the Passover is taken from its being a sign of the liberation from Egypt, or the fact that circumcision is a sign of the covenant (*pactum*) God had with Abraham, pertains to a literal reason.

Reply to objection 2: This objection would go through if the ceremonial precepts had been given solely in order to prefigure the future and not in order to worship God in the present.

Reply to objection 3: It was explained above (q. 96, a. 6) that there are general reasons for human laws, but not reasons for their particular conditions; rather, the particular conditions stem from the judgment of those who institute the laws. So, too, many of the particular determinations found in the ceremonies of the Old Law have only a figurative reason and not a [specific] literal reason, even though they do have a general literal reason.

Article 3

Can appropriate reasons be assigned
for the ceremonies that involve sacrifices?

It seems that appropriate reasons cannot be assigned for the ceremonies that involve sacrifices:

Objection 1: What was offered in sacrifice were things necessary for sustaining human life, e.g., certain animals and breads. But God does not need such sustenance—this according to Psalm 49:13 ("Will I eat the flesh of bullocks? Or will I drink the blood of goats?"). Therefore, it was inappropriate for sacrifices of this sort to be offered to God.

Objection 2: The only animals offered in divine sacrifice were (a) three kinds of quadrupeds, viz., oxen, sheep, and goats, and (b), among the birds, the turtledove and the dove generally speaking, while the sparrow was sacrificed in the specific case of the cleansing of a leper. But there are many other animals more noble than these. Therefore, since whatever is best ought to be given to God, it seems that it should not have been just these things that had to be offered to God as sacrifices.

Objection 3: Just as man has dominion from God over the birds and the beasts, so too he has dominion over the fish. Therefore, it was inappropriate for fish to be excluded from the divine sacrifices.

Objection 4: It is commanded indifferently that doves and turtledoves be offered. Therefore, just as it is commanded that the young of the doves be offered, so too it should be commanded that the young of the turtledoves be offered.

Objection 5: As is clear from what is said in Genesis 1, God is the author of the life not only of men but also of the animals. But death is opposed to life. Therefore, what should have been offered to God were living animals instead of animals that had been killed—especially because in Romans 12:1 the Apostle likewise admonishes that we should present our bodies "as a living sacrifice, holy and pleasing to God."

Objection 6: If animals were offered to God in sacrifice only after they had been killed, then it does not seem to make any difference how they were killed. Therefore, it was inappropriate for the manner of immolation to be set down—especially in the case of birds, as in Leviticus 1:15–16.

Objection 7: Every defect in an animal is a path to corruption and death. Therefore, if animals that had already been killed were being offered to God, then it was inappropriate to prohibit the sacrifice of a defective animal, e.g., a lame or blind or otherwise unclean animal.

Objection 8: Those who offer victims to God ought to partake of those victims—this according to the Apostle in 1 Corinthians 10:18 ("Are not they that eat of the sacrifices partakers of the altar?"). Therefore, it was inappropriate for certain parts of the victims—viz., the blood, the fat, the breastbone, and the right shoulder—to be withheld from those who were offering the sacrifice.

Objection 9: Just as holocausts were offered in honor of God, so too were peace-offerings and sin-offerings. But no female animal was offered to God in a holocaust, even though holocausts were made with both quadrupeds and birds. Therefore, it was inappropriate for female animals to be offered as peace-offerings and sin-offerings, and yet for birds not to be offered as peace-offerings.

Objection 10: All peace-offerings seem to be of the same type. Therefore, no distinction should have been drawn among them, as Leviticus 7:15–16 does in mandating that the flesh of some peace-offerings cannot be eaten a day later, whereas the flesh of others can be.

Objection 11: All sins alike involve a turning away from God. Therefore, a single type of sacrifice should have been offered for all sins in order to be reconciled with God.

Objection 12: All the animals that were offered in sacrifice were offered in a single way, viz., after having been killed. Therefore, it does not seem appropriate that offerings of things that grow in the earth should have been made in diverse ways. For instance, sometimes an offering was made of grain, sometimes of flour, and sometimes of bread, where the bread was sometimes cooked in an oven, sometimes in a pan, and sometimes on a grill.

Objection 13: All things that we have use of are such that we should acknowledge them as coming from God. Therefore, it was unfitting that, besides animals, the only things offered to God were bread, wine, oil, incense, and salt.

Objection 14: Bodily sacrifices express the heart's interior sacrifice, by which a man offers his own spirit to God. But in an interior sacrifice there is more of sweetness, which is represented by honey, than of sharpness, which is represented by salt; for Ecclesiasticus 24:27 says, "My spirit is sweet beyond honey." Therefore, it was inappropriate to prohibit in sacrifices the use of honey and leaven, which make bread tasty, and to prescribe instead the use of salt, which is sharp, and incense, which has a bitter taste.

Therefore, it seems that the things having to do with the ceremonies of the sacrifices do not have a reasoned cause.

But contrary to this: Leviticus 1:13 says, "The priest shall offer all the gifts and burn them upon the altar for a holocaust and a most sweet savor to the Lord." But according to Wisdom 7:28, "God loves no one except he who dwells with wisdom," from which one can infer that whatever is acceptable to God is imbued with wisdom. Therefore, the ceremonies of the sacrifices were imbued with wisdom, i.e., they had reasoned causes.

I respond: As was explained above (a. 2), there are two kinds of reasons for the ceremonies of the Old Law, viz., (a) *literal* reasons, given that the ceremonies are ordered toward the worship of God, and (b) *figurative* or *mystical* reasons, given that the ceremonies are ordered toward prefiguring Christ. The ceremonies having to do with sacrifices can be appropriately assigned reasons of both kinds.

Insofar as the sacrifices are ordered to the worship of God, there are two reasons that can be specified for them:

The first reason is that the sacrifices represent that ordering of the mind toward God which the one offering the sacrifice is incited to. Now the correct ordering of the mind to God involves (a) a man's acknowledging that all the things he has are from God as their first principle and (b) his ordering all those things to God as their ultimate end. This was represented in the oblations and sacrifices by the fact that a man offered some of his own things to honor God, as if acknowledging that he had them from God. Accordingly, in 1 Paralipomenon 39:14 David said, "All things are yours, and we have given you what we received from your hand." So in offering sacrifices man was professing that God is the first principle of the creation of things and the ultimate end to whom all things should be directed.

Now because the correct ordering of the mind to God involves the human mind's (a) not recognizing any first author of things other than God alone and (b) not setting up any other being as its own last end, the Law prohibits offering sacrifices to any being other than God—this according to Exodus 22:20 ("Anyone who sacrifices to gods besides the Lord alone shall be put to death"). And so the second reason that can be specified for the ceremonies involving sacrifice is that through ceremonies of this sort men were restrained from offering sacrifices to idols. Moreover, this is why the precepts concerning the sacrifices were given to the Jewish people only after they had fallen into idolatry by worshiping the molten calf; it was as if these sacrifices were instituted in order that a people eager to offer sacrifices should offer such sacrifices to God rather than to idols. Hence, Jeremiah 7:22 says, "For I spoke not to your fathers, and I commanded them not, in the day that I brought them out of the land of Egypt, concerning the matter of burnt offerings and sacrifices."

Now among all the gifts that God gave to the human race once it had already fallen through sin, the principal one was that He gave His own Son. Hence, John 3:16 says, "God so loved the world as to give His only-begotten Son, so that whoever believes in Him may not perish, but may have eternal life." And so the most powerful sacrifice is the one by which Christ "offered Himself to God . . . for an odor of sweetness," as Ephesians 5:22 puts it. Because of this, all the other sacrifices were offered in the Old Law in order that they might be figures of this one singular and principal sacrifice, in the way that the imperfect is a figure of the perfect. Hence, in Hebrews 10:11 the Apostle says that a priest of the Old Law "offered many times the same sacrifices, which are never able to take away sins," whereas Christ "offered one sacrifice for sins" for all times. And since the reason for a figure is taken from what it is a figure of, it follows that the reasons for the figurative sacrifices of the Old Law are to be taken from the true sacrifice of Christ.

Reply to objection 1: God did not want sacrifices of this sort for the sake of the things themselves that were offered, as if He stood in need of them; hence, Isaiah 1:11 says, "I did not want holocausts of rams, and the fat of fatlings, and the blood of calves and lambs and goats." Rather, as has been explained, He wanted them offered to Himself (a) in order to prevent idolatry, (b) in order to signify the appropriate ordering of the human mind toward God, and (c) in order to be a figure of the mystery of human redemption accomplished by Christ.

Reply to objection 2: In all the respects just mentioned, there was an appropriate reason why the animals in question—and not others—were offered to God in sacrifice.

First, in order to prevent idolatry. For the idolaters offered all the other animals to their gods or used them for their sorceries (*maleficia*), whereas among the Egyptians, with whom they had lived, it was an abomination to kill the animals in question, and so the Egyptians did not offer them in sacrifice to their own gods. Hence, Exodus 8:26 says, "We shall sacrifice the abominations of the Egyptians to the Lord our God." For the Egyptians worshiped sheep and venerated goats, since demons appeared in the shape of these animals, whereas they used oxen for agriculture, which they held to be something sacred.

Second, this was appropriate in two ways for the ordering of the mind toward God:

(a) First, because animals of the sort in question are especially the ones that human life is sustained by and, along with this, they are the cleanest animals and eat the cleanest food. By contrast, other animals are such that they either live in the wild and are not commonly thought of as useful to men or, if domesticated, then, like the pig and the goose, eat unclean food. But only what is pure should be offered to God. On the other hand, the birds in question were specifically offered to God because they were found in abundance in the promised land.

(b) Second, because purity of mind is signified by the immolation of animals of the sort in question. For as the Gloss on Leviticus 1 says, "We offer a calf when we conquer the pride of the flesh; we offer a lamb when we correct our irrational movements; we offer a goat when we conquer our lasciviousness; we offer a turtledove when we preserve our chastity; we offer unleavened bread when we eat the unleavened bread of sincerity." Moreover, the turtledove clearly signifies charity and simplicity of mind.

Third, these animals were appropriately offered as figures of Christ. For the Gloss on the same passage says, "Christ is offered in the calf as a figure of the power of the cross; He is offered in the lamb as a figure of His innocence; He is offered in the ram as a figure of His sovereignty; He is offered in the goat as a figure of the sinful flesh. What is shown in the turtledove and the dove is the conjoining of the two natures"—or, alternatively, the turtledove signifies chastity and the dove signifies charity— "and the flour is a figure of the sprinkling of believers with the water of Baptism."

Reply to objection 3: Since they live in the water, fish are more distant from man than are the other animals, which live in the air, as man does. Again, when fish are taken from the water, they immediately die, and so they could not be offered in the temple in the way the other animals were.

Reply to objection 4: Among the turtledoves, the older ones are better than the younger, whereas it is just the opposite in the case of the doves. And so, as Rabbi Moses puts it, they were told to offer turtledoves and the young of the doves, because everything that is the best should be given to God.

Reply to objection 5: The animals offered in sacrifice were killed because animals that have been killed are useful to man, insofar as God has given them to man for food. And so they were consumed by fire, because it was through fire that, having been cooked, they were apt for human use. Again, the killing of the animals signified the destruction of sins, and also signified that men deserved to be killed for their sins—as if the animals were being killed in place of the men in order to signify the expiation of sins.

Moreover, the killing of these animals signified the killing of Christ.

Reply to objection 6: The Law set down a specific way of killing the immolated animals in order to exclude the other ways by which idolaters sacrificed animals to their idols.

Alternatively, as Rabbi Moses puts it, "The Law chose a type of killing by which the animals being killed would suffer the least." This excluded (a) cruelty (*immisericordia*) on the part of those offering the sacrifice and (b) the mangling (*deterioratio*) of the animals killed.

Reply to objection 7: Defective animals are normally held in contempt by men, and so it was forbidden that they be offered in sacrifice to God. Because of this, it was also forbidden "to offer the price of a prostitute or the price of a dog in the house of God" (Deuteronomy 23:18). And for this same reason they did not offer animals that were not yet seven days old; for such animals were, so to speak, abortive—not as yet fully firmed up because of their tender age.

Reply to objection 8: There were three kinds of sacrifice:

One kind was totally consumed by fire, and this was called a *holocaust* (*holocaustum*). For a sacrifice of this sort was offered to God specifically to show reverence to His majesty and love for His goodness, and it corresponded to *the state of perfection in fulfilling His counsels*. And so the sacrifice was totally consumed by fire, in order that just as the entire animal, reduced to smoke, ascended upward, so this might signify that the whole man and all that belonged to him were subject to the Lord God and were to be offered to Him.

The second kind of sacrifice was a *sin-offering* (*sacrificium pro peccatis*), which was offered to God because of the need for the forgiveness of sins and which corresponded to *the state of those doing penance as satisfaction for their sins*. The offering was divided into two parts: one part of it was consumed by fire, and the other part went for the use of the priests in order to signify that the expiation of sins is accomplished by God through the ministry of the priests. The only exception occurred when the sacrifice was being offered for the sins of all the people or specifically for the sins of the priests. On such occasions the whole offering was consumed by fire. For it would have been unfitting for the priests to have use of what had been offered for their sins in such a way that nothing sinful should remain in them. For this would not have been satisfaction for their sins. After all, if the offering were handed over for the use of those whose sins it had been offered for, this would seem to be equivalent to their not having made an offering at all.

The third kind of sacrifice was called a *peace-offering* (*hostia pacifica*), which was offered to God either as a thanksgiving (*pro gratiarum actione*) or for the well-being (*salus*) and prosperity of those making the offering, in return for a favor already received or to be received in the future, and which corresponds to *the state of those proficient in the fulfillment of the commandments*. These offerings were divided into three parts: (a) one part was burned in honor of God, (b) another part went for the use of the priests, and (c) the third part went for the use of those making the offering. This was in order to signify that (a) man's well-being proceeds from God, (b) under the direction of God's ministers, and (c) with the cooperation of the very men who are being saved.

Now it was a general rule that the blood and fat did not go either for the use of the priests or for the use of those making the offering; instead, the blood was poured out at the foot of the altar in honor of God, while the fat was burned up in the fire.

One reason for this was to prevent idolatry, since idolaters drank the blood of sacrificial victims and ate their fat—this according to Deuteronomy 32:38 ("Of the victims [of the idols] they ate the fat, and drank the wine of their drink offerings").

A second reason was to give shape to a humane way of life. For the use of the blood was forbidden to them in order that they might abhor the shedding of human blood; hence, Genesis 9:4–5 says, "Flesh with blood you shall not eat; for I will require the blood of your lives." And the use of the fat was forbidden to them in order to stave off licentiousness; hence, Ezechiel 34:3 says, "You killed that which was fat."

A third reason was to show reverence for God. For blood is especially necessary for life and, because of this, the soul is said to exist in the blood (see Leviticus 17:11). Fat, on the other hand, points to an abundance of food. And so in order to show that life and every adequate supply of goods come to us from God, the blood was poured out and the fat burned in honor of God.

A fourth reason is that it prefigured the shedding of Christ's blood and the abundance of charity with which He offered Himself to God on our behalf.

The priests were given the breast and right shoulder from the peace-offerings in order to prevent the type of divination that is called spatulamancy (*spatulamantia*), since divinations were made in the shoulder-blades (*in spatulis*) of sacrificed animals, as well as in their breastbones.

And so these things were taken away from those who made the offerings. This practice also signified that the priest needed (a) 'wisdom of the heart' (*sapientia cordis*) in order to instruct the people, and this is signified by the breast, which covers the heart, as well as (b) the fortitude to endure their defects, and this is signified by the right shoulder.

Reply to objection 9: Since the holocaust was the most perfect among the sacrifices, only the male was offered in a holocaust. For the female is an imperfect animal.

Now turtledoves and doves were offered because of the poverty of those making the offering; for they were unable to offer the bigger animals. Moreover, since the peace-offerings were offered spontaneously and no one was forced to offer them unwillingly, birds of this sort were offered not in the peace-offerings, but rather in the holocausts and sin-offerings, which had to be offered at certain times. In addition, these birds fit in with the perfection of the holocausts because they fly high in the sky, and they fit in with the sin-offerings because of their sad singing.

Reply to objection 10: The holocaust was the chief among the sacrifices, since the entire offering was consumed by fire in honor of God, and none of it was eaten. The second place in holiness was held by the sin-offering, which was eaten only in the court, by the priests, and on the very day of the sacrifice. The third place was held by the peace-offerings of thanksgiving, which were eaten on the same day, but anywhere in Jerusalem. And the fourth place was had by peace-offerings made with a private vow (*ex voto*); the meat from these sacrifices could be eaten on the next day as well.

The reason for this ordering is that man is obligated to God (a) most of all because of His majesty; (b) second, because of the offenses committed against Him; (c) third, because of favors already received; and (d) fourth, because of favors hoped for.

Reply to objection 11: As was explained above (q. 73, a. 10), sins are made more serious by the status of the sinner. And so the offerings mandated for the sins of a priest or a ruler are different from those mandated for the sins of a private person.

But notice that, as Rabbi Moses points out, "the graver the sin was, the lower the species of animal offered for it. Hence, the goat, which is a very low animal, was offered for idolatry, which is the gravest sin, whereas a calf was offered for a sin of ignorance on the part of a priest, and a ram was offered for a sin of negligence on the part of a ruler."

Reply to objection 12: In the case of sacrifices, the Law wished to take into account the poverty of those making the offering, so that someone who could not afford a four-footed animal might at least offer a bird, and someone who could not afford a bird might at least offer bread, and someone who could not afford bread might at least offer flour or grain.

The figurative reason for this is that the bread signifies Christ, who is the living bread, as John 6:41 says. Under the law of nature Christ was like grain in the faith of the patriarchs; and then He was like flour in the teaching of the Law of the prophets; and then He was like formed bread-dough after He assumed His human nature; and then He was cooked by a fire, i.e., He was formed by the Holy Spirit in the oven of the virgin's womb, and He was also cooked in a baking pan through the hardships (*labores*) He endured in the world; and on the cross He was, as it were, consumed by fire on a grill.

Reply to objection 13: Among the things that grow from the earth, those that are useful to man are either (a) for eating, and from these bread was offered, or (b) for drinking, and from these wine was offered, or (c) for seasoning, and from these oil and salt were offered, or (d) for healing, and from these incense, which is aromatic and gives strength, was offered.

Now the bread is a figure of Christ's flesh; the wine is a figure of His blood, through which we have been redeemed; the oil is a figure of Christ's grace; the salt is a figure of His knowledge; and the incense is a figure of His prayer.

Reply to objection 14: The reason why honey was not offered in sacrifices to God was that it used to be offered in sacrifices to idols, and also in order to prevent any sort of carnal delight or pleasure in those who intended to make sacrifice to God.

The reason why leaven was not offered was to prevent spoiling. And perhaps it, too, used to be offered in sacrifices to idols.

On the other hand, salt was offered because it prevents spoiling, and sacrifices to God ought to be unspoiled. Also, salt signifies the discretion of wisdom as well as the mortification of the flesh.

Incense was offered in order to signify the devotion of mind required in those making the offering, and also to signify the odor of a good reputation. For incense is rich and fragrant. Moreover, since the 'sacrifice of jealousy' (*sacrificium zelotypiae*) proceeded not from devotion but instead from suspicion, incense was not offered in this sort of sacrifice (see Numbers 5:15).

Article 4

Can appropriate reasons be assigned for the ceremonies that involve the sacred things?

It seems that appropriate reasons cannot be assigned for the ceremonies that involve the sacred things:

Objection 1: In Acts 17:24 Paul says, "God, who made the world, and all things therein; He, being Lord of heaven and earth, dwells not in temples made with hands." Therefore, it was inappropriate for the tabernacle or temple to be instituted under the Old Law for the worship of God.

Objection 2: The status of the Old Law was altered only by Christ. But the tabernacle signified the status of the Old Law. Therefore, it should not have been altered by the building of a temple.

Objection 3: The divine law should be principally concerned with inducing men to worship God. But as is clear in the New Law, the making of many altars and many temples contributes to an increase in the worship of God. Therefore, it seems that even in the Old Law there should have been many temples or tabernacles, and not just a single temple or single tabernacle.

Objection 4: The tabernacle or temple was ordered toward the worship of God. But it is especially God's oneness and simplicity that should be venerated. Therefore, it does not seem to have been appropriate for the tabernacle or temple to be divided by veils.

Objection 5: The power of the first mover, who is God, is first apparent in the East (*in parte orientis*), where the first motion begins. But the tabernacle was instituted for the adoration of God. Therefore, it should have faced toward the East rather than the West.

Objection 6: In Exodus 20:4 the Lord commanded that they should "not make . . . a graven thing, nor the likeness of anything." Therefore, it was improper for there to have been graven images of the Cherubim in the tabernacle or temple. Similarly, there seems to have been no appropriate reason for the ark or the propitiatory or the candelabra or the table or the two altars to be there.

Objection 7: In Exodus 20:24 the Lord commanded, "You shall make an altar of earth unto me," and again, "You shall not go up by steps unto my altar." Therefore, it was inappropriate to command later on that the altar be made of wood covered with gold or bronze and of such a height that it could not be ascended except by means of steps. For Exodus 27:1–2 says,

"You shall make also an altar of setim wood, which shall be five cubits long and as many wide . . . and three cubits high . . . and you shall cover it with brass." And Exodus 30:1,3 says, "You shall make . . . an altar to burn incense of setim wood . . . and you shall overlay it with the purest gold."

Objection 8: There should be nothing superfluous in the works of God, since there is nothing superfluous in the works of nature. But a single covering (*operimentum*) is sufficient for one tabernacle or house. Therefore it was inappropriate for the tabernacle to have many coverings, viz., curtains, blankets made of the hair of goats, ram skins dyed red, and violet-colored skins (see Exodus 26).

Objection 9: Exterior consecration signifies interior holiness, whose subject is the soul. Therefore, since the tabernacle and its vessels were inanimate corporeal things, it was inappropriate for them to be consecrated.

Objection 10: Psalm 33:2 says, "I will bless the Lord at all times, His praise will always be in my mouth." But the solemn feasts (*solemnitates*) were instituted in order to praise God. Therefore, it was inappropriate for certain set days to be instituted for celebrating the feasts.

So, then, it seems that there were no appropriate reasons for the ceremonies involving the sacred things.

But contrary to this: In Hebrews 8:4 the Apostle says, "Those who offer gifts according to the law . . . serve as an example and shadow of heavenly things. As Moses was told when he was finishing the tabernacle: 'See to it that you make all things according to the pattern which was shown to you on the mountain.'"

I respond: The whole of the exterior worship of God was principally ordered toward men's holding God in reverence. However, human affection is such that things that are common and not distinctive in relation to other things are less revered, whereas things that have some mark of excellence in distinction from other things are more revered and admired. Because of this, it has been the custom among men that kings and princes, who should be held in reverence by their subjects, dress in more expensive clothes and have bigger and more beautiful houses to live in.

For this reason, it was necessary that special times and special places and special vessels and special ministries should be ordered toward the worship of God, so that men's minds might thereby be led to a greater reverence for God.

Similarly, as has been explained (a. 2), the status of the Old Law was instituted in order that it might be a figure of the mystery of Christ. But that which is a figure of another must itself be something determinate in order to represent a likeness of that other. And so, again, it was necessary for special things to be observed in those matters that involve the worship of God.

Reply to objection 1: The worship of God involves two things, viz., the God who is being worshiped and the men who are doing the worshiping. The God who is being worshiped is not Himself confined to any corporeal place, and hence it is not because of Him that a tabernacle or temple must be fashioned. By contrast, the men worshiping Him are corporeal, and it is because of them that a special tabernacle or temple must be instituted for the worship of God—and this for two reasons.

First, when they come together at such a place with the thought that the place has been set aside for the worship of God, they come with greater reverence.

Second, the arrangement of the tabernacle or temple signifies certain things that bear upon the excellence of the divine nature or of the humanity of Christ.

Thus, in 3 Kings 8:27 Solomon says, "If heaven and the heavens of heavens cannot contain You, how much less this house which I have built for You?" And after this he adds, "Let Your eyes be open upon this house . . . of which You said, 'My name shall be there', . . . so that You may hear the prayer of Your servant and of Your people Israel." From this it is clear that the house of the sanctuary was instituted not in order to capture God, as if He might live there as in a place, but rather in order that (a) the name of God might dwell there, i.e., in order that the knowledge of God might be made manifest in that place through the things that were said and done there, and in order that (b) out of reverence for the place, the prayers made there would be heard more readily because of the devotion of those praying.

Reply to objection 2: In the time before Christ the status of the Old Law was not altered with respect to the fulfillment of the Law, which was accomplished only through Christ. However, it was altered with respect to the condition of the people who were living under the Law.

For at first the people were living in the desert and had no fixed dwelling place. After that, they waged various wars against the neighboring Gentiles. Finally, at the time of David and Solomon the people lived in a very peaceful state. And it was at that time that the temple was first built on the site that Abraham, instructed by God, had designated for sacrifice. For Genesis 22:2 says that Lord commanded Abraham to offer his son "for a holocaust upon one of the mountains which I will show you." And afterwards it says that he named this place 'The Lord Sees'—as if it were in accord with God's foreknowledge that this place had been chosen for divine worship. It is for this reason that Deuteronomy 12:5–6 says, "You shall come to the place which the Lord your God shall choose . . . and you shall offer . . . your holocausts and victims."

However, before the time of David and Solomon it would have been inappropriate to designate a place for building the temple, and this for the three reasons Rabbi Moses puts forth: first, so that the Gentiles would not appropriate that place for themselves; second, so that the Gentiles would not destroy that place; and, third, so that the tribes would not all want to have that place in their own territory, with quarrels and disputes arising as a result. And so the temple was not built until the people had a king who could stop the quarreling.

Before that time, a tabernacle that could be carried to different places had been ordained for the worship of God—as if there was not yet a determinate place for divine worship. And this is the literal reason for the difference between the tabernacle and the temple.

Now one possible figurative reason is that this signified our twofold status. For the tabernacle, which is mutable, signifies the state of our present mutable life, whereas the temple, which is fixed and stable, signifies the state of the future life, which is completely unchangeable. And because of this it is said that when the temple was being built, no sound of hammers or saws was heard, and this was to signify that all disturbances will be far removed from the future state.

An alternative reason is that the tabernacle signifies the status of the Old Law, whereas the temple constructed by Solomon signifies the status of the New Law. Hence, only Jews worked on the construction of the tabernacle, whereas even Gentiles from Tyre and Sidon cooperated in the building of the temple.

Reply to objection 3: Both a literal and a figurative reason can be given for the fact that there is just one temple or tabernacle.

The literal reason is to prevent idolatry. For the Gentiles used to build different temples to different gods, and so in order to strengthen in the minds of men a faith in God's oneness, God willed that sacrifices to Himself should be offered in just one place. Again, He did this in order to show that it was not because of itself that bodily worship was acceptable to Him. And so they were kept from offering sacrifices at just any time or place. By contrast, worship under the New Law, whose sacrifice contains spiritual grace, is acceptable to God in its own right, and this is why the multiplication of altars and temples is accepted under the New Law.

However, as regards those things that had to do with the spiritual worship of God and consisted in the teaching of the Law and the prophets, even under the Old Law there were different places set aside where they would come together to praise God. These were called 'synagogues', just as now there are places called 'churches' where the Christian people congregate to praise God. And so among us the church has taken the place of both the temple and the synagogue, since the very sacrifice of the Church is spiritual, and so there is no distinction among us between the place of sacrifice and the place of teaching.

A possible figurative reason is that the oneness of the temple signifies the oneness of the Church, whether the Church militant or the Church triumphant.

Reply to objection 4: Just as the oneness of God or the oneness of the Church is represented by the oneness of the tabernacle or temple, so the distinctions within the tabernacle or temple represent the distinctions among the things which are subject to God and out of which we rise up to venerate God.

Now the tabernacle was divided into two parts. The one part was called the 'Holy of Holies' and was situated to the West, and the other was called 'The Holy Place' and was situated to the East. Again, in front of the tabernacle there was a court.

There are two reasons for this division.

The first reason is that the tabernacle is ordered toward the worship of God. For the divisions within the tabernacle are a figure of the different parts of the world. The part called the 'Holy of Holies' was a figure of the higher world, i.e., the world of spiritual substances, whereas the part called the 'Holy Place' represented the corporeal world. And this is why the Holy Place was divided off from the Holy of Holies by a veil divided into four colors designating the four elements, viz., (a) flaxen (*byssum*), signifying *earth*, since linen, i.e., flax, grows from the earth; (b) purple (*purpura*), signifying *water*, since the purple tint was made from a certain shellfish found in the sea; (c) violet (*hyacinthus*), signifying *air*, since it has the color of the atmosphere; and (d) twice-dyed scarlet (*coccus bis tinctus*), signifying *fire*. The reason for this is that the matter composed of the four elements is a barrier by which the incorporeal substances are veiled from us. And so only the high priest entered the inner tabernacle, i.e., the Holy of Holies, and this just once a year, in order to signify that man's final perfection is to enter into that higher world. By contrast, the priests entered the outer part, i.e., the Holy Place, every day—though not the people, who went only as far as the court. For while the people can perceive corporeal things, only the wise are able, by their study, to grasp the inner natures (*rationes*) of those things.

As for the figurative reasons, the outer tabernacle, called the Holy Place, signifies the status of the Old Law, as the Apostle says in Hebrews 9:6–7. For the priests always entered the outer tabernacle in carrying out the duties associated with the sacrifices.

By contrast, the inner tabernacle, called the Holy of Holies, signifies either heavenly glory or the spiritual status of the New Law, which is a sort of beginning of future glory. Christ led us into this status, and a figure of this was the fact that the high priest entered into the Holy of Holies by himself.

Now the veil was a figure of the hiddenness of the spiritual sacrifices within the old sacrifices. And as for the fact that the veil was decorated with four colors, the flaxen signified the purification of the flesh (*carnis puritatem*), the purple signified the sufferings that the saints have endured for the sake of God, the twice-dyed scarlet signified the twofold love of God and neighbor, and the violet signified heavenly contemplation (*caelestis meditatio*).

Now the people and the priests were related in different ways to the status of the Old Law. For the people concentrated on the corporeal sacrifices that were offered in the court. The priests, on the other hand, took into account the reasons behind the sacrifices and had a more explicit faith concerning the mysteries of the Christ. And so they entered the outer tabernacle, which was divided off from the court by a veil, because certain things about the mystery of the Christ which were veiled from the people were made known to the priests. However, as Ephesians 3:5 says, these things were not revealed to them in full, as they would later be revealed in the New Testament.

Reply to objection 5: Adoration toward the West was introduced in the Law in order to prevent idolatry. For all the Gentiles worshiped toward the East out of reverence for the sun. Hence, Ezechiel 8:16 says, "Some had their backs toward the temple of the Lord, and their faces to the East, and they adored in the direction of the sun's rising." Hence, in order to prevent this, the tabernacle had the Holy of Holies situated to the West, so that they worshiped toward the West.

This can also serve as a figurative reason, since the whole status of the prior tabernacle was ordered toward being a figure of the death of Christ, which is signified by the West—this according to Psalm 67:5 ("He ascends unto the West, the Lord is His name").

Reply to objection 6: Both literal and figurative reasons can be given for the things that were contained in the tabernacle.

The literal reasons, of course, have to do with their relation to the worship of God.

Since, as was explained above, the *inner tabernacle*, called the 'Holy of Holies', signified the higher world of spiritual substances, there were three things contained in that inner tabernacle. One was the ark of the covenant (*arca testamenti*), in which there was a golden vase containing manna, the rod of Aaron that had flowered, and the tablets on which the ten precepts of the Law had been written. This ark was situated between the two Cherubim, who were looking at each other. And above the ark there was a sort of table, called the 'propitiatory', which was located over the wings of the Cherubim and was being held up, as it were, by the Cherubim themselves—as if one were to imagine that this table was the seat of God. The reason the table was called the 'propitiatory' is that the people received propitiation when the high priest prayed. And it was held up by the Cherubim, who were bowing down to God, whereas the ark of the covenant served as the footstool, as it were, of the One sitting on the propitiatory.

These three things signify three things that exist in that higher world.

First there is *God*, who exists above all things and is incomprehensible to every creature. And in order to represent His invisibility, no likeness of Him was placed there. Instead, a representation of His seat was placed there, because a creature's being subject to God is comprehensible, just like a seat's being subject to the one sitting on it. Again, there are *spiritual substances* called 'angels' in that higher world, and they are signified by the two Cherubim. They are looking at each other in order to signify their concord with one another—this according to Job 25:2 ("He makes concord in high places"). And the reason why there was not just one Cherub was to signify the multitude of heavenly spirits and to prevent their being worshiped by those who were commanded to worship the one God alone. Again, *conceptions* (*rationes*) of all the things that are brought to completion in our world are contained in some sense in that intelligible world—in the way that conceptions of effects are contained in their causes and that conceptions of his artifacts are contained in a craftsman. And this was signified by the ark, which, by the three things it contained, represented the three most powerful things in human affairs, viz., wisdom, which was represented by the tablets of the covenant; political power (*potestas regi-minis*), which was represented by Aaron's rod; and life, which was represented by the manna that sustained life. An alternative explanation is that these three items represented three of God's attributes, viz., wisdom, in the tablets; power, in the rod; and goodness, in the manna, both because of its sweetness and because it was given to the people out of God's mercy and so was conserved in memory of God's mercy.

Figures of these three things are likewise found in Isaiah's vision (see Isaiah 6). For he saw the Lord exalted and elevated on His throne, and he saw the Seraphim attending Him, and the house was filled with the glory of God. And so the Seraphim proclaimed, "All the earth is full of the glory of God." And thus, as has been explained, the likenesses of the Seraphim were placed there not to be worshiped—something forbidden by the first precept of the Law—but instead, as has been explained, as a sign of their ministry.

On the other hand, the *outer tabernacle*, which signifies the present world, likewise contained three things, viz., the *altar of incense* (*altare thymiamatis*), which was directly across from the ark; the *table of proposi-tion* (*mensa propositionis*), with the twelve loaves of bread on it, which was positioned toward the North; and the *candelabra*, which was positioned toward the South. These three items seem to correspond to the three things contained in the ark, but they represented them in a more evident way. For the conceptions of things have to be given a more evident manifestation than their existence in the minds of God and the angels in order for wise men to be able to grasp them, where the wise men are signified by the priests entering the tabernacle. The candelabra signified, as a visible sign, the wisdom that was expressed in intelligible words on the tablets. The altar of incense signified the role of the priests in leading the people back to God, and this was likewise signified by the rod. For the sweet-smelling incense, which signified the holiness of a people acceptable to God, was lit on that altar; as Apocalypse 8:3–4 puts it, the smoke of aromatic herbs signifies the "prayers of the saints" (*iustificationes sanctorum*). The dignity of the priests was appropriately signified in the ark by the rod and in the inner tabernacle by the altar of incense, because the priest is a mediator between God and the people, ruling over the people by God's power, which is signified by the rod. And he offers, as it were, the fruit of his rule, viz., the holiness of the people, on the altar of incense. Now the table signifies the nourishment of life, just as the manna does—though the former is a more common and coarse sort of nourishment, while the latter is sweeter and more subtle. The candelabra was appropriately positioned toward the South and the table toward the North, since, as *De Caelo et Mundo* 2 says, the South is the right-hand part of the world, whereas the North is the left-hand part. And wisdom pertains to the right, as do other spiritual goods, whereas temporal nourishment pertains to the left—this according to Proverbs 3:16 ("In her left hand are riches and glory"). Moreover, the power of the priesthood occupies a middle place between temporal things and spiritual wisdom, since both spiritual wisdom and temporal goods are dispensed through this power.

Now these things can be assigned another and more literal reason.

The ark contained the tablets of the Law in order to prevent the Law from being forgotten; hence, Exodus 24:12 says, "I will give you two stone tablets, and the Law and commandments which I have written, that you might teach them to the children of Israel." Aaron's rod was placed there in order to suppress the dissension of the people against Aaron's priesthood; hence, Numbers 17:10 says, "Carry back the rod of Aaron into the tabernacle of the testimony, that it may be kept there for a token of the rebellious children of Israel." The manna was preserved in the ark as a reminder of the favors God had bestowed on the children of Israel in the desert; hence, Exodus 16:32 says, "Fill an omer with it, and let it be kept unto generations to come hereafter, that they may know the bread, wherewith I fed you in the wilderness." The candelabra was set up to give honor to the tabernacle, since a house's magnificence includes its being well lit. For the candelabra had seven arms to signify, as Josephus says, the seven planets by which the whole world is illumined, and the reason why the candelabra was positioned toward the South was that the course of the planets is from our South. The altar of incense was set up so that the tabernacle would continually have sweet-smelling smoke (*fumus boni odoris*)—both because of the veneration due the tabernacle and also as a remedy for the stench that necessarily arose from the outflow of blood and the killing of the animals. For things that smell bad are despised as vile, whereas things with a good odor are more highly valued by men. The table was set up to signify that the priests who served the temple were supposed to have their food in the temple; hence, as Matthew 12:4 says, only the priests were allowed to eat the twelve loaves of bread that were placed on the table as a memorial of the twelve tribes. Now the table was not placed exactly in the middle in front of the propitiatory. This was in order to prevent an idolatrous rite, since on the feasts of the moon the Gentiles put a table in front of the idol of the moon; hence, Jeremiah 7:18 says, "The women knead the dough, to make cakes to the queen of heaven."

In the *court outside the tabernacle* there was an altar of holocausts, on which sacrifices were offered to God from among the things possessed by the people. And so the people who offered sacrifices by the hand of the priests could be present in the court. But only the priests, whose role was to offer the people to God, could go up to the inner altar, on which the very devotion and holiness of the people was offered to God. The altar of holocausts was placed in the court outside the tabernacle in order to prevent idolatrous worship, since the Gentiles set up altars within their temples to offer sacrifices to their idols.

Now figurative reasons can be assigned for all these things on the basis of the tabernacle's relation to Christ, of whom it is a figure. Note that in order to signify the imperfection of the figures in the Law, diverse figures were set up in the temple to signify Christ.

For He is signified by the propitiatory, since, as 1 John 2:2 puts it, He Himself is "a propitiation for our sins." And it was appropriate for the propitiatory to be held up by the Cherubim, since it is written of Him that all the angels of God adore Him, as Hebrews 1:6 says. He is likewise signified by the ark, since just as the ark was made of setim wood, so Christ's body consists of the purest members. The ark was overlaid with gold, since Christ was full of wisdom and charity, which are signified by gold. Inside the ark there was a golden urn, i.e., a holy soul, containing manna, i.e., all the plenitude of divinity. Inside the ark there was also the rod, i.e., priestly power, since He was made a priest forever. The tablets of the covenant were also there, in order to signify that Christ Himself is the lawgiver. Christ Himself is also signified by the candelabra, since He says, "I am the light of the world," and the seven lights signify the seven gifts of the Holy Spirit. He is spiritual food—this according to John 6:41 ("I am the living bread"), while the twelve loaves signify the twelve apostles, or their teaching. Alternatively, the candelabra and the table can signify the teaching and faith of the Church, which likewise gives light and spiritual renewal. Christ is also signified by the two altars, the altar of holocausts and the altar of incense. For it is through Him that we must offer to God all the works of the virtues, or all the things by which we afflict our flesh and which are offered, as it were, on the altar of holocausts, along with those things which, with a greater perfection of mind and through the spiritual desires of the perfect, are offered to God in Christ as on the altar of incense—this according to Hebrews 13:15 ("By Him therefore let us offer the sacrifice of praise always to God").

Reply to objection 7: The Lord commanded that the altar be constructed in order to offer gifts and sacrifices both in honor of God and for the sustenance of the ministers who served in the tabernacle. Now there are two commands given by the Lord concerning the construction of the altar.

The first occurs at the beginning of the Law in Exodus 20, where the Lord commanded that the altar be made of earth or at least of uncut stones and, again, that they not make the altar so high that it would be necessary to ascend it by means of steps. This was out of hatred for idolatrous worship, since the Gentiles constructed ornate and towering altars to their idols, and they believed there to be something holy and divine in their altars. It was for the same reason that the Lord commanded in Deuteronomy 16:21, "You shall plant no grove, nor any tree near the altar of the Lord your God." For the idolaters used to offer sacrifices under trees because it was pleasant and shady there.

There was also a figurative reason for these precepts. For in Christ, who is our altar, we should confess the true nature of flesh with respect to His humanity, and this corresponds to making an altar of earth. And with respect to His divinity, we should confess His equality with the Father, and this corresponds to not ascending the altar by means of steps. Nor should we allow near to Christ the Gentile teaching which leads to licentiousness.

However, once the tabernacle had been fashioned in honor of God, then there was no reason to fear such occasions of idolatry. And so the Lord commanded that the altar of holocausts, which would be visible to all the people, should be made out of bronze, and that the altar of incense, which only the priests would see, should be made out of gold. Nor was bronze so precious that the people would be moved to idolatry because of it.

However, since Exodus 20:26 adds—as a reason for the precept 'You shall not ascend my altar by steps'— ". . . lest your nakedness be revealed," one has to think that this precept was likewise instituted to prevent idolatry. For on the feasts of Priapus the Gentiles uncovered their genitals before the people. But later on the priests were ordered to use loincloths to cover their genitals, and so there was no danger in building an altar so high that at the hour of sacrifice the priests offering the sacrifices would ascend the altar by wooden steps—not permanent steps but portable ones.

Reply to objection 8: The main body of the tabernacle consisted of boards standing on end, which were covered on the inside by curtains of four different colors, viz., twisted flaxen, violet, purple, and twice-dyed scarlet. But these curtains covered only the sides of the tabernacle, whereas the roof of the tabernacle was one covering of violet-colored skins and, over that, another covering of red ram-skins, and, over that, a third covering of goat-skin blankets that not only covered the roof of the tabernacle but came down all the way to the ground and covered the outside of the boards of the tabernacle.

The general literal reason behind these coverings was to decorate and protect the tabernacle, in order that it might be treated with reverence. As for specific reasons, according to some the curtains signified the starry heaven, which is dotted with the different stars; and the blankets signified the waters that are above the firmament; and the red-colored skins signified the empyrean heaven, where the angels reside; and the violet-colored skins signified the heaven of the Holy Trinity.

On the other hand, the figurative reasons for these things are as follows: The boards out of which the tabernacle was built signify Christ's faithful ones, out of whom the Church is built. The walls are covered on the inside with curtains of four different colors because the faithful are decorated interiorly with four virtues: for as the Gloss puts it, "The twisted flax signifies the flesh striving after chastity, the violet signifies the mind desiring heavenly things, the purple signifies the flesh subject to the passions, and the twice-dyed scarlet signifies the mind shining forth from among the passions with the love of God and neighbor. As for the coverings on the roof, the violet-colored skins signify the prelates and doctors, in whom the celestial way of life should shine forth; the red-colored skins signify a readiness for martyrdom; and the goat-skin blankets—which, as the Gloss says, were exposed to the wind and the rain—signify austerity of life and perseverance against enemies.

Reply to objection 9: The sanctification of the tabernacle and its vessels had as its literal reason that they might be treated with great reverence, given that through this consecration they were being assigned to the worship of God.

On the other hand, the figurative reason is that this sanctification signifies the spiritual sanctification of the living tabernacle, viz., the tabernacle of the faithful from whom the Church of Christ is built.

Reply to objection 10: As can be seen from Numbers 28 and 29, in the Old Law there were seven periodic solemn feasts (*solemnitates temporales*) and one continuous solemn feast.

For there was, as it were, a continuous feast, since a lamb was sacrificed every day in the morning and in the evening, and this continuous feast of continual sacrifice represented the perpetuity of God's happiness.

Now the first of the periodic feasts was the one that was repeated every seventh day, and this was the solemn feast of the Sabbath, which, as explained above (q. 100, a. 5), was celebrated in memory of the creation of things.

The second solemn feast was repeated every month, viz., the feast of the New Moon (*festum Neomeniae*), which was celebrated to commemorate the work of divine governance. For things here below vary mainly according to the moon's motion, and so this feast was celebrated at the time of the new moon—and not at the time of the full moon, in order to prevent the idolatrous worship that offered sacrifices at the time of the full moon.

The other five feasts were celebrated once a year, and they recalled favors that had been specially given to that people. The feast of the Passover (*festum Phase*) was celebrated in the first month, in order to commemorate the favor of the liberation from Egypt, while the feast of Pentecost (*festum Pentecostes*) was celebrated fifty days later, in order to recall the favor of the giving of the Law. The other three feasts were celebrated in the seventh month, the whole of which was solemn among them in the same way that the seventh day was. On the first day of the seventh month was the feast of Trumpets (*festum Tubarum*), in memory of the liberation of Isaac, when Abraham found the ram caught by its horns, which were represented by the horns that they sounded. The feast of Trumpets was, as it were, an invitation to prepare oneself for the next feast, which was celebrated on the tenth day. This was the feast of Atonement (*festum Expiationis*), in memory of that favor by which, at the prayer of Moses, God forgave (*propitiatus est*) the sin of the people worshiping the calf. After this, the feast of Booths (*festum Scenopegiae*), i.e., the feast of Tabernacles, was celebrated for seven days to commemorate the favor of God's protecting them and leading them through the desert, where they lived in tents. Hence, on that feast they had to have the fruit of the most beautiful tree, i.e., the citron, and a tree of dense foliage, i.e., the myrtle, which is fragrant, and the branches of palm trees, and the willows of the brook, which keep their greenness for a long time. All of these are found in the promised land (*terra promissionis*), and signify that God had led them through the arid terrain of the desert into a delightful land. On the eighth day another feast was celebrated, viz., the feast of Assembly and Collection (*festum Coetus atque Collectae*), in which the necessary expenses for divine worship were collected from the people. This signified the union of the people and the peace bestowed on them in the promised land.

Now the figurative reasons for these feasts are as follows: The continual sacrifice of the lamb is a figure of the perpetuity of Christ, who is the Lamb of God—this according to Hebrews 13:8 ("Jesus Christ yesterday and today, and the same for ever"). The Sabbath signifies the spiritual rest given to us through Christ, as Hebrews 4 says. The feast of the New Moon, which is the beginning of a new moon, signifies the illumination of the primitive Church by Christ through His preaching and miracles. The feast of Pentecost signifies the descent of the Holy Spirit on the apostles, whereas the feast of Trumpets signifies the preaching of the apostles. The feast of Atonement signifies the washing away of the sins of the Christian people, whereas the feast of Tabernacles signifies their journey in this world, in which they walk by advancing in virtue. The feast of Assembly and Collection signifies the congregation of the faithful in the kingdom of heaven, and that is why this feast was called "most holy." And these last three feasts were continuous with one another because, as Psalm 83 says, it is necessary for those whose vices have been forgiven to make progress in virtue until they arrive at the vision of God.

Article 5

Can appropriate reasons be assigned
for the sacraments of the Old Law?

It seems that appropriate reasons cannot be assigned for the sacraments of the Old Law:

Objection 1: What is done in divine worship should not be similar to the observances of the idolaters; for Deuteronomy 12:31 says, "You shall not do in like manner to the Lord your God. For they have done to their gods all the abominations which the Lord abhors." But in their worship, the worshipers of idols used to cut themselves to the point of drawing blood; for 3 Kings 18:28 says, "They cut themselves after their manner with knives and lancets, until they were all covered with blood." For this reason the Lord commanded in Deuteronomy 14:1, "You shall not cut yourselves, nor shave your heads over the dead." Therefore, it was inappropriate for circumcision to have been instituted in the Law.

Objection 2: What is done in divine worship should be upright and serious—this according to Psalm 34:18 ("I will praise You in a serious people"). But it seems to smack of a certain levity that men should eat in haste.

Therefore, it was inappropriate for Exodus 12 to command that they should eat the paschal lamb in haste. In addition, other rules that were instituted concerning the eating of the lamb seem to have no reason at all behind them.

Objection 3: The sacraments of the Old Law were figures of the sacraments of the New Law. But the paschal lamb signifies the sacrament of the Eucharist—this according to 1 Corinthians 5:7 ("Christ our Pasch is sacrificed"). Therefore, there should also have been sacraments in the Law that prefigured the other sacraments of the New Law such as Confirmation, Extreme Unction, Matrimony, and the others.

Objection 4: One can be purified only of impurities. But in God's eyes, nothing corporeal is considered unclean; for every corporeal entity is a creature of God and, as 1 Timothy 4:4 says, "Every creature of God is good, and nothing is to be rejected that is received with thanksgiving." Therefore, it was inappropriate for them to have to be purified because of contact with a human corpse or with a similar kind of bodily infection.

Objection 5: Ecclesiasticus 34:4 asks, "What can be made clean by the unclean?" But the ashes of a burnt red heifer (see Hebrews 9:13) were unclean; for Numbers 19:7ff. says that the priest who killed the red heifer was rendered impure until evening, and likewise the one who burned it and the one who collected its ashes. Therefore, it was inappropriate for there to have been a precept in the Law according to which the unclean were purified by the sprinkling of these ashes.

Objection 6: Sins are not anything corporeal that can be moved from one place to another; nor can a man be cleansed of his sins by anything unclean. Therefore, it was inappropriate that, in order to expiate the sins of the people, the priest would confess the sins of the children of Israel over a goat which would then carry them into the desert, whereas through another goat, which the priests used for purification and which they burned along with a calf outside the camp, they were rendered unclean, so that they had to wash their clothes and their bodies with water.

Objection 7: That which has already been made clean does not need to be made clean again. Therefore, it was inappropriate that after a man's leprosy, or even his house, had been made clean, another purification should be made, as Leviticus 14 has it.

Objection 8: Spiritual uncleanness cannot be washed away by corporeal water or by shaving. Therefore, it seems that there is no reason for the Lord to have commanded in Exodus 30:18–20 that a brass washbasin with its own base be fashioned for the washing of the hands and feet of the priests who were about to enter the tabernacle, or for Him to have commanded in Numbers 8:7 that the Levites be sprinkled with the water of purification and shave all the hair off their bodies.

Objection 9: What is greater should not be sanctified by what is lesser. Therefore, it was inappropriate for the consecration of the higher and lower priests (Leviticus 8) and of the Levites (Numbers 8) to be done with bodily ointment and corporeal sacrifices and corporeal oblations.

Objection 10: 1 Kings 16:7 says, "Men see those things that appear, but the Lord beholds the heart." But the things that appear outwardly in a man are his bodily disposition and his clothes. Therefore, it was inappropriate for special vestments to be assigned to the higher and lower priests (Exodus 28). And there seems to be no reason why anyone should be excluded from the priesthood because of bodily defects, in the way stated in Leviticus 21:17–18: "Whoever of your seed throughout their families has a blemish, he shall not offer bread to his God; neither shall he approach to minister to Him if he is blind or lame."

Therefore, it seems that there were no reasons behind the sacraments of the Old Law.

But contrary to this: Leviticus 20:8 says, "I am the Lord your God, who sanctifies you." But nothing comes from God without a reason; for Psalm 103:24 says, "You have made all things with wisdom." Therefore, in the sacraments of the Old Law, which were ordered toward the sanctification of men, there was nothing that did not have a reasoned cause behind it.

I respond: What are properly called sacraments are things that were done to the worshipers of God by way of a consecration through which they were in some sense set off (*deputabantur*) for the worship of God. Now the worship of God pertained in a general way to the whole people and in a specific way to the priests and Levites, who were the ministers of divine worship. And so among the sacraments of the Old Law, some pertained in general to all the people, whereas others pertained specifically to the ministers.

With respect to both groups, there were three requirements:

The first is being initiated (*institutio*) into the state of worshiping God. This general initiation with respect to everyone was accomplished through *circumcision*, without which no one was admitted to anything having to do with the Law. With respect to the priests, on the other hand, the initiation was accomplished through the *consecration of the priests*.

The second requirement was the exercise (*usus*) of what pertained to divine worship. With respect to the people, this consisted in the eating of the Paschal meal, which, as is clear from Exodus 12:43–45, no one uncircumcised was admitted to. With respect to the priests, it consisted in the offering of sacrifices (*oblatio victimarum*) and in the eating of the loaves of proposition and other items set aside for the use of the priests.

The third requirement was the removal of whatever might impede someone from divine worship, viz., impurities. And so with respect to the people, certain purifications from exterior impurities were instituted, along with rites for the atonement for sins; and with respect to the priests, the washing of the hands and feet was instituted, along with the shaving of the hair.

For all these sacraments there were both (a) literal reasons, insofar as the sacraments were ordered toward the worship of God for that time period, and (b) figurative reasons, insofar as they were ordered toward being figures of Christ. This will become clear as we go through them one by one.

Reply to objection 1: The main literal reason behind circumcision was to give witness to faith in the one God. For since Abraham was the first to separate himself from the non-believers (*infideles*), leaving his home and his relatives, he was the first to receive circumcision. The reason for this is set forth by the Apostle in Romans 4:9–11: "He received the sign of circumcision, a seal of the justice of the faith that he had while still uncircumcised." More specifically, we read, "Abraham's faith was reputed to justice . . ." because "he believed in hope against hope"—i.e., he believed in the hope of grace against the hope of nature—"that he would become the father of many nations," even though he was old and his wife was an old woman and barren. And in order that this witness, along with the imitation of Abraham's faith, should be strengthened in the hearts of the Jews, they received a sign in their flesh which they could not forget about. Hence, Genesis 17:13 says, "My covenant (*pactum*) shall be in your flesh for a perpetual covenant (*foedus*)."

Now the reason why it was done on the eighth day was that before then a boy is very delicate and could suffer gravely from it and is not yet considered strong enough (*solidatum*). Hence, even animals were not offered before their eighth day. On the other hand, the reason why it was not delayed longer was that some boys might refuse the sign of circumcision because of the pain, and also that some parents, given that their love for their sons would increase after constant contact with them and after the boys had grown, would prevent them from being circumcised.

A second possible reason was to reduce concupiscence in the bodily member in question.

A third reason was to give affront to the sacred rites of Venus and Priapus, in which that bodily part was honored.

Moreover, the Lord prohibited only the sort of slashing that took place in the worship of idols, and circumcision was not similar to that.

On the other hand, the figurative reason for circumcision was that it was a figure of the removal of corruption which was to be brought about by Christ and which will be perfectly completed on the eighth day, i.e., the time of resurrection. And it was because all the corruption of sin and punishment came to us through our carnal origin from the sin of our first parent that this circumcision was done to the body's generative member. Hence, the Apostle says in Colossians 2:11, "You are circumcised with a circumcision not made by hand, in despoiling of the body of the flesh, but in the circumcision of our Lord Jesus Christ."

Reply to objection 2: The literal reason for the Paschal meal was to commemorate the favor by which God led them out of Egypt. Hence, through the celebration of this meal they professed that they belonged to that people whom God had taken to Himself out of Egypt. For when they were liberated from Egypt, they were commanded to sprinkle the lamb's blood on the threshold of their houses, as if proclaiming that they rejected the rites of the Egyptians, who worshiped the ram. Hence, by sprinkling or rubbing the lamb's blood on their door-posts, they were freed from the danger of being exterminated that threatened the Egyptians.

Now in their flight from Egypt there were two elements of note, viz., (a) their haste in going, since the Egyptians implored them to leave quickly, according to Exodus 12:33, and (b) the fact that those who did not hurry to leave with the crowd were threatened with the danger of being killed by the Egyptians if they remained behind.

Their haste was signified in two ways:

First, it was signified by *what* they ate. For they were commanded to eat unleavened bread, as a sign of the fact that the bread "could not rise with the Egyptians pressing them to leave" (Exodus 12:39). And they were commanded to eat meat that had been roasted over a fire, since that was a quicker way to prepare it, and they were commanded not to separate the bone from the meat, since someone in a hurry does not have time to break the bones off.

Second, it was signified by *how* they ate. For Exodus 12:11 says, "You shall gird your loins, and you shall have shoes on your feet, holding your staffs in your hands; and you shall eat quickly." This obviously signifies men who are ready to go on a journey. The same point is involved in this command that is given to them: "In one house shall you eat, and you shall not carry any of its meat outside" (Exodus 12:46). That is, because of their haste they do not have time to send out portions to one another. Again, the hardship that they had suffered in Egypt was signified by the bitter herbs (*lactuae agrestes*).

Now the figurative reasons behind the Paschal meal are clear. The sacrifice of the paschal lamb signified the sacrifice of Christ—this according to 1 Corinthians 5:7 ("Christ our paschal lamb has been sacrificed"). The lamb's blood, which freed them from the destroyer (*exterminator*) when it was sprinkled on the door-posts of their houses, signifies the faith in Christ's passion which is found in the hearts and minds of the faithful and through which they are freed from sin and death—this according to 1 Peter 1:18 ("You were redeemed by the precious blood of the unspotted lamb"). They ate the meat to signify the eating of the body of Christ in the sacrament. The meat was roasted over a fire to signify the passion, or perhaps Christ's charity. They ate it with unleavened bread to signify the pure way of life that belongs to the faithful who receive the body of Christ—this according to 1 Corinthians 5:8 ("Let us feast with the unleavened bread of sincerity and truth"). The bitter herbs were added as a sign of the repentance of sinners that is required of those who receive the body of Christ. Their loins had to be girded by the cincture of chastity, whereas the shoes on their feet signify the example given by our dead ancestors (*patres*). The staffs held in their hands signify pastoral care. Moreover, they are commanded to eat the paschal lamb in one house, i.e., in the Catholic Church, and not in gatherings of heretics.

Reply to objection 3: Some of the sacraments of the New Law had corresponding sacraments in the Old Law that were figures of them.

For example, Baptism, which is the sacrament of faith, corresponds to circumcision; hence, Colossians 2:11–12 says, "You have been circumcised in the circumcision of our Lord Jesus Christ and buried with Him in Baptism." The Eucharist in the New Law corresponds to the meal of the paschal lamb, while the sacrament of Penance corresponds to all the purifications under the Old Law. Again, the sacrament of Orders corresponds to the consecration of the high-priests and priests.

On the other hand, the sacrament of Confirmation, which is a sacrament of the fullness of grace, cannot have any corresponding sacrament in the Old Law; for the time of fullness had not yet arrived, because "the Law brought no one to perfection" (Hebrews 7:19). The same holds for Extreme Unction, which is an immediate preparation for one's entrance into glory, whereas the way to glory was not yet open under the Old Law, because the price for it had not yet been paid.

Matrimony did, to be sure, exist in the Old Law as a natural institution (*officium naturae*), but not as the sacrament of the union of Christ and the Church, since the Church had not yet come into existence. Hence, a decree of divorce (*libellus repudii*) was granted under the Old Law—which is contrary to the nature of the sacrament.

Reply to objection 4: As has been explained, the purifications under the Old Law were ordered toward removing impediments to divine worship. There are two kinds of worship, viz., *spiritual worship*, which consists in devoting one's mind to God, and *corporeal worship*, which consists in sacrifices, offerings, and other things of this sort.

Men are impeded in spiritual worship through the sins by which men were said to be polluted, e.g., idolatry, homicide, adultery, and incest. Men were purified of this sort of pollution by certain sacrifices or offerings made either communally on behalf of the whole multitude or for the sins of individuals. These carnal sacrifices did not in their own right have the power to expiate sins; rather, they signified the future expiation of sins through Christ. For the ancients, too, participated in Christ by professing their faith in a redeemer through the figures of their sacrifices.

On the other hand, men were impeded in their exterior worship through certain corporeal impurities that were thought of as first existing in the men and then also in other animals and in their clothes and houses and vessels. In men the uncleanness was thought of as stemming in part from the men themselves and in part from their contact with unclean things. As for men themselves, what was considered unclean was anything that already had some sort of corruption or had been exposed to corruption. And so since death is a kind of corruption, a man's corpse was considered unclean. Similarly, since leprosy occurs because of a corruption of bodily fluids (*humores*) that erupt externally and infect others, lepers were also considered unclean. The same held for women who were having a flow of blood—either through illness or else through nature, whether during their menstrual periods or at the time of conception. For the same reason, men were considered unclean when having an emission of seminal fluid—whether through sickness or nocturnal emission or sexual intercourse. For every bodily fluid flowing from a man or a woman in one of these ways has a certain unclean taint. Again, one was also unclean from having contact with anything unclean.

There were both literal and figurative reasons for these types of uncleanness.

The literal reason was to promote reverence for what had to do with divine worship, because when men are unclean, they do not normally touch precious objects, and also because sacred things are more venerated when access to them is rare. For since one could only rarely avoid all impurities of the sort in question, it happened that men could only rarely approach to touch those things that had to do with divine worship; and so when they did approach, they did so with more reverence and humility of mind.

In some of these cases the literal reason was so that men would not stay away from divine worship in order to avoid contact with lepers or other sick people whose diseases were loathsome and contagious. Again, in some cases the reason was to prevent idolatry, since in their rites the Gentiles sometimes used human blood and seminal fluid.

Now all types of corporeal uncleanness were purified either through the mere sprinkling of water or, in the case of more serious impurities, through some sacrifice to expiate the sin from which the indispositions (*infirmitates*) arose.

On the other hand, the figurative reason for these impurities was that the forms of exterior uncleanness were figures of different types of sin. For instance, the uncleanness of a corpse signifies the uncleanness of sin, which is the death of the soul. The uncleanness of leprosy signifies the uncleanness of heretical doctrine, because heretical doctrine is contagious, just as leprosy is, and also because there is no false doctrine that does not mix truths with falsehoods, just as on the surface of a leprous body there is a distinction between unclean parts of the flesh and healthy parts. The uncleanness of a woman with a flow of blood signifies the uncleanness of idolatry, because of the stream of blood from immolated victims [in idolatrous rites]. The uncleanness of a man's loss of seminal fluid signifies the uncleanness of fruitless speech (*vana locutio*), since "the seed (*semen*) is the word of God" (Luke 8:11). The uncleanness of sexual intercourse and of a woman giving birth signifies the uncleanness of original sin. The uncleanness of a menstruating woman signifies the uncleanness of a mind weakened by sensual pleasure.

In general, uncleanness contracted by touching an unclean thing signifies the uncleanness of consenting to the sin of another—this according to 2 Corinthians 6:17 ("Exit from among them and be separate, and do not touch what is unclean"). This type of uncleanness by touching also extended to non-living things, since whatever someone who was unclean touched in any way was itself unclean. In this respect, the Law attenuated the superstition of the Gentiles, who claimed that uncleanness is contracted not only by touching someone unclean, but also by speaking with him or looking at him—as Rabbi Moses reports about a menstruating woman. This signified in a mystical way what Wisdom 14:9 says, "To God, the wicked and his wickedness are alike hateful."

Now there was also a certain kind of uncleanness that non-living things had in their own right, in the way that the uncleanness of leprosy existed in a house or in clothes. For just as the disease of leprosy occurs in men because of corrupted fluids that putrefy and corrupt the flesh, so too because of corruption and because of excessive moistness or dryness, corrosion sometimes occurs in the stones of a house or even in clothing. And so the Law called this sort of corruption 'leprosy', and on the basis of it a house or piece of clothing would be judged unclean—because, as has been explained, every sort of corruption is relevant to uncleanness, and also because the Gentiles worshiped household gods in order to combat this sort of corruption. And so the Law commanded that houses in which persistent corruption of this sort existed should be destroyed and that clothes of this sort should be burned, in order to remove an occasion for idolatry.

There were also certain kinds of uncleanness with respect to vessels, spoken of in Numbers 19:15: "The vessel that has no cover or binding over it shall be unclean." The reason for this uncleanness is that something unclean could easily fall into such vessels and they could in that way be made unclean. This precept, too, was meant to discourage idolatry. For the idolaters believed that if mice or lizards or something of this sort that they sacrificed to their idols suddenly fell into a vessel or into water, they would become more pleasing to their gods. Even now some girls leave vessels uncovered in honor of the nocturnal spirits called the Janae.

The figurative reasons for these impurities are as follows: A leprous house signifies the assembly of heretics. A leprous piece of linen clothing signifies the perversity of the habits arising from a bitterness of mind, whereas a leprous piece of wool clothing signifies the perversity of flatterers. A leprous warp signifies vices of the soul, whereas a leprous woof signifies carnal sins; for the soul is in the body as the warp is in the woof. The vase that has no cover or binding signifies a man who has no covering of taciturnity and who is not constrained by any strictness of discipline.

Reply to objection 5: As was explained above, there were two kinds of uncleanness under the Law. The one kind involved a corruption of mind or body, and this was the more serious kind of uncleanness. The other kind merely involved touching something unclean, and this was less serious and expiated by a more simple rite. The first kind of uncleanness was expiated by a sacrifice for sins, since every type of corruption proceeds from sin and signifies sin, whereas the second kind of uncleanness was expiated simply by the sprinkling of a certain sort of water. Numbers 19 talks of this water of expiation. For in that place the Lord commands them to take a red heifer in memory of the sin they committed when they adored the calf. And it says a heifer rather than a calf because that is what the Lord used to call the assembly (*synagoga*)—this according to Hosea 4:16 ("Israel has gone astray like a wanton heifer"). Perhaps this was because they worshiped heifers in the manner of the Egyptians—this according to Hosea 10:5 ("They worshiped the heifers of Beth-aven"). Out of detestation for the sin of idolatry, the heifer was sacrificed outside the camp, and whenever a sacrifice was made for the expiation of the sins of the multitude, it was burned as a whole outside the camp. And in order to signify that through this sacrifice the people were cleansed from the totality of their sins, the priest dipped his finger into the heifer's blood and sprinkled it "over against the entrance of the tabernacle seven times" (Numbers 19:4) because the number *seven* signifies a totality. The sprinkling itself also had to do with the renunciation of idolatrous rites in which the blood was not poured out but instead collected, and the men gathered around it to have a meal in honor of the idols. Then the blood was burned in the fire. This was either because God had appeared to Moses in a fire and the Law had been given in the midst of fire, or because the burning of the blood signified that idolatry had to be completely rooted out, along with everything having to do with idolatry, just as the heifer was cremated "with her skin and her flesh, her blood and dung being delivered to the flames" (Numbers 19:5).

Also, "cedar wood, hyssop, and twice-dyed scarlet" (Numbers 19:6) were added to the fire to signify that just as cedar wood does not easily putrefy, and twice-dyed scarlet does not lose its color, and hyssop retains its smell even after it has been dried out, so too this sacrifice was for the preservation of the people itself and of its uprightness and devotion. Hence, the ashes of the heifer are said to be "reserved for the multitude of the children of Israel" (Numbers 19:9). Alternatively, according to Josephus, they signified the four elements: the cedar was added to the fire in order to signify earth, because of its earthiness; hyssop signified air, because of its smell; and scarlet signified water for the reason that purple did, because of the tints that are derived from the water—and this was meant to express that the sacrifice was being offered to the creator of the four elements.

And because this sort of sacrifice was offered for the sin of idolatry, and in detestation of idolatry, the one who did the burning and the one who collected the ashes and the one who sprinkled the water with which the ashes had been mixed were all considered unclean, in order to show that anything that had to do in any way with idolatry was to be rejected as unclean. Now the three of them were purified of this uncleanness merely by the washing of their clothes, and they did not need to be sprinkled with water because of this sort of uncleanness, since this would have involved an infinite regress. For the one who sprinkled the water became unclean, and so if he sprinkled himself, he would remain unclean; but if someone else sprinkled him, then that one would remain unclean, and, again, the one who sprinkled that one would remain unclean, and so on *ad infinitum*.

Now the figurative reason for this sacrifice is that the red heifer signifies Christ with respect to the weakness He has taken on (*secundum infirmitatem assumptam*), which the feminine gender designates. The color of the heifer signifies the blood of His passion. The red heifer was of full age, because every operation of Christ's is perfect. There was no blemish in the heifer and it did not carry a yoke, because Christ did not carry the yoke of sin. It is commanded that the heifer be led to Moses, because they imputed to it the transgression of the Mosaic Law in the violation of the Sabbath. It was commanded that it be handed over to Eleazar the priest, because Christ was handed over to the hands of the priests to be killed. It was sacrificed outside the camp, because Christ suffered outside the gates. The priest dipped his finger into the heifer's blood because the mystery of Christ's passion is to be meditated on and imitated with prudence, which the finger signifies. The blood was sprinkled against the tabernacle, through which the assembly is signified, either in order to condemn non-believing Jews or to purify the believing Jews. And it was sprinkled seven times either because of the seven gifts of the Holy Spirit or because of the seven days, in which the whole of time is understood.

Then there are all the things to be burned by the fire, i.e., to be understood spiritually, that have to do with Christ's Incarnation. The skin and flesh signify Christ's exterior action. The blood signifies the subtle interior virtue that gives life to His exterior actions. The dung signifies His weariness, His thirst, and everything else related to His weakness. Of the three added things, the cedar wood signifies the height of hope or of contemplation, the hyssop signifies humility or faith, and the twice-dyed scarlet signifies the twofold charity—for it is through these things that we should adhere to the suffering Christ. The ashes of the fire are collected by "a man that is clean," because the relics of Christ's passion found their way to Gentiles who were not culpable in the death of Christ. The ashes were placed in water for the expiation because by virtue of Christ's passion Baptism has the power to wash away sins. The priest who performed the sacrifice and burned the heifer, along with the priest who burned it and collected the ashes and the priest who sprinkled the water, were all unclean, either because (a) the Jews became unclean from the killing of Christ, through whom our sins are forgiven, and this right up to evening, i.e., until the end of the world, when the remnant of Israel will be converted, or because (b), as Gregory explains in *Pastoralis*, those who deal with holy things in order to cleanse others contract certain impurities themselves, and this right up to evening, i.e., to the end of this life.

Reply to objection 6: As has been explained, the sort of uncleanness that stemmed from the corruption of mind or body was expiated through sacrifices made for sin. Now special sacrifices were made for the sins of individuals, but because some were negligent with regard to the expiation of such sins and impurities, or even failed to offer expiation out of ignorance, it was decreed that once a year, on the tenth day of the seventh month, a sacrifice of expiation should be offered for the whole people.

Since, as the Apostle points out in Hebrews 7:28, "the law makes men who have infirmity priests," it was necessary that the priest first offer a calf on his own behalf for his own sins, in memory of the sin Aaron committed in the production of the golden calf, along with a ram in a holocaust in order to signify that the priest's preeminence (*praelatio*), which the ram signifies as the leader of the flock, was ordered toward honoring God.

Then he offered two goats for the people.

One of the goats was sacrificed for the sins of the multitude. For the goat is a foul-smelling animal, and the clothes made from its skin have a pungent smell, and this signified the stench and impurity and pangs of sin. Now the blood of this sacrificial goat, along with the blood of the calf, was carried into the Holy of Holies and sprinkled over the whole sanctuary in order to signify that the tabernacle was being washed clean of the impurities of the children of Israel. But the corpses of the goat and the calf which had been sacrificed for sin had to be burned in order to signify the destruction (*comsumptio*) of sin. However, this burning did not take place on the altar, since only the holocausts were totally consumed by fire on the altar. This is why it was commanded that the corpses of the goat and the calf be burned outside the camp in detestation of sin. This is what was done whenever a sacrifice was offered for some particular grave sin or for a multitude of sins.

However, the other goat was sent off into the desert, not to be offered to the demons whom the Gentiles used to worship in desert places, since [the children of Israel] were not allowed to make sacrifices to the demons, but rather to signify the effect of the immolated sacrifice. And so the priest imposed his hand on the goat's head while confessing the sins of the children of Israel, as if the goat were carrying those sins off into the desert where he would be eaten by beasts—bearing, as it were, the punishment for the sins of the people. The goat was said to be carrying the sins of the people either because its being sent out signified the forgiveness of the sins of the people or because a piece of paper on which the sins had been written was tied to its head.

The figurative reason for these things were as follows: The calf signifies Christ because of His power (*propter virtutem*), the ram signifies Him because He is the leader of the faithful, and the goat signifies Him because of "the likeness of sinful flesh" (Romans 8:3). And Christ Himself was sacrificed for the sins of both the priests and the people, since through His passion both the great and the small (*maiores et minores*) were washed of their sins. Now the blood of the calf and the goat was carried into the sanctuary by the high priest because through the blood of Christ's passion the entrance into the kingdom of heaven is opened up to us. Their corpses were burned outside the camp, because "Christ suffered outside the gates," as the Apostle puts it in Hebrews 13:12. On the other hand, the goat that was sent out can signify either (a) Christ's divine nature itself (*ipsa divinitas*), which goes off into solitude when Christ the man undergoes His suffering—not changing its place, but having its power restrained—or (b) evil desire, which we should cast off from ourselves while offering our virtuous actions (*virtuosos motus*) to the Lord.

As for the uncleanness of those who burned these sacrifices, the figurative reason is the same one given above in the case of the sacrifice of the red heifer.

Reply to objection 7: The rite of the Law did not cleanse a leper from the stain of leprosy, but rather declared him to be cleansed. This is shown in Leviticus 14:3–4, where it says of the priest, "When he finds that the leprosy has been cleansed, he shall command him to be purified." Therefore, the leprosy had already been cleansed, whereas he was said to be purified insofar as he was restored by the priest's decree to the fellowship of men and to divine worship. (However, it sometimes happened that when the priest was mistaken in this judgment, the bodily leprosy was cleansed by a divine miracle through the rite of the Law.)

Now there were two purifications for the leper, First, he was judged to be clean, and, second, as clean, he was restored after seven days to the fellowship of men and to divine worship.

In the first purification, the leper who was to be cleansed offered on his own behalf "two living sparrows . . . cedar wood, and scarlet, and hyssop" (Leviticus 14:4), in such a way that the one sparrow and the hyssop were tied to the cedar wood with a scarlet thread, so that the cedar wood was like the handle of a sprinkler, while the hyssop and sparrow were the part of the sprinkler that was dipped into the blood of the other sparrow, which had been "immolated . . . over living waters" (Leviticus 14:5). He offered these four things to counter the four defects of leprosy. The cedar wood, which is a tree not subject to putrefaction, was offered to counter the putrefaction; the hyssop, which is a fragrant plant, was offered to counter the stench; the live sparrow was offered to counter the numbness; and the scarlet, which has a vivid color, was offered to counter the lurid color of leprosy. The live sparrow was sent off flying into the plain because the leper was being restored to his original freedom.

On the eighth day the leper was admitted to the divine worship and restored to the fellowship of men—though he first shaved the hair off his whole body and washed his clothes, since leprosy rots one's hair and infects one's clothes and makes them smell bad. Afterwards, a sacrifice was offered for his sins, since leprosy was often inflicted because of sin. Some blood from the sacrifice was put on the tip of the ear of the one who was being cleansed "and on the thumb of his right hand and on the big toe of his right foot" (Leviticus 14:14), because it is in these parts of the body that leprosy is first diagnosed and felt. Three liquids were used in this rite, viz., blood, to counter the corruption of the blood; oil, to signify the healing of the disease; and living water, to wash away the filth.

The figurative reasons were as follows: The two sparrows signify Christ's divinity and humanity. One of them, viz., the humanity, is immolated in an earthen vessel over living waters, because the waters of Baptism are consecrated by the passion of Christ. The other sparrow, viz., the impassible divinity, remained alive, because the divinity cannot die; and it flew away, because it could not be bound by the passion. Now as noted above, this living sparrow—along with the cedar wood and scarlet (or cochineal) and hyssop, i.e., faith, hope, and charity—was dipped into the water for sprinkling, since we are baptized in faith in the God-man (*in fide Dei et hominis*). Through the water of Baptism, or the water of tears, the man washes his clothes, i.e., his deeds, and all his strands of hair, i.e., his thoughts. The tip of the right ear of the one who is being cleansed is tinged with the blood and the oil in order to guard his hearing against corrupting words, whereas his right thumb and big toe are tinged in order that his action might be holy.

There is nothing special to be said about any of the other things involved in this purification, or in the purification of other kinds of uncleanness, over and beyond what has been said about the other sacrifices for sins or for crimes.

Reply to objections 8 and 9: Just as the people were initiated (*instituebatur*) for divine worship through circumcision, so the ministers were initiated for divine worship through a special purification or consecration. In this way they were perceived as being separated off from the others in the sense of being set aside specially, in preference to the others, for the ministry of divine worship. Everything that was done to them in their consecration or initiation had to do with showing that they had a certain prerogative of cleanness and power and dignity. And so three things were done in the initiation of the ministers: first, they were purified; second, they were vested (*ornabantur*) and consecrated; and third, they were assigned (*applicabantur*) to the exercise of the ministry.

As Leviticus 8 [and Numbers 8] have it, all of them were purified in general through a washing with water and through certain sacrifices, while the Levites (*Levitae*) in particular shaved all the hair off their bodies.

The consecration of the high priests (*pontifices*) and priests (*sacerdotes*) was done in the following order: First, after they had been washed, they were clothed with certain special vestments to signify their dignity. The high priest in particular was anointed on the head with the oil of unction in order to signify that the power of consecrating flowed from him to the others, just as the oil flowed from his head to the lower parts of his body—this according to Psalm 132:2 ("Like the precious ointment on the head that ran down upon the beard, the beard of Aaron").

The Levites, on the other hand, did not have a consecration other than being offered to the Lord by the children of Israel through the hands of the high priest, who prayed for them.

As for the lower priests (*sacerdotes minores*), only their hands, which were to be used for the sacrifices, were consecrated. In addition, the tip of their right ear, the big toe of their right foot, and the thumb of their right hand were tinged with the blood of an immolated animal. This was done in order that (a) they would be obedient to the Law of God in the offering of sacrifices (this was signified by the intinction of the right ear), and in order that (b) they would be solicitous and prompt in carrying out the sacrifices (this was signified by the intinction of the big toe of the right foot and the thumb of the right hand). They, along with their vestments, were sprinkled with the blood of an immolated animal, in memory of the blood of the lamb through which they had been liberated from Egypt. Moreover, in their consecration the following sacrifices were offered: (a) a calf for sin, in memory of the remission of the sin of Aaron in the fashioning of the [golden] calf; (b) a ram for a holocaust, in memory of the offering of Abraham, whose obedience the high priest was expected to imitate; (c) a ram of consecration, which was, as it were, a peace-offering in memory of the liberation from Egypt through the blood of the lamb; and (d) a basket of loaves of bread, in memory of the manna bestowed upon the people.

As for the assignment to the ministry, the fat of the ram and its right shoulder and a piece of bread twisted off from one of the loaves were placed in their hands, in order to show that they accepted the power of making offerings to the Lord. The Levites, on the other hand, were assigned to their ministry by being sent into the tabernacle of the covenant in order to take care of the vessels of the sanctuary.

The figurative meaning of these things was as follows: Those who are to be consecrated to the spiritual ministry of Christ must first be purified by the water of Baptism and the water of tears of faith in Christ's passion, which is an expiative and cleansing sacrifice. And they should shave all the hairs off their bodies, i.e., they should shave off all evil thoughts. They should also be vested with the virtues and consecrated by the oil of the Holy Spirit and by being sprinkled with the blood of Christ. And they should in this way be ordered toward exercising their spiritual ministries.

Reply to objection 10: As has been explained (a. 4), the intention of the Law was to induce reverence for divine worship, and this in two ways: first, by excluding from divine worship anything that could have been contemptible; second, by affixing to divine worship everything that seemed relevant to giving honor. And if this norm was observed in the case of the tabernacle and the vessels and the animals to be sacrificed, it had to be observed all the more in the case of the ministers themselves.

And so to remove any contempt for the ministers, it was commanded that they not have any bodily blemish or defect, since men of this sort are apt to be held in contempt by others. Because of this, it was also prescribed that those to be assigned to the ministry of God would come not in a haphazard way from just any family (*genus*), but would instead come by a succession of generation from a particular stock, so that in this way they might be thought of as more distinctive and more noble.

To ensure that they would be held in reverence, special ornate vestments and a special consecration were likewise provided for them—this is the general reason for their ornate vestments. As for specific reasons, note that the high priest had eight ornate vestments:

First, he had a linen tunic (*vestis linea*).

Second, he had a violet tunic (*tunica hyacinthia*), at whose bottom edges there was a circle of little bells and "pomegranates of violet, and purple, and scarlet twice dyed" (Exodus 39:23).

Third, he had a humeral veil (*superhumorale*) that covered his shoulders and the front part of his body down to waist. The humeral veil was composed of gold, violet, purple, twice-dyed scarlet, and twisted linen, and on the shoulders it had two onyx-stones on which were inscribed the names of the sons of Israel.

Fourth, he had a breastpiece (*rationale*) made of the same material. It was square and positioned on the breast, and it was fastened to the humeral veil. On this breastpiece there were twelve precious stones separated into four rows, and the names of the sons of Israel were likewise inscribed on these stones. This was to signify that (a) the high priest was to bear the burden of the whole people, given that he was carrying their names on his shoulders, and that (b) he should constantly be thinking about their well-being, given that he was carrying them on his breast—having them, as it were, in his heart. The Lord also commanded that doctrine and truth (*doctrinam et veritatem*) be put on the breastpiece. For certain points concerning the truth of justice and the truth of doctrine were written on the breastpiece. (The Jews, however, imagine that there was a stone on the breastpiece that changed colors according to the different things that were going to happen to the sons of Israel, and they call this stone 'Truth and Doctrine'.)

Fifth, there was the belt (*balteus*), i.e., girdle (*cingulus*), of the four colors mentioned above.

Sixth, there was the tiara (*tiara*), i.e., miter (*mitra*), made of linen.

Seventh, hanging on his forehead there was a thin piece of gold metal (*lamina aurea*) that had the name of the Lord on it.

Eighth, there were "the linen loincloths (*femoralia linea*) to cover the flesh of their nakedness" (Exodus 28:42) when they climbed up to the sanctuary or climbed up to the altar.

Of these eight ornate vestments, the lower priests had four, viz., the linen tunic, the loincloth, the belt, and the tiara.

Some give literal reasons for these ornate vestments, claiming that the arrangement of the world is signified in them, as if the high priest were declaring that he is the minister of the creator of the world. Hence Wisdom 18:24 says, "The world was described on the vestments of Aaron." For the loincloth was a figure of the earth, in which linen grows. The circularity of the belt signified the ocean that surrounds the earth. The color of the purple tunic signified the atmosphere, its little bells signified claps of thunder, and the pomegranates signified flashes of lightning. The humeral veil signified by its variety the stars of the heavens, and the two onyx-stones signified the two hemispheres or, alternatively, the sun and the moon. The twelve gems on the breast, which were positioned on the breastpiece, signify the twelve signs of the zodiac, since the heavens contain explanations of earthly things—this according to Job 38:33 ("Do you know the order of heaven, and can you set down the reason thereof on the earth?"). The miter or tiara signified the empyrean heaven, and the piece of gold metal signified God presiding over all things.

The figurative reasons are obvious. The blemishes or defects from which the priests should be immune signify the different vices and sins which they ought to lack. For a priest is not permitted to be blind, i.e., ignorant. Nor is he allowed to be lame, i.e., unstable and tending in many different directions. Nor is he allowed to have a nose that is too small or too big or crooked, i.e., he should not through a lack of discretion do too much or too little or engage in depraved acts; for the nose signifies discretion, because it distinguishes smells. Nor is he allowed to have a broken foot or hand, i.e., he is not allowed to lose the habit of acting well or of progressing toward virtue. He is also rejected if he has a large belly or is hunchbacked, since these signify a love of earthly things. If he is bleary-eyed, then his mind is darkened by carnal desire; for bleary eyes stem from a flow of the humors. He is likewise rejected if he has a pearl-like white spot in his eye, i.e., if in his own mind he presumes that he has the brightness of moral uprightness. He is also rejected if he has a chronic scab, i.e., lustfulness of the flesh (*petulantia carnis*). And he is also rejected if he has a skin disease (*impetigo*) that covers his body without pain and destroys the beauty of his body; this signifies avarice. Also, he is rejected if he has a rupture or is overweight, since this gives rise to a heaviness of evil in his heart, even if he does not express it in his deeds.

The ornate vestments signify the virtues of the ministers of God. Now there are four virtues that are necessary for all ministers, viz., chastity, which is signified by the loincloth; purity of life, which is signified by the linen tunic; the moderation of discretion, which is signified by the girdle; and rectitude of intention, which is signified by the tiara covering the head.

But before all these, the high priests should have four things. First, they should have the constant remembrance of God in their contemplation, and this is signified by the thin piece of gold metal on their forehead with the name of God on it. Second, they should bear the weaknesses of the people, and this is signified by the humeral veil. Third, they should have the people in their hearts and in their breasts through the solicitude of charity, and this is signified by the breastpiece. Fourth, they should have a heavenly way of life through works of perfection, and this is signified by the violet tunic. That is also why the violet tunic has the golden bells at its edges, signifying the teaching of divine things that must be joined to the high priest's heavenly way of life. The adjoined pomegranates signify unity of faith and agreement in good morals, since his teaching ought to be interconnected in such a way that the unity of faith and peace is not ruptured by it.

Article 6

Are there reasoned causes for the ceremonial observances?

It seems that there are no reasoned causes for the ceremonial observances:

Objection 1: As the Apostle says in 1 Timothy 4:4: "Every creature of God is good, and nothing received with thanksgiving is to be rejected." Therefore, it was inappropriate to prohibit, as Leviticus 11 and Deuteronomy 14 do, the eating of certain foods regarded as unclean.

Objection 2: Just as animals are given as food for man, so too are plants; hence, Genesis 9:3 says, ". . . even as I have given you the green plants, so I have given all meat to you." But the Law did not single out any plants as unclean, even though some of them were especially harmful, e.g., the poisonous ones. Therefore, it seems that no animals should have been prohibited as unclean, either.

Objection 3: If the matter from which something is generated is unclean, then by parity of reasoning that which is generated from it should be unclean. But meat is generated from blood. Therefore, since not all meats were prohibited as unclean, then by parity of reasoning neither should blood—or fat, which is generated from blood—have been prohibited as unclean.

Objection 4: In Matthew 10:28 and Luke 12:4 the Lord says, "Do not fear those who kill the body . . . since after death there is nothing else for them to do"—which would not be true if a man were harmed by something that came from his corpse. *A fortiori*, it does not matter how one cooks the meat of an animal that has already been killed. Therefore, it seems unreasonable for Exodus 23:19 to say, "You shall not cook a kid in the milk of his mother."

Objection 5: Among men and animals, it is the ones that come forth first (*primitiva*) that are mandated to be offered to the Lord, since they are more perfect. Therefore, it is inappropriate for Leviticus 19:23 to command, "When you shall have come into the land and shall have planted fruit trees in it, you shall take away their foreskins (*praeputia*) [*read*: their first fruits], and they shall be unclean for you, and you shall not eat of them."

Objection 6: A man's clothing is something separate from his body. Therefore, it should not have been the case that certain specific types of clothing were forbidden to the Jews—for instance, Leviticus 19:19 says, "You shall not wear a garment that is woven of two sorts of cloth," and Deuteronomy 22:5 says, "A woman shall not be clothed with men's apparel, neither shall a man use women's apparel," and later on in verse 11, "You shall not wear a garment that is woven of wool and linen together."

Objection 7: Being mindful of God's commandments has to do not with the body, but with the heart. Therefore, it was inappropriate for Deuteronomy 6 to command, "You shall tie the precepts of God as a sign on your hand . . . and they shall be written on the threshold of your doors." And it was inappropriate for Numbers 15:38–39 to command, "They shall make themselves fringes in the corners of their garments, on which they will put violet ribbons to remind them of the commandments of God."

Objection 8: In 1 Corinthians 9:9 the Apostle says, "God is not concerned about oxen," and, as a consequence, neither is He concerned about other non-rational animals. Therefore, it was inappropriate for Deuteronomy 22:6 to command, "If you are walking along and you find a bird's nest, you shall not take the mother with her young." And it was inappropriate for Deuteronomy 25:4 to command, "You shall not muzzle the ox that is threshing." And it was inappropriate for Leviticus 19:19 to command, "You shall not make your cattle mate with beasts of any other kind."

Objection 9: The Law made no distinction between clean plants and unclean plants. Therefore, *a fortiori*, there should have been no distinctions made with respect to the cultivation of plants. Therefore, it was inappropriate for Leviticus 19:19 to command, "You shall not sow your field with different kinds of seeds." And it was inappropriate for Deuteronomy 22:9–10 to command, "You shall not sow your vineyard with different kinds of seeds. . . . You shall not plow with an ox and an ass together."

Objection 10: We notice that inanimate things are especially subject to the power of men. Therefore, it was inappropriate to restrict a man, as the precept of the Law found in Deuteronomy 7:25–26 does, from taking the silver and gold from which idols had been made, or from taking the other things found in the temples of the idols. Likewise, the command in Deuteronomy 23:13, "Digging a hole in the earth, they shall cover their excrement with dirt," seems ridiculous.

Objection 11: Piety is especially required in the priests. But piety seems to involve one's being concerned with the burial of one's friends; hence, Tobias is praised for this, as Tobias 1:20–25 attests. Similarly, piety sometimes also involves a man's taking a prostitute for his wife, since in this way he frees her from sin and from a bad reputation. Therefore, it seems inappropriate that these things should be forbidden to the priests in Leviticus 21.

But contrary to this: Deuteronomy 18:14 says, "But you are otherwise instructed by the Lord your God." From this one can gather that observances of the sort in question were instituted by God as the special prerogative of this people. Therefore, these observances are not unreasonable or without due cause.

I respond: As has been explained (a. 5), the Jewish people were set aside in a special way for divine worship; and, among the people, the priests were set aside in a special way. And just as the other things assigned to divine worship ought to have some sort of special character that involves the honored status (*honorificentia*) of divine worship, so too in the way of life of the people, and especially of the priests, there ought to be certain special elements, whether spiritual or corporeal, that are congruent with divine worship.

Now worship under the Law was a figure of the mystery of Christ, and so all their actions were a figure of things having to do with Christ—this according to 1 Corinthians 10:11 ("All these things happened to them in figure"). And so the reasons for the observances in question can be assigned in two ways: first, according to their fittingness for divine worship; and, second, insofar as they prefigured something in the life of Christians.

Reply to objection 1: As was explained above (a. 5), there were two kinds of pollution or uncleanness observed under the Law, viz., (a) the uncleanness of sin, through which the soul is polluted, and (b) the uncleanness of any sort of corruption through which the body is in some way defiled.

If we are talking about the first kind of uncleanness, then no types of food are unclean, or able to defile a man, according to their nature; hence, Matthew 15:11 says, "It is not what goes into his mouth that defiles a man, but rather it is what comes out of his mouth that defiles a man," and this is understood as talking about sins. However, certain foods are incidentally able to defile a man, viz., insofar as they are eaten out of disobedience or contrary to a vow or from excessive sensual desire, or insofar as they promote lust, for which reason some men abstain from wine and meat.

Now as regards corporeal uncleanness, i.e., the uncleanness of corruption, the meat of certain animals is unclean either because (a) the animals feed on unclean things, as the pig does, or because (b) they live in an unclean way, as do animals that live underground, such as moles and mice and others of this sort, and hence have a foul smell, or because (c) their meat generates corrupted humors in human bodies because of its moistness or dryness. And so the people were forbidden to eat the meat of animals having soles, i.e., uncloven hoofs, because of their earthiness. Similarly, they were forbidden to eat the meat of animals that have many clefts in their feet, since these are fierce and sun-scorched, e.g., lion meat and others of this sort. And for the same reason, they were forbidden to eat certain birds of prey, which have excessive dryness, along with certain water fowls, because of their excessive moistness. The same held for certain fish that do not have fins and scales, e.g., eels and others, and this because of their excessive moistness. On the other hand, they were permitted to eat animals that ruminate and have a cloven hoof, since these animals have well-digested humors and a balanced composition; for they are not too moist, which is signified by their hoofs, or too earthy, given that they have a cloven and not a continuous hoof. Among the fish, they were allowed to eat the fish that are drier, which is signified by the fact that they have scales and fins, since it is in this way that the moist composition of fish is tempered. Among the birds, they were permitted to eat the more temperate ones, such as hens, partridges, and others of this sort.

A second reason [for the prohibitions] was the detestation of idolatry.

For the Gentiles, and especially the Egyptians, among whom they had been brought up, sacrificed these forbidden animals to their idols or used them for sorcery (*ad maleficia*). On the other hand, they did not eat the animals that the Jews were permitted to eat; instead, they worshiped those animals as gods or abstained from them for other reasons, as was explained above (a. 3, ad 2).

A third reason was to prevent excessive concern about food. This is why they were permitted to eat animals that could be easily and promptly obtained. However, they were generally forbidden to eat the blood and fat of any animal. The prohibition of blood was meant (a) to prevent cruelty, in order that they might hate the shedding of human blood, as was explained above (a. 3, ad 8), and (b) to prevent idolatrous rites, since the custom of the idolaters was to come together around the collected blood in order to have a meal in honor of the idols to whom they thought the blood was especially acceptable. This is why the Lord commanded that the blood be poured out and covered with dust. For this reason they were also forbidden to eat suffocated or strangled animals, because their blood was not separated from their flesh, or because the animals suffered greatly in that kind of death and the Lord wanted to prohibit cruelty even with respect to brute animals, so that having shown kindness (*exercitium pietatis*) even to beasts, the people might withdraw further from cruelty to men. They were forbidden to eat fat, because (a) the idolaters ate it in honor of their gods, and because (b) it was burned in honor of God, and because (c) blood and fat do not make for good nutrition—this is the explanation Rabbi Moses gives. Now the reason for the prohibition of the eating of sinews is expressed in Genesis 32:32, where it says, "The children of Israel, unto this day, eat not the sinew, because Jacob touched the sinew of his thigh and it shrank."

The figurative reason for these prohibitions is that particular sins are signified by all the prohibited animals, and it is as a figure of those sins that the animals are prohibited. Hence, in *Contra Faustum* Augustine says, "If someone asks about the pig and the lamb, both are clean by nature, since every creature of God's is good; however, by signification the lamb is clean and the pig is unclean. It is as if one were to say that both of the words 'foolish' and 'wise' are clean with respect to the nature of the sounds and letters and syllables out of which they are composed, and yet by signification the one is clean and the other is unclean." For the animal that ruminates and has a cloven hoof is clean by signification, since the cleft in the hoof signifies the distinction between the two Testaments, or between the

Father and the Son, or between the two natures in Christ, or the distinction between good and evil—whereas the rumination signifies meditation on the Scriptures and the sound interpretation of the Scriptures, where anyone who lacks either of these things is spiritually unclean.

The same holds in the case of fish. The ones that have scales and fins are clean by signification, since the fins signify the sublime life, i.e., contemplation, whereas the scales signify the difficult life—and each of these is necessary for spiritual cleanness.

In the case of birds, certain kinds are specifically prohibited. For in the eagle (*aquila*), which flies high, pride is prohibited, and in the griffin (*gryps*), which is inimical to horses and men, the cruelty of the powerful is prohibited. The seahawk (*haliaeetos*), which feeds on small birds, signifies those who prey upon the poor, whereas the kite (*milvus*), which makes special use of deception, signifies fraudulent men. The vulture (*vultur*), which follows an army with the expectation of eating the corpses of the dead, signifies those who desire men to die or to have conflicts with one another, so that they can thereby profit. Raven-like animals (*animalia corvini generis*) signify those who are sullied by sensual desire or who are devoid of good affections, since the raven, once it had been sent off from the ark, did not return. The ostrich (*struthiocamelus*), which cannot fly even though it is a bird, but is always close to the ground, signifies those who, fighting for God, entangle themselves in worldly affairs. The night-raven (*nycticorax*), which sees well at night but cannot see in the daytime, signifies those who are astute in temporal matters but dull in spiritual matters. The seagull (*larus*), which both flies in the air and swims in the sea, signifies those who revere both circumcision and Baptism or, alternatively, those who wish to fly through contemplation and yet to live in the waters of sensual desire. The hawk (*accipiter*), which helps men in catching prey, signifies those who serve the powerful in preying upon the poor. The owl (*bubo*), which seeks its food at night and hides during the day, signifies the lustful, who seek to remain hidden in the night-time works they do. The sea-dove (*mergulus*), which by nature stays under water for long periods of time, signifies the gluttonous, who immerse themselves in the waters of delicacies. The ibis (*ibis*) is an African bird with a long beak which feeds on snakes and is perhaps the same as the stork (*ciconia*); it signifies the envious, who feed upon the ills of others as upon snakes. The swan (*cygnus*) is dazzling white in color and with its long neck extracts its food from the depths of the earth or water; and it can signify men who seek earthly profit with an external veneer of virtue. The pelican (*onocrotalus*) is a bird of the Orient with a long beak, whose jaws have sacks in which it first stores its food, and after an hour sends it to its belly; it signifies the greedy, who collect the necessities of life with excessive solicitude. The purple swamphen (*porphyrio*), beyond the manner of other birds, has one wide foot for swimming and one cloven foot for walking, since in the water it swims like a duck (*anas*), and on dry ground it walks like a partridge (*perdix*); it drinks only when it chews, since it moistens its food with water, and it signifies those who do not want to do anything at another's bidding but want to do only what has been moistened with the water of their own will. The herodio (*herodio*), commonly called the falcon (*falco*), signifies those whose feet are "quick to the shedding of blood" (Psalm 13:3). The plover (*charadrius*), which is a garrulous bird, signifies the loquacious, whereas the hoopoe (*upupa*), which nests in dung and eats stinking excrement and simulates a moan in its song, signifies the sadness of the world, which works death in unclean men. The bat (*vespertilio*), which flies close to the ground, signifies those who, gifted in worldly knowledge, are wise only about worldly things.

In the case of the fowls and quadrupeds, the only permitted ones are those that have longer back legs, so that they are able to leap. By contrast, the others, which stay closer to the ground, are prohibited, because those who misuse the doctrine of the four Evangelists and are not uplifted by it are considered unclean.

In the case of the blood and the fat and the nerves, what is being understood as prohibited are cruelty and voluptuousness and a bravado for sinning (*fortitudo ad peccandum*).

Reply to objection 2: Men ate plants and other things growing from the earth even before the flood, but the eating of meat seems to have been introduced after the flood. For Genesis 9:3 says, "I have given you all the meat, even as I have given you the green plants." This is because the eating of things that grow in the earth bespeaks a certain simplicity of life, whereas the eating of meat bespeaks certain pleasures and cares in living. For the earth generates plants spontaneously, and things growing in the earth are procured in great volume with a modicum of effort, whereas a great effort is necessary for eating animals or even for catching them. And so the Lord, wishing to lead His people to a more simple way of life, forbade them to eat many things in the genus of animals, but not in the genus of things growing in the earth.

An alternative reason is that animals were sacrificed to idols, whereas things growing in the earth were not.

Reply to objection 3: The reply to the third objection is obvious from what has been said.

Reply to objection 4: Even if the kid that has been killed does not know how its own flesh is being cooked, there still seems to be a certain cruelty in the mind of the cook if the mother's milk, which was given to the kid for nutrition, is used in the consumption of its meat.

Alternatively, one can point out that in the feasts of their idols the Gentiles cooked the meat of the kid in this way in order either to sacrifice it or to eat it. This is why Exodus 23, after it has previously talked about the celebration of the solemn feasts in the Law, adds, "You shall not cook a kid in the milk of his mother."

The figurative reason for this prohibition is that it prefigured the fact that Christ, who is a kid because of the "likeness of sinful flesh" (Romans 8:3), was not to be cooked, i.e., killed, by the Jews in His mother's milk, i.e., at the time of His infancy.

An alternative reply is that it signifies that the kid, i.e., the sinner, is not to be cooked in his mother's milk, i.e., he is not to be soothed with blandishments.

Reply to objection 5: The Gentiles offered first fruits, which they considered lucky, to the gods, or even burned them in order to do certain forms of magic. And so the precept is that the people should consider the fruits of the first three years to be unclean. For in a period of three years almost all the trees of that land produce fruit from either seeding or grafting or planting. However, it rarely happens that the stones inside the tree fruits or the hidden seeds are planted; for these take more time to produce fruit, whereas the Law had an eye toward what happened for the most part. Now the fruits of the fourth year were offered to God as the first of the clean fruits, whereas the fruits from the fifth year and beyond were eaten.

The figurative reason was that this prefigured the fact that after the three stages of the Law—one of which lasted from Abraham to David, the second from David to the Babylonian exile, and the third from the Babylonian exile to Christ—Christ, who is the fruit of the Law, was to be offered to God.

An alternative figurative reason is that we should put the first of our own works under suspicion, because of our imperfection.

Reply to objection 6: As Ecclesiasticus 19:27 says, "A man's clothing shows what he is." And so the Lord wanted His people to be distinguished from other peoples not only by the sign of circumcision, but also by a distinctive way of dressing (*habitus*).

There were two reasons why they were forbidden to wear a garment sewn together from wool and linen, and why the women were forbidden to wear men's clothes, and vice versa.

First, to prevent idolatrous worship. For in the worship of their gods the Gentiles used various vestments made of diverse materials. Moreover, in the worship of Mars the women put on men's armor, while, conversely, in the worship of Venus men used women's clothing.

The second reason is to fend off lust. For all kinds of disordered sexual intercourse are excluded [by the prohibition of] various mixtures of clothing. A woman dressing in men's clothing, or vice versa, is an incentive to sensual desire and provides an occasion for lust.

The figurative reason is that what is forbidden in the case of a garment sewn together from wool and linen is the combination of the simplicity of innocence, of which the wool is a figure, with the subtlety of malice, of which the linen is a figure. It is also prohibited that a women should take upon herself the office of teaching or any of the other functions of a man, or that a man should descend to the softness of women.

Reply to objection 7: As Jerome says in *Super Matthaeum*, "The Lord commanded that they make violet fringes in the four corners of their garments in order to mark the people of Israel off from other peoples." Hence, in this way they professed that they were Jews, and so by looking at this sign they were induced to be mindful of their Law.

Now the words "You shall tie them on your hand, and they will be always before your eyes" were misinterpreted by the Pharisees when they wrote the Decalogue of Moses on scrolls and tied it on their foreheads like a crown, so that it would move before their eyes. The Lord's intention, however, was that the precepts should be tied to their hand, i.e., to their actions, and that the precepts should be before their eyes, i.e., in meditation. Also, in the case of the violet strips which were inserted inside their cloaks, what is signified is the heavenly intention that ought to be joined to all our works.

Still, one could claim that since these people were carnal and stiff-necked, they had to be stirred to the observance of the Law through sensible things of this sort.

Reply to objection 8: There are two kinds of human affect, the one involving reason and the other involving the passions.

With respect to the affect of reason, it does not matter what a man does with brute animals, since all of them have been subjected to his power by God—this according to Psalm 8:8 ("You have subjected all things under his feet"). In this regard, the Apostle says that God is not concerned about oxen because God does not require of man what he does to the oxen or other animals.

However, with respect to the affect of passion, human affect is moved even with respect to the other animals. For since the passion of pity (*misericordia*) arises from the sufferings of others, and since brute animals are also able to sense pain, the affect of pity can arise in a man even with respect to the sufferings of animals. It follows that one who is able to feel the affect of pity with respect to animals is thereby more disposed toward the affect of pity with respect to men; hence, Proverbs 12:10 says, "The just man has regard for the lives of his beasts, but the innards of the wicked are cruel." And so the Lord, in order that He might call the Jewish people, who were prone to cruelty, back to pity, wished them to be moved to pity even for brute animals and prohibited them from doing to animals certain things that seem to involve cruelty. Thus, He forbade them to cook a kid in its mother's milk, or to muzzle an ox threshing grain, or to kill a mother with her children.

Still, one could also claim that it was out of a detestation of idolatry that they were forbidden to do these things. For the Egyptians considered it evil for oxen that were threshing to eat any of the grain. Again, certain magicians used an incubating mother together with her captured young ones for securing fertility and good fortune in the nurturing of children; also, among the fortune-tellers it was considered good fortune to find a mother incubating young ones.

As for the [prohibition against] mixing animals of differing species, there were three possible literal reasons:

First, detestation of the idolatry of the Egyptians, who used differing mixtures in the service of the planets, which according to their different conjunctions have diverse effects on diverse kinds of things.

The second reason was to prevent sexual intercourse that is contrary to nature.

The third reason is the general one of removing occasions for sensual desire. For animals of different species do not easily mate with one another unless this is procured by men, and the movement of sensual desire is excited in men when they witness animals having sexual intercourse. Hence, as Rabbi Moses reports, among the Jewish traditions there is a precept according to which men should avert their eyes from animals that are having sexual intercourse.

The figurative reasons for these things are as follows: The necessities of life should not be taken from the ox who is threshing, i.e., from the preacher who bears the sheaves of doctrine, as the Apostle puts it in 1 Corinthians 9:4. Again, we should not hold fast the mother along with her young, since in certain matters the spiritual meaning, i.e., the young, should be held on to while the literal observance, i.e., the mother, is over-ridden. Again, as beasts of burden, i.e., ordinary people, we are forbidden to have sexual intercourse, i.e., to have close connections, with living things of a different kind, i.e., with Gentiles or Jews.

Reply to objection 9: As far as the literal reason is concerned, all these agricultural mixtures were prohibited in renunciation of idolatry. For in their veneration of the stars, the Egyptians concocted different mixtures of seeds and animals and clothes, representing the different conjunctions of the stars.

An alternative reply is that all mixtures of the sort in question were prohibited in renunciation of sexual intercourse that is contrary to nature.

Still, these prohibitions have a figurative reason behind them. For the passage "You shall not sow your vineyard with diverse seeds" is to be understood spiritually to mean that strange doctrine is not to be sown within the Church, which is a spiritual vine. And similarly, the field, i.e., the Church, is not to be sown with diverse seeds, i.e., with both Catholic doctrine and heretical doctrine. Nor is to be plowed simultaneously with an ox and a donkey, since he who is foolish is not to join with him who is wise in preaching; for the one impedes the other.

Reply to objection 10: [*There is no reply in the manuscripts to objection 10.*]

Reply to objection 11: In their rites the magicians and priests of the idols used the bones or flesh of dead men. And so, in order to root out idolatrous worship, the Lord commanded that the lower priests, who ministered in the sanctuary for fixed periods, should not be defiled with death, except for the deaths of those close to them, viz., their father or mother or persons related to them in like manner.

The high priest, however, had always to be prepared for the ministry of the sanctuary, and so he was absolutely forbidden to approach the dead, no matter how closely related they were.

Again, the priests were also commanded to take a virgin as a wife, and not to marry a prostitute or divorced woman. This was meant to induce reverence for the priests, whose dignity might seem to be diminished by such a marriage, and also because of the sons, for whom the mother's shame would be a source of ignominy—something to be especially avoided insofar as the

dignity of the priesthood would be conferred on them according to familial succession.

In order to prevent idolatrous rites, they were also forbidden to shave
their heads or beards or to make incisions in their flesh. For the priests of
the Gentiles shaved their heads and beards; hence, Baruch 6:30 says, "The
priests sit . . . with their garments rent, and their heads and beards shaven."
Also, in the worship of their idols "they cut themselves with knives and
lances," as 3 Kings 18:28 reports. Hence, the contraries of these things
were mandated for the priests of the Old Law.

The spiritual reasons behind these precepts are as follows: The priests
had to be entirely immune from dead works, i.e., the works of sin. And they
should also not shave, i.e., put off wisdom, or rid themselves of their
beards, i.e., rid themselves of wisdom, or tear their vestments or cut their
flesh, i.e., incur the vice of schism.

QUESTION 103

The Duration of the Ceremonial Precepts

The next thing to consider is the duration of the ceremonial precepts. On this topic there are four questions: (1) Were there ceremonial precepts before the Law? (2) Did the Law have the power to give justification? (3) Did the ceremonial precepts cease to apply after Christ came? (4) Is it a mortal sin to observe the ceremonial precepts in the time after Christ?

Article 1

Did the ceremonies of the Law exist before the Law existed?

It seems that the ceremonies of the Law existed before the Law did:

Objection 1: As was explained above (q. 102, a. 3), sacrifices and holocausts have to do with the ceremonies of the Old Law. But there were sacrifices and holocausts before the Law; for Genesis 4:3–4 says, "Cain offered gifts to the Lord from the fruits of the earth, whereas Abel offered gifts from the first-born of his flock and from their fat." Again, Noah offered holocausts to the Lord, as Genesis 18:20 states; and Abraham did so, too, as Genesis 22:13 reports. Therefore, the ceremonies of the Old Law existed before the Law existed.

Objection 2: The construction and anointing (*injunctio*) of an altar have to do with the ceremonies relating to the sacred things. But these things existed before the Law did; for Genesis 13:18 says, "Abraham built an altar to the Lord," and Genesis 28:18 says of Jacob, "He took the stone . . . and set it up as a monument (*vitulus*), pouring oil over it." Therefore, the ceremonies of the Law existed before the Law existed.

Objection 3: Among the sacraments of the Law the primary one (*primum*) seems to have been circumcision. But as is clear from Genesis 17:10ff., circumcision existed before the Law did. Likewise, the priesthood existed before the Law did; for Genesis 14:18 says, "Melchisedech was a priest of the most high God." Therefore, the ceremonies of the sacraments existed before the Law existed.

Objection 4: As was explained above (q. 102, a. 6), the distinction between clean and unclean animals has to do with the ceremonies of the observances. But this distinction existed before the Law did; for Genesis 7:2–3 says, "Take seven and seven of all the clean animals, but two and two of the unclean animals." Therefore, the ceremonies of the Law existed before the Law existed.

But contrary to this: Deuteronomy 6:1 says, "These are the precepts and ceremonies that the Lord your God has commanded that I should teach you." But they would not have needed to be taught about them if these ceremonies had already existed. Therefore, the ceremonies of the Law did not exist before the Law existed.

I respond: As is clear from what has been said (q. 102, a. 2), the ceremonies of the Law were ordered toward two things, viz., worshiping God and being figures of Christ.

Now whoever worships God must worship Him in specific ways that bear upon exterior worship. But this specification (*determinatio*) of divine worship involves ceremonies in the same way that, as was explained above (q. 99, a. 4), the specification of how we are ordered to our neighbor involves judicial precepts. And so just as it was common among men for there to be judicial precepts that were not instituted by God's authority but were instead ordained by human reason, so too there were certain ceremonies that were specified not by the authority of any law but rather solely by the will and devotion of the men who were worshiping God.

However, since even before the Law existed there were certain outstanding men empowered with a prophetic spirit, it is plausible to believe that they were led by a divine instinct—by a private law, as it were—to a certain set way (*ad aliquem certum modum*) of worshiping God which was appropriate for interior worship and which was also fit to signify the mysteries of Christ that other actions of theirs were also figures of—this according to 1 Corinthians 10:11 ("All things happened to them in figure").

Therefore, there were ceremonies before the Law existed, but they were not the ceremonies of the Law, since they were not instituted through any legislation.

Reply to objection 1: Before the Law existed, the ancients offered oblations and sacrifices and holocausts out of the devotion of their own will, insofar as it seemed fitting to them that in those things which they had received from God and which they offered out of reverence for God, they should give witness (*protestarentur*) to the fact that they were worshiping God, who is the source and end of all things.

Reply to objection 2: They likewise instituted certain sacred things because it seemed fitting to them that there should be some places that were set off from others and tied to divine worship.

Reply to objection 3: The sacrament of circumcision was established by God's command before the Law existed. Hence, circumcision can be called a sacrament of the Law only in the sense that it was observed under the Law and not in the sense that it was instituted by the Law. This is why our Lord says in John 7:22, "Circumcision is not from Moses, but from his fathers."

Likewise, among those who worshiped God the priesthood existed according to a human specification before the Law existed, since they gave this dignity to the first-born.

Reply to objection 4: Before the Law existed, the distinction between clean and unclean animals did not exist as far as eating was concerned, since Genesis 9:3 says, "Everything that moves and lives will be food for you." Rather, the distinction existed only with respect to the offering of sacrifices, since they offered certain specific animals as sacrifices.

However, if there was any distinction among animals that pertained to eating, this was not because the eating of the animals was illegal—for it was not forbidden by any law—but rather because of abhorrence or custom, just as even now we see that certain foods that are eaten in some lands are abhorred in others.

Article 2

Did the ceremonies of the Old Law have the power to confer justification at the time of the Law?

It seems that the ceremonies of the Old Law had the power to confer justification (*habuerint virtutem justificandi*) at the time of the Law:

Objection 1: Expiation from sin and the consecration of a man have to do with justification. But Exodus 29:21 says that the priests and their vestments were consecrated through the sprinkling of blood and anointing with oil, while Leviticus 16:16 says that through the sprinkling of the blood of the heifer the priest expiated the sanctuary from the impurities of the children of Israel and from their deceits and sins. Therefore, the ceremonies of the Old Law had the power to confer justification.

Objection 2: That by which a man is pleasing to God pertains to justification—this according to Psalm 10:8 ("The Lord is just, and He loved just acts"). But some men were pleasing to God because of the ceremonies—this according to Leviticus 10:19 ("How could I have been pleasing to the

Lord in the ceremonies with the mind of a sad man?") Therefore, the ceremonies of the Old Law had the power to confer justification.

Objection 3: What belongs to the worship of God involves the soul as well as the body—this according to Psalm 18:8 ("The Law of the Lord is pure, converting souls"). But as Leviticus 14 points out, lepers were cleansed by the ceremonies of the Old Law. Therefore, *a fortiori*, the ceremonies of the Old Law were capable of cleansing the soul by conferring justification on it.

But contrary to this: In Galatians 2:21 the Apostle says, "If a law had been given that was capable of conferring justification, then Christ would have died for nothing (*gratis*)," i.e., for no reason. But this is absurd. Therefore, the ceremonies of the Old Law did not confer justification.

I respond: As was explained above (q. 102, a. 5), there were two kinds of uncleanness under the Old Law. The one kind was spiritual, and this is the uncleanness of sin (*immunditia culpae*). The other kind, by contrast, was corporeal (*immunidita corporalis*) and took away one's fitness for divine worship; this is the sense in which a leper was unclean, or one who touched something associated with death. Uncleanness of this kind was nothing other than a certain irregularity (*irregularitas*).

The ceremonies of the Old Law had the power to cleanse this second kind of uncleanness, since these ceremonies were remedies applied by legal ordinance to remove those sorts of uncleanness, like the ones mentioned above, which had been induced by a statute of the Law. This is why in Hebrews 9:13 the Apostle says, "The blood of goats and bulls and the sprinkled ashes of a heifer sanctify those who are defiled as far as the cleansing of the flesh is concerned." And just as the uncleanness that was washed away by these ceremonies was an uncleanness of the flesh rather than of the mind, so shortly before the cited passage (Hebrews 9:10) the Apostle calls these ceremonies 'justifications of the flesh' (*iustitiae carnis*). "They are justifications of the flesh," he says, "imposed during the time of correction."

However, these ceremonies did not have the power to expiate uncleanness of the mind, i.e., the uncleanness of sin. This is because the expiation from sins could never have been brought about except through Christ, who "takes away the sins of the world," as John 1:29 says; and since the mystery of Christ's incarnation and passion had not yet been accomplished in reality, the ceremonies of the Old Law were unable in their own right to have a real power that flowed from the incarnate and suffering Christ in the way that the sacraments of the New Law do. And so these ceremonies were unable to wash away sin. As the Apostle puts it in Hebrews 10:4, "It was impossible for sins to be removed by the blood of bulls and goats." This is what in Galatians 4:9 the Apostle calls "those empty and weak elements"—weak because they cannot wash away sin, whereas the weakness arises from the fact that they are empty, i.e., from the fact that they do not contain grace in their own right.

Still, at the time of the Law the mind of the faithful ones was able, through faith, to be joined to Christ incarnate and suffering, and so the faithful were justified by their faith in Christ. The observance of the ceremonies in question was a kind of profession of this faith, insofar as the ceremonies were figures of Christ. And the reason that sacrifices were offered for sins in the Old Law was not that the sacrifices themselves washed away sin, but rather that they were a kind of profession of that faith which did wash away sin. The Law itself lends support to this claim by its mode of speaking; for Leviticus 4–5 says that in the offering of sacrifices for sin the priest "will pray for him and his sin will be forgiven"—as if to say that the sin is forgiven not by the power of the sacrifices, but rather because of the faith and devotion of those offering the sacrifices. Note, however, that the fact that the ceremonies of the Old Law expiated corporeal impurities was itself a figure of the expiation of sins that is made through Christ.

So, then, it is clear that the ceremonies under the status of the Old Law did not themselves have the power to confer justification.

Reply to objection 1: The sanctification of the priests and their sons and of their vestments, or of any other things, through the sprinkling of blood was nothing other than a deputation for divine worship and a removal of impediments to the purity of the flesh, as the Apostle puts it. This was done as a prefigurement of the sanctification by which Jesus sanctified the people by His own blood.

Similarly, the expiation in question should be thought of as removing corporeal impurities and not sins. Hence, the sanctuary, which was not capable of sinning (*culpae subiectum esse non poterat*), is likewise said to be expiated.

Reply to objection 2: In the ceremonies the priests were pleasing to God because of their obedience and devotion and because of their faith in the reality prefigured by the ceremonies—and not because of the ceremonies themselves considered in their own right.

Reply to objection 3: The ceremonies that had been instituted for the cleansing of a leper were not ordered toward removing the uncleanness of the disease of leprosy. This is clear from the fact that these ceremonies were applied only to someone who was already cleansed of the disease; hence, Leviticus 14:3–4 says, "When the priest, upon leaving the camp, finds that the leprosy has been cleansed, he will command that the one *who is purified* should offer, etc."—and not "*who is about to be purified.*" From this it is clear that the priest was set up as the judge of an already cleansed leper and not of a leper who was about to be cleansed.

Ceremonies of this sort were used to remove an uncleanness of irregularity. However, they say that sometimes, if the priest happened to make a mistake in his judgment, the leper was miraculously cleansed by God through His divine power—and not through the power of the sacrifices. In the same way, as Numbers 5:27 reports, the thigh of the adulterous woman rotted when she drank the water upon which the priest had "heaped curses."

Article 3

Did the ceremonies of the Old Law cease with the coming of Christ?

It seems that the ceremonies of the Old Law did not cease with the coming of Christ:

Objection 1: Baruch 4:1 says, "This is the book of God's commandments and the law which lasts forever." But the ceremonies of the Law are part of the Law. Therefore, the ceremonies of the Law were to last forever.

Objection 2: A cleansed leper's offering belongs to the ceremonies of the Law. But even in the Gospel a cleansed leper is ordered to make offerings of this sort. Therefore, the ceremonies of the Old Law did not cease when Christ came.

Objection 3: As long as a cause remains, its effect remains. But the ceremonies of the Old Law had certain reasoned causes insofar as they were ordered toward divine worship, even beyond the fact that they were ordered toward being figures of Christ. Therefore, the ceremonies of the Old Law were not supposed to cease.

Objection 4: As was explained above (q. 102, a. 4), circumcision was instituted as a sign of Abraham's faith, and the observance of the Sabbath was instituted to recall the favor of creation, and the other solemn feasts of the Law were instituted to recall others of God's favors. But Abraham's faith should be imitated even by us; and the favor of creation, along with God's other favors, should always be recalled. Therefore, it is even less the case that circumcision and the solemn feasts of the Law should cease.

But contrary to this: In Colossians 2:16–17 the Apostle says, "Let no man judge you in meat or in drink, or with respect to a feast day or the new moon or the Sabbaths, which are a shadow of things to come." And Hebrews 8:13 says, "In saying 'a new [covenant]', He has made the former [covenant] old, and that which decays and grows old is near its end."

I respond: As was explained above (q. 102, aa. 1 and 2), all the ceremonial precepts of the Old Law were ordered toward the worship of God. Now exterior worship should be proportioned to interior worship, which consists in faith, hope, and charity. Hence, exterior worship should be diversified in a way corresponding to the diversity of interior worship.

Now one can distinguish three states (*status*) of interior worship:

The first state is that in which faith and hope are had both (a) with respect to heavenly goods and also (b) with respect to the means by which we are led to those heavenly goods, where both of these are seen as something future. This is the state of faith and hope under the Old Law.

The second state of interior worship is that in which faith and hope are had (a) with respect to heavenly goods as something future, but (b) with respect to the means by which we are led to those goods as something present or past. This is the state of the New Law.

The third state is that in which both things are had as something present, and nothing is believed in or hoped for as something absent. This is the state of the blessed in heaven (*status beatorum*). Thus, in the state of the blessed nothing that has to do with divine worship is figurative; instead, there is only the act of thanksgiving and the voicing of praise. Thus, Apocalypse 21:22 says of the city of the blessed, "I saw no temple in it, for the Lord, the almighty God, is its temple, and the Lamb."

Therefore, by parity of reasoning, it was fitting that the ceremonies of the first state, which were figures of the second and third states, should cease when the second state arrived, and that other ceremonies should be introduced which corresponded to the state of divine worship for that later time, in which the heavenly goods are something future, but the divine favors by which we are led to the heavenly goods are something present.

Reply to objection 1: The Old Law is said to be eternal in an absolute and unqualified way with respect to its moral precepts. On the other hand, as far as its ceremonial precepts are concerned, it is eternal with respect to the truth that the ceremonies are figures of.

Reply to objection 2: The mystery of the redemption of the human race was completed in Christ's passion; hence, in John 19:30 our Lord says, "It is consummated" (*consummatum est*). As a sign of this, we read that during Christ's passion the veil of the temple was rent (Matthew 27:51).

And so before Christ's passion, when Christ was preaching and working miracles, the Law and the Gospel were running side by side, since the mystery of Christ had already begun but had not yet been consummated. And it was for this reason that our Lord ordered the leper to observe the ceremonies of the Law.

Reply to objection 3: The literal reasons given above (q. 102) for the ceremonies have to do with divine worship, which was worship with faith in something yet to come. And so when He who was to come had already come, the first state of worship ceased and all the reasons were ordered toward the second state of worship.

Reply to objection 4: Abraham's faith was commended because he trusted God's promise about his future seed, in which all nations were to be blessed. And so as long as this was still something future, Abraham's faith had to be professed in circumcision. However, after it had already been accomplished, the same reality was declared by another sign, viz., Baptism, which was in this regard the successor to circumcision—this according to the Apostle in Colossians 2:11–12 ("You have been circumcised with a circumcision made not by hand in the despoiling of the body's flesh, but rather with the circumcision of our Lord Jesus Christ, buried with Him in Baptism").

Moreover, the Sabbath, which signified the first creation, is changed to Sunday (*dies dominicus*), on which the new creature, begun in the Christ's resurrection, is commemorated.

Likewise, the other solemn feasts of the Old Law are succeeded by the new solemn feasts, since the favors granted to that people signify the favors granted to us through Christ. Hence, the feast of the Passover is succeeded by the feast of the passion and resurrection of Christ. The feast of Pentecost on which the Old Law was given is succeeded by the feast of Pentecost on which the Law of the Spirit of life was given. The feast of the New Moon is succeeded by the feast of the Blessed Virgin on which the illumination of the sun, i.e., Christ, first appeared through the outpouring of grace. The feast of Trumpets is succeeded by the feasts of the apostles. The feast of the Atonement is succeeded by the feasts of the martyrs and confessors. The feast of Tabernacles is succeeded by the feast of the consecration of a church. The feast of the Assembly and Collection is succeeded by the feast of the angels, or also by the feast of All Saints.

Article 4

Can the ceremonial precepts be observed without mortal sin after Christ's passion?

It seems that the ceremonial precepts can be observed without mortal sin after Christ's passion:

Objection 1: It is unbelievable that the apostles committed mortal sin after having received the Holy Spirit. For as Luke 24:49 says, by His fullness "they were endowed with power from on high." But after the coming of the Holy Spirit the apostles observed the Law. For Acts 16:3 says that Paul circumcised Timothy, and Acts 21:26 says that Paul, acting on the advice of James, "took the men and, having been purified with them, entered the temple, announcing the fulfillment of the day of purification while an offering was being made for each of them." Therefore, the ceremonial precepts can be observed without mortal sin after Christ's passion.

Objection 2: The ceremonial precepts include avoiding contact with Gentiles. But the first shepherd (*pastor*) of the Church observed this precept; for Galatians 2:12 says that when certain men came to Antioch, Peter withdrew from the Gentiles and separated himself from them. Therefore, the ceremonies of the Law can be observed without mortal sin after Christ's passion.

Objection 3: The commands of the apostles did not lead men into sin. But by a decree of the apostles it was decided that the Gentiles should observe certain of the ceremonial precepts (*quaedam de ceremoniis*) of the Law; for Acts 15:28–29 says, "It has seemed good to the Holy Spirit and to us to lay no further burden upon you than these necessary things: that you abstain from what has been sacrificed to idols, and from blood, and from things strangled, and from fornication." Therefore, the ceremonies of the Law can be observed without sin after Christ's passion.

But contrary to this: In Galatians 5:2 the Apostle says, "If you are circumcised, Christ shall profit you nothing." But nothing rules out Christ's fruit except mortal sin. Therefore, being circumcised, along with observing the other ceremonies of the Law, is a mortal sin after Christ's passion.

I respond: All the ceremonies were a sort of profession of that faith which the interior worship of God consists in. A man can profess this interior faith by deeds as well as by words, and in both sorts of profession, a man commits a mortal sin if he professes something false.

Now even though the faith we have in Christ is the same faith that the ancient fathers had, nonetheless, because they came before Christ whereas we come after Christ, this same faith is signified with different words by us and by them. For they say, "Behold, a virgin will conceive and bring forth a son," where the verbs are future-tense, whereas we represent this same thing with past-tense verbs by saying, "She conceived and brought forth a son."

Similarly, the ceremonies of the Old Law signified the Christ as someone who would be born and would suffer, whereas our sacraments signify Him as someone who has been born and has suffered. Therefore, just as someone would commit a mortal sin if he now, in professing his faith, claimed that the Christ will be born—something that the ancients said in a pious and faith-filled manner—so too someone would commit a mortal sin if he now observed those ceremonies which the ancients observed in their pious and faith-filled manner. This is what Augustine says in *Contra Faustum*: "'Will be born', 'will suffer', and 'will rise' —which those [old] sacraments in a sense resounded with—are no longer permitted. Instead, it is proclaimed that He has been born, that He has suffered, and that He has risen—which the sacraments performed by Christians now resound with."

Reply to objection 1: Jerome and Augustine seem to have had differing views on this matter.

Jerome distinguished two periods of time. The one period occurred before Christ's passion, and in this period the ceremonial precepts of the Law were neither dead (*mortua*), in the sense of not having obligatory or expiatory force in their own way, nor deadly (*mortifera*), because those observing them did not thereby sin. However, immediately after Christ's passion, the ceremonial precepts of the Law began to be not only dead, i.e., lacking in power and obligation, but also deadly, in the sense that if anyone observed them, he was committing a mortal sin. For this reason, Jerome claims that after Christ's passion the apostles never in truth observed the ceremonial precepts of the Law, but instead observed them only by a sort of pious simulation, and this in order not to give scandal to the Jews and thus impede their conversion. The simulation is not to be understood in such a way that they did not in truth perform the relevant actions, but rather is to be understood to mean that they did not perform them in such a way as to observe the ceremonial precepts of the Law—as, for instance, if someone were to cut off the foreskin of the male member for the sake of health and not for the sake of observing the legal ceremony of circumcision.

However, because it seems implausible that the apostles should have hidden, out of concern for scandal, those very things that have to do with the truth of life and doctrine, and that they should have made use of a simulation in matters that involve the salvation of the faithful, Augustine more appropriately distinguishes three periods of time. One occurred before Christ's passion, and in this period the ceremonial precepts of the Law were neither dead nor deadly. A second occurs after the time of the spread of the Gospel, and in this period the ceremonial precepts of the Law were both dead and deadly. The third period was the time between the other two, viz., from Christ's passion to the spread of the Gospel, and during this period the ceremonial precepts of the Law were, to be sure, dead, because they did not have power and because no one was obliged to observe them, but they were nonetheless not deadly, because those who had been converted to Christ from among the Jews were able to observe them licitly as long as they did not place their hope in them in such a way that they considered them necessary for salvation, i.e., as long as they did not believe that faith in Christ was unable to justify them in the absence of the ceremonies of the Law. However, there was no reason for those who were converted to Christ from among the Gentiles to observe the ceremonial precepts of the Law.

Accordingly, Paul circumcised Timothy because Timothy had been born of a Jewish mother, whereas he decided not to circumcise Titus, since Titus had been born of Gentiles. However, in order to show the difference between the rites of the Law and the rites of the Gentiles, the Holy Spirit did not want the observance of the ceremonies of the Law to be immediately forbidden for those who had been converted from among the Jews, in the way that the Gentile rites were forbidden for those who had been converted from among the Gentiles. For the rites of the Gentiles were repudiated as altogether illicit and had always been prohibited by God. By contrast, the rites of the Law ceased because they had been fulfilled through Christ's passion; for they had been instituted by God as a figure of the Christ.

Reply to objection 2: According to Jerome, Peter put up the pretense of withdrawing from the Gentiles in order to avoid scandalizing the Jews, of whom he was the Apostle. Hence, in this he did not in any way sin. Paul, on the other hand, likewise put up the pretense of reprehending him in order to avoid scandalizing the Gentiles, of whom he was the Apostle.

Augustine, however, disproves this view by appeal to the fact that in the canonical Scriptures, viz., in Galatians 2:11, in which one cannot believe that there is anything false, Paul says that Peter was reprehensible. Hence, it is true that Peter sinned and that Paul corrected him in reality and did not just pretend to correct him.

Still, Peter did not sin in observing the Law for that time period, since he was permitted to observe the Law as someone converted from among the Jews. Instead, he sinned by being excessively diligent in his observance of the Law in order not to scandalize the Jews, with the result that he scandalized the Gentiles instead.

Reply to objection 3: Some have claimed that this prohibition by the apostles should be understood not in a literal sense but in a spiritual sense, so that the prohibition of blood stands for the prohibition of homicide, and the prohibition of what is suffocated stands for the prohibition of robbery and violence, and the prohibition of what has been sacrificed stands for the prohibition of idolatry, and the prohibition of fornication stands for the prohibition of what is bad *per se*. This opinion is accepted by certain Glosses, which expound precepts of this sort in a mystical sense.

However, since homicide and robbery were thought of as being against the law even among the Gentiles, it would not have been necessary for a special commandment to be given about this matter to those who had been converted to Christ from paganism.

Hence, others have claimed that the foods were prohibited literally not because of the observances of the Law but in order to suppress gluttony. Hence, in *Super Ezechiel*, commenting on 44:31 ("The priests shall not eat of anything that is dead"), Jerome says that the passage in question condemns priests who, out of gluttonous desire, do not keep these precepts in the case of thrushes and other things of this sort.

However, since there are foods that are greater delicacies and more conducive to gluttony, there does not seem to be any reason why the particular foods in question were prohibited rather than others.

Therefore, one should reply, in keeping with a third opinion, that the foods in question were prohibited literally not with an eye toward observing the ceremonies of the Law, but rather in order to strengthen the union of Gentiles and Jews who were living together. For as a matter of ancient custom, blood and strangled meat were abominable to the Jews, whereas the eating of things that had been sacrificed to idols could generate among the Jews the suspicion that the Gentiles were relapsing into idolatry. And so these things were forbidden for the period in which it was necessary to bring Gentiles and Jews together for the first time (*de novo*). However, as time went on and the cause ceased to be present, the effect also ceased to be present—once the truth of the Gospel teaching became evident, where our Lord teaches that "nothing that enters through the mouth makes a man unclean" (Matthew 15:11) and 1 Timothy 4:4 says, "Nothing is to be rejected that is received with thanksgiving."

On the other hand, fornication was specifically prohibited because the Gentiles did not consider it a sin.

QUESTION 104

The Judicial Precepts of the Old Law

Next we have to consider the judicial precepts. First, we have to consider them in general and, second, we have to consider the reasons for them.

On the first topic there are four questions: (1) What are the judicial precepts? (2) Are the judicial precepts figurative? (3) How long do they endure? (4) What are the kinds of judicial precepts?

Article 1

Does the nature of the judicial precepts consist in their directing a man in his relations with his neighbor?

It seems that the nature of the judicial precepts does not consist in their directing a man in his relations with his neighbor (*ordinantia ad proximum*):

Objection 1: The judicial precepts (*praecepta iudicialia*) take their name from judicial proceedings (*iudicium*). But there are many other things by which a man is directed in his relations with his neighbor and which do not involve any judicial proceeding. Therefore, it is not the case that these precepts are called judicial because they direct a man in his relations with his neighbor.

Objection 2: As was explained above (q. 99, a. 4), the judicial precepts are distinct from the moral precepts. But there are many moral precepts by which a man is directed in his relations with his neighbor, as is clear from the seven precepts of the second tablet. Therefore, it is not the case that precepts are called judicial by reason of the fact that they direct a man in his relations with his neighbor.

Objection 3: As was explained above (q. 99, a. 4 and q. 101, a. 1), the judicial precepts bear upon our neighbor in the same way that the ceremonial precepts bear upon God. But among the ceremonial precepts there are some that have to do with one's own self, e.g., the observances regarding food and clothing that were discussed above (q. 102, a. 6). Therefore, it is not the case that precepts are called judicial by virtue of the fact that they direct a man in his relations with his neighbor.

But contrary to this: Ezechiel 18:8 lists among the good works of the just man: ". . . if he judges accurately (*iudicium fecerit verum*) between one man and another." But the judicial precepts take their name from judicial proceedings (*iudicium*). Therefore, it seems that the precepts that are called judicial are those that involve directing men in their relations with one another.

I respond: As is clear from what was said above (q. 99, a. 4), certain precepts of the Law have their binding force (*vis obligandi*) from the very dictate of reason—i.e., in virtue of the fact that natural reason dictates that such-and-such is to be done or is to be avoided. Precepts of this sort are called *moral* precepts, because human morals (*mores humani*) come from reason.

By contrast, other precepts do not have their binding force from the very dictate of reason; for, considered in themselves, they do not absolutely speaking have the character of what ought to be done or ought not to be done. Instead, they have their binding force from some statute, either divine or human (*ex aliqua institutione divina vel humana*). Certain specifications (*determinationes*) of the moral precepts are of this sort. Thus, if the moral precepts are given a specification by divine statute in those matters in which man is ordered toward God, then the resulting precepts are called *ceremonial* precepts. On the other hand, if the moral precepts are given a specification in matters that involve the ordering of men to one another, then the resulting precepts are called *judicial* precepts.

Therefore, the nature of the judicial precepts consists in two things, viz., (a) the fact that they have to do with directing men in their relations with one another, and (b) the fact that they have binding force not just from reason, but from statutes.

Reply to objection 1: Judicial proceedings are conducted as the official duty of certain rulers (*principes*) who have the power to pass judgment. Now a ruler has the role of bringing order not only to what comes under litigation, but also to the voluntary contracts made among men and to everything that involves the communal life and governance of the people. Hence, the judicial precepts include not only those matters that involve disputes requiring judicial proceedings but also any matter that involves the ordering of men to one another and that is subject to the determination of the ruler as the supreme judge.

Reply to objection 2: This argument goes through in the case of those precepts that direct a man in his relations with his neighbor and that have their binding force solely from the dictate of reason.

Reply to objection 3: It is likewise the case that among the precepts that direct one toward God, some are moral, i.e., are dictated by reason itself as informed by faith—e.g., that God is to be loved and worshiped—whereas others are ceremonial, i.e., they have binding force only by divine ordinance.

Now what pertains to God are not just the sacrifices offered to God, but also anything relevant to one's fitness for making offerings and for worshiping God. For men are directed toward God as their end, and so it is relevant to the worship of God, and thus to the ceremonial precepts, that a man should have a certain sort of fitness (*idoneitas*) with respect to divine worship.

By contrast, a man is not directed to his neighbor as his end in such a way that he must be, within his very self, at the disposal of his neighbor (*ut oporteat eum disponi in seipso in ordine ad proximum*). For this is the way in which servants are related to their masters—where, according to the Philosopher in *Politics* 1, "servants, in all that they are, belong to their masters." And so there are no judicial precepts that direct a man within himself; instead, all precepts of that sort are moral. For reason, which is the principle of the moral precepts, plays the same role within a man—i.e., with respect to the things pertaining to his very self—that a ruler or judge plays within a city.

Still, note that because the relation of a man to his neighbor falls [directly] under reason to a greater degree than does the relation of a man to God, there are more moral precepts by which a man is directed in his relations with his neighbor than there are moral precepts by which he is directed toward God. It is for this reason, too, that in the Law there are more ceremonial precepts than there are judicial precepts.

Article 2

Are the judicial precepts figures of anything?

It seems that the judicial precepts are not figures of anything:

Objection 1: It seems proper to the ceremonial precepts to be instituted as a figure of something. Therefore, if the judicial precepts were likewise figures of something, then there would be no difference between the judicial precepts and the ceremonial precepts.

Objection 2: Just as the Jewish people were given certain judicial precepts, so other peoples among the Gentiles were given judicial precepts, too. However, the judicial precepts of those other peoples were not figures of anything, but instead laid down what ought to be done. Therefore, the judicial precepts of the Old Law do not seem to have been figures of anything, either.

Objection 3: What pertains to the worship of God had to be handed down by means of figures, since, as was explained above (q. 101, a. 2), the things of God exceed our reason. By contrast, what has to do with our neighbor does not exceed our reason. Therefore, it is unnecessary for the judicial precepts, which direct us in our relations with our neighbor, to be figures of anything.

But contrary to this: In Exodus 21 the precepts are explained by means of both an allegorical sense and a moral sense (*allegorice et moraliter*).

I respond: There are two ways in which a precept can be a figure of something:

In the first way, a precept is a figure primarily and *per se*, i.e., it is instituted mainly in order to be a figure of something. This is the way in which the ceremonial precepts are figurative, since they were instituted in order to be figures of things having to do with the worship of God and the mystery of Christ.

On the other hand, certain precepts are figurative not primarily and *per se*, but in a derivative way (*in consequenti*). This is the way in which the judicial precepts of the Old Law are figurative. For they were instituted not for the purpose of being figures of anything, but rather for the purpose of regulating the condition (*status*) of the Jewish people in accordance with justice and equity. However, the judicial precepts were figures of something in a derivative way, viz., insofar as the overall condition (*totus status*) of the people who were disposed by these precepts was itself figurative— this according to 1 Corinthians 10:11 ("All things happened to them in figure").

Reply to objection 1: As has been explained, the ceremonial precepts were figurative in a way different from that in which the judicial precepts were figurative.

Reply to objection 2: The Jewish people had been chosen by God in order that the Christ should be born from them. And so, as Augustine puts it in *Contra Faustum*, the overall condition of that people had to be prophetic and figurative. Because of this, it was also the case that the judicial precepts given to that people were figurative to a greater degree than the judicial precepts given to other peoples. For instance, that people's wars and deeds are given a mystical interpretation, unlike the wars and deeds of the Assyrians and the Romans—even though the latter are far more famous among men.

Reply to objection 3: If, within that people, the directing of a man in his relations with his neighbor is considered merely by itself, then it is accessible to reason (*pervius rationi*). However, it surpassed reason insofar as it was ordered toward the worship of God. And it is on this score that it was figurative.

Article 3

Do the judicial precepts of the Old Law have perpetual binding force?

It seems that the judicial precepts of the Old Law have perpetual binding force (*perpetuam obligationem habeant*):

Objection 1: The judicial precepts (*praecepta iudicialia*) have to do with the virtue of justice, since a legal judgment (*iudicium*) is an execution of justice. But as Wisdom 1:15 says, justice is "everlasting and undying (*perpetua et immortalis*)." Therefore, the binding force of the judicial precepts is perpetual.

Objection 2: A divine statute (*institutio divina*) is more stable than a human statute. But the judicial precepts of the codes of human law have perpetual binding force. Therefore, *a fortiori*, so do the judicial precepts of divine law.

Objection 3: In Hebrews 7:18 the Apostle says, "The previous Law (*mandatum*) was set aside because of its weakness and unprofitableness." This is true of the ceremonial Law, which, as the Apostle says in Hebrews 9:9–10, "could not make one perfect in conscience except only with respect to food and drink and various types of ritual washing and rules governing the flesh." By contrast, the judicial precepts were useful and effective for the purpose to which they were ordered, viz., to establish justice and equity among men. Therefore, the judicial precepts of the Old Law were not set aside, but still have force.

But contrary to this: In Hebrews 7:12 the Apostle says, "Once the priesthood is transferred (*translatum*), the Law must be transferred as well." But the priesthood is transferred from Aaron to Christ. Therefore, the whole of the Law is transferred. Therefore, it is not the case that the judicial precepts still have binding force.

I respond: The judicial precepts did not have perpetual binding force, but were set aside with the coming of Christ—though in manner different from that in which the ceremonial precepts were set aside.

For the ceremonial precepts were set aside in such a way that they are not only dead but also deadly for those observing them after Christ, especially after the spread of the Gospel. By contrast, the judicial precepts are, to be sure, dead, since they do not have binding force, and yet they are not deadly. For if a ruler were to command that these judicial precepts should be observed in his domain, he would not thereby sin—unless, perhaps, the precepts were observed or were to be observed as if they had their binding force from the institution of the Old Law. For this sort of intention in observing them would be deadly.

The explanation for this difference between the ceremonial precepts and the judicial precepts can be gathered from what was said above (a. 2). For it was claimed that the ceremonial precepts are figurative primarily and *per se*, in the sense that they were instituted primarily to be figures of the mysteries of the Christ understood as something future. And so to observe them now is prejudicial to the truth of the Faith, since we now confess that these mysteries have been accomplished. By contrast, the judicial precepts were instituted not in order to be figures, but in order to mold the state of the people that was ordered toward the Christ. And so when the status of that people changed because Christ had already come, the judicial precepts lost their binding force; for as Galatians 3:24 says, the Law was a teacher leading them to the Christ.

Still, since the judicial precepts are ordered not toward being figures of anything, but rather toward something's being done, the observance of those precepts is not itself, absolutely speaking, prejudicial to the truth of the Faith. However, the intention to observe the judicial precepts because of the binding power of the Law is indeed prejudicial to the truth of the Faith. For it implies that the former people's state still persists and that the Christ has not yet come.

Reply to objection 1: To be sure, justice must always be observed. But the specification of what is just by human or divine decree must vary with the different states of men.

Reply to objection 2: The judicial precepts instituted by men have perpetual binding force as long as the relevant state of the regime persists. But if a city or nation devolves into another regime, then the laws must change. For instance, as is clear from the Philosopher in his *Politics*, it is not the case that the same laws are appropriate for both a democracy, which is rule by the people (*potestas populi*), and an oligarchy, which is rule by the rich (*potestas divitum*). So, too, once the status of the people in question changed, the judicial precepts had to change.

Reply to objection 3: The judicial precepts disposed the people toward justice and equity in a way appropriate for their status. But after Christ, the status of that people had to change, since now in Christ there would be no distinction between Gentile and Jew, as there had been before. For this reason, the judicial precepts also had to change.

Article 4

Can the judicial precepts be divided into set kinds?

It seems that the judicial precepts cannot be divided into set kinds:

Objection 1: The judicial precepts direct men in their relations with one another. But the things that need to be directed among men and are part of human practice do not fall under set kinds, since there are infinitely many of them. Therefore, the judicial precepts cannot have set kinds.

Objection 2: The judicial precepts are specifications of the moral precepts. But the moral precepts do not seem to admit of set kinds, except insofar as they are traced back to the precepts of the Decalogue. Therefore, the judicial precepts do not have set kinds.

Objection 3: Since the ceremonial precepts have set kinds, their division is based on the Law, as when some are called sacrifices and some are called observances. But there is no division of the judicial precepts that is based on the Law. Therefore, it seems that the judicial precepts do not have set kinds.

But contrary to this: Where there is order, there must be distinctions. But the notion of order is especially relevant to the judicial precepts, through which the people in question were ordered. Therefore, the judicial precepts ought especially to have set kinds.

I respond: Since law is, as it were, the craft (*ars*) of instituting or ordering human life, it follows that just as in any craft there is a set distinction among the rules of the craft, so too in any law there must be a set division of the precepts; otherwise, confusion would by itself destroy the law's usefulness. Accordingly, one should claim that the judicial precepts of the Old Law, through which men were ordered in their relations with one another, have divisions corresponding to the divisions of human ordering.

Now within a given people there are four orderings: (a) the ordering of the rulers of the people to their subjects, (b) the ordering of the subjects to one another, (c) the ordering of the people themselves to outsiders (*ad extraneos*), and (d) the ordering of domestic relations, e.g., father to son, wife to husband, master to servant. It is according to these four orderings that the judicial precepts of the Old Law can be divided:

(a) Some precepts are given that have to do with the institution of the rulers and their duties, and with the respect that ought to be shown for them; and this is one part of the judicial precepts.

(b) Again, some precepts are given that have to do with the citizens' relations with one another, e.g., precepts concerning buying and selling, and precepts concerning judgments and penalties. And this is the second part of the judicial precepts.

(c) Again, some precepts are given that have to do with outsiders, e.g., precepts concerning wars against enemies and precepts concerning the manner in which travelers and strangers are to be received. And this is the third part of the judicial precepts.

(d) Again, in the Law some precepts are given that have to do with domestic common life, e.g., precepts concerning servants and wives and children. And this is the fourth part of the judicial precepts.

Reply to objection 1: The things that have to do with the ordering of men to one another are, to be sure, infinitely many. However, as has been explained, they can still be reduced to certain set kinds of things according to the differences among human relations.

Reply to objection 2: As was explained above (q. 100, a. 3), the precepts of the Decalogue are first in the genus of morals, and so the other moral precepts are appropriately divided by reference to them. By contrast, the judicial and ceremonial precepts have a different sort of binding force that comes not from natural reason but solely by decree. And so their divisions have a different explanation.

Reply to objection 3: The Law bases the division of the judicial precepts on the very things that are ordered by the judicial precepts in the Law.

QUESTION 105

The Reasons for the Judicial Precepts

Next we have to consider the reasons for the judicial precepts. On this topic there are four questions: (1) What are the reasons for the judicial precepts that have to do with the rulers? (2) What are the reasons for the ones that have to do with the common life of men with one another? (3) What are the reasons for the ones that have to do with outsiders? (4) What are reasons for the ones that have to do with domestic life?

Article 1

Did the Old Law give appropriate direction concerning the rulers?

It seems that the Old Law did not give appropriate direction (*inconvenienter ordinaverit*) concerning the rulers:

Objection 1: As the Philosopher says in *Politics* 3, "The governance of the people depends principally on the highest ruling office." But the Law does not say how the highest ruler should be appointed. By contrast, it does say something about the lower rulers in Exodus 18:21–22 ("Provide wise men from among the whole people"), Numbers 11:16–17 ("Gather to me seventy men from among the elders of Israel"), and Deuteronomy 1:13 ("Give me wise and knowledgeable men from among yourselves," and so on). Therefore, the Old Law did not give sufficient direction concerning the rulers of the people.

Objection 2: As Plato says, "It belongs to the best to do the best." But the best arrangement for a city or for any people is that it should be governed by a king, since governance (*regimen*) of this sort is the best representation of the divine governance by which God rules the world. Therefore, the Law should have set up a king for the people from the beginning, and it should not have left this up to the choice of the people, as Deuteronomy 17:14–15 does ("When you shall say, 'I will set a king over me', then you will set him over you," and so on).

Objection 3: As Matthew 12:25 says, "Every kingdom divided against itself will be laid waste," and this became clear from experience in the case of the Jewish people, among whom the division of the kingdom was a cause of devastation. But the Law should principally tend toward what contributes to the common welfare. Therefore, the Law should have forbidden the division of the kingdom between two kings. Nor should this division have been introduced by divine authority, in the way that, according to 3 Kings 11, it was introduced by the Lord's authority through the prophet Ahijah the Shilonite.

Objection 4: Just as the priests are ordained (*instituuntur*) in order to benefit the people in those things that have to do with God, as is clear from Hebrews 5, so too the rulers are constituted in order to benefit the people in human affairs. But certain things on which their livelihood depends—e.g., tithes and first fruits and many other such things—are allotted to the priests and Levites under the Law. Therefore, in the same way, certain things necessary for sustenance should have been directed to the rulers of the people, especially in light of the fact that they were forbidden to accept gifts, as is clear from Exodus 23:8 ("You shall not accept gifts, which make even prudent men blind and subvert the words of the just").

Objection 5: Just as a monarchy (*regnum*) is the best kind of government (*regimen*), so a tyranny is the worst corruption of government. But in setting up a king, the Lord instituted a tyrannical rule; for 1 Kings 8:11 says, "This will be the right of the king who is to rule over you: that he should take your sons," and so on. Therefore, the Law did not appropriately provide for the regulation of the rulers.

But contrary to this: In Numbers 24:5 the people of Israel is commended for the elegance of its order ("How beautiful are your tabernacles, O Jacob, and your tents, O Israel"). But the beauty of a people's order depends on its rulers being instituted in the right way. Therefore, through the Law this people was set up correctly with respect to its rulers.

I respond: There are two points to notice regarding the fitting institution (*ordinatio*) of the rulers in a city or among a people.

The first is that everyone should have some role in governance (*principatus*), since, as *Politics* 2 points out, the peaceful existence (*pax*) of a people is thereby maintained, and everyone loves and safeguards an arrangement of this sort.

The second point has to do with the type of political arrangement (*species regiminis*), i.e., the manner in which the ruling offices are constituted. Even though, as the Philosopher points out in *Politics* 3, there are various types of political arrangements, the preeminent types are monarchy (*regnum*), in which a single ruler governs in accord with virtue (*principatur secundum virtutem*), and aristocracy (*aristocratia*), i.e., rule by the best, in which a small number govern in accord with virtue.

Hence, the best manner of constituting the ruling offices occurs in a city or region in which (a) there is a single person who is placed in authority on the basis of virtue (*secundum virtutem*) and presides over everyone, and in which (b) under him there are certain others who govern in accord with virtue, and yet in which (c) this political arrangement involves everyone (*ad omnes pertinet*), both because the rulers can be chosen *from among* everyone and also because they are chosen *by* everyone. This is the best political arrangement, with a good mixture of (a) *monarchy*, insofar as there is a single preeminent ruler, and (b) *aristocracy*, insofar as many govern in accord with virtue, and (c) *democracy*, i.e., rule by the people, insofar as the rulers can be chosen from among the people and the choice of rulers falls to the people (*ad populum pertinet electio principium*).

This was the arrangement instituted by divine law. For Moses and his successors governed the people as single rulers over all, which is a certain type of monarchy. Moreover, the seventy-two elders were chosen for their virtue; for Deuteronomy 1:15 says, "I took from your tribes men who were wise and honorable, and I made them rulers." And this was similar to aristocracy. On the other hand, it was democratic in that (a) these rulers were chosen from among all the people (Exodus 18:21: "Provide wise men from among the whole people") and (b) the people chose them (Deuteronomy 1:15: "Give me wise men from among yourselves," and so on). Hence, it is clear that the Law established the best arrangement for the rulers.

Reply to objection 1: The people in question were ruled under God's special care; this is why Deuteronomy 7:6 says, "The Lord your God chose you to be His special people." And so the Lord reserved to Himself the institution of the highest ruler. And this is just what Moses asked for in Numbers 27:16: "May the Lord, the God of the spirits of all flesh, provide a man to preside over this multitude." And so Joshua was appointed by God's command to govern after Moses. And we read, with respect to each of the judges who succeeded Joshua, that "God raised up a savior for the people," and that "the spirit of the Lord" was in them, as is clear from Judges 3. And so, as is clear from Deuteronomy 17:15 ("You shall appoint him king whom the Lord your God chooses"), the Lord did not hand over to the people the choice of a king, but instead reserved it for Himself.

Reply to objection 2: As long as it is not corrupt, monarchy is the best political arrangement for a people. However, because of the great power that is granted to a king, monarchy easily degenerates into tyranny unless the one who is granted such power is completely virtuous. For as the Philosopher says in *Ethics* 4, it is only the virtuous who bear good fortune well.

Now complete virtue is found in only a few cases, and the Jews were particularly cruel and prone to greed—vices through which men especially fall into tyranny. And so at the beginning the Lord did not establish for them a king with full power, but instead instituted a judge and a governor to watch over them. Later on, however, at the request of the people, He granted them a king—though indignantly, so to speak, as is clear from what He said to Samuel in 1 Kings 8:7 ("It is not you they have rejected, but me, lest I rule over them").

However, as regards the institution of a king, He did make arrangements from the beginning, first of all, for the manner of choosing a king. In this regard, He made two specifications, viz., (a) that in choosing a king they should wait for the Lord's judgment, and (b) that they should not make anyone from another nation king, since such kings have no affective ties to the nation over which they preside and, as a result, do not take care of the people. Second, He prescribed how the kings, once appointed, should behave with respect to themselves, viz., that they should not accumulate chariots or horses or wives or even great wealth, since a strong desire for these things makes rulers fall into tyranny and abandon justice. He also specified how they should behave with respect to God, viz., that they should always be reading and meditating on God's Law, and that they should always live in the fear of God and in obedience to Him. He also specified how they should behave with respect to their subjects, viz., that they should not hold them in contempt out of pride or oppress them, and also that they should not deviate from justice.

Reply to objection 3: The division of the kingdom and the multiplication of kings was given to the people less as something for their benefit than as a punishment for the many instances of dissension that they directed against David's just kingdom. Hence, Hosea 13:11 says, "I will give you a king in my anger," and Hosea 8:4 says, "They themselves ruled, but not because of me; they became rulers, and I did not know it."

Reply to objection 4: The priests were appointed to sacred affairs through a succession of birth. And the reason was that they would be held in greater reverence if not just anyone from among the people could become a priest; and the honor they received contributed to the reverence for divine worship. And so they had to be granted certain special provisions in the form of tithes and first fruits, as well as oblations and sacrifices, so that they might live off of those things.

By contrast, the rulers, as has been explained, were taken from the people as a whole, and so they had certain possessions of their own that they could live off of. Also, and especially, the Lord forbade the king to have extravagant wealth or showy magnificence, both because (a), given these things, it would difficult for him not to be led into pride and tyranny, and also because (b) if the rulers were not extravagantly rich, and if ruling were arduous and full of anxiety, then ordinary people would not aspire to rule—and in this way one cause of rebellion (*seditio*) was removed.

Reply to objection 5: It is not the case that this right was being given to the king by divine institution; rather, the passage is foretelling the usurpation by the kings, who establish this unjust right as they degenerate into tyranny and plunder their subjects.

This interpretation is clear from what is added at the end—viz., ". . . and you will be his servants"—which properly has to do with tyranny, since tyrants rule their subjects as if they were servants. Hence, Samuel uttered these words in order to deter them from asking for a king. For what follows is this: "The people refused to listen to the voice of Samuel."

Still, it can happen that even a good king, in the absence of tyranny, takes away the sons and makes them tribunes and centurions, and demands many things from his subjects—and this in order to procure the common good.

Article 2

Were appropriate judicial precepts given with respect to the common life of the people?

It seems that appropriate judicial precepts were not given with respect to the common life of the people:

Objection 1: Men cannot live peacefully with one another if one takes what belongs to another. But this seems to be encouraged in the Law; for Deuteronomy 23:24 says, "Having entered your neighbor's vineyard, eat as many grapes as you please." Therefore, the Old Law did not appropriately provide for peace among men.

Objection 2: As the Philosopher points out in *Politics* 2, a chief reason why many cities and kingdoms are destroyed is that their possessions fall to women. But this very thing was introduced in the Old Law; for Numbers 27:8 says, "When a man dies without a son, his inheritance shall pass to his daughter." Therefore, the Law did not appropriately provide for the welfare of the people.

Objection 3: As *Politics* 1 says, human society is mainly conserved by the fact that men provide one another with the things they need through buying and selling. But as is clear from Leviticus 25:28, the Old Law undermined the effect of commerce (*virtus venditionis*) by commanding that possessions that had been sold should revert to the seller during the fiftieth year, the year of the Jubilee. Therefore, the Law did not appropriately direct the people on this matter.

Objection 4: Human needs are met especially by the fact that men are ready to lend. Yet this readiness is undermined when borrowers do not return what they have taken; hence, Ecclesiasticus 29:10 says, "Many have refused to lend, not out of wickedness, but because they were afraid of being defrauded without cause." But the Law encourages just this. For, first of all, Deuteronomy 15:2 commanded, "One to whom something is owed by his friend or neighbor or brother shall not ask for it back, because it is the Lord's year of remission," and, again, Exodus 22:15 says that if a borrowed animal dies while its owner is present, the borrower does not have to make restitution (*reddere*). Second, the security the lender has because of the promised collateral (*pignus*) is undermined; for Deuteronomy 24:10ff. says, "When you demand of your neighbor something that he owes you, you shall not go into his house to take away the promised collateral," and, again, "The promised collateral shall not pass the night with you, but you shall give it back to him immediately." Therefore, the Law did not give sufficient direction in the case of lending.

Objection 5: There is a very great risk of being defrauded of what one has deposited for safekeeping (*depositum*), and so the greatest caution has to be exercised; hence, 2 Maccabees 3:15 says, "The priests . . . called upon Him from heaven who made the law concerning things deposited for safekeeping, that He would preserve them safe for those who had deposited them." But in the precepts of the Old Law little caution is shown in the case of things deposited for safekeeping. For Exodus 22:10–11 says that when something deposited for safekeeping is lost, one should accept the oath of the one with whom the thing was deposited. Therefore, the Law's direction on this matter was inappropriate.

Objection 6: Just as a wage laborer hires out his services, so too some rent out their houses or other possessions. But it is not necessary that a tenant (*conductor*) immediately pay the rent on a house he has rented. Therefore, it was excessively harsh for Leviticus 19:13 to command, "The wages owed to your wage laborer shall not remain in your hands all the way until morning."

Objection 7: Since there is a frequent need for judgments, there should be easy access to a judge. Therefore, it was inappropriate for the Law to prescribe in Deuteronomy 17:8–9 that those seeking judgment for their cases should all proceed to a single fixed place.

Objection 8: It is possible not only for two people, but also for three or more, to agree to lie. Therefore, it was inappropriate for Deuteronomy 19:15 to say, "Every word that comes from the mouth of two or three witnesses shall stand."

Objection 9: Punishment should be determined according to the measure of the fault (*culpa*); hence, Deuteronomy 25:2 says, "According to the measure of the sin shall the measure also of the lashes be." But the Law established unequal punishments for certain equal faults. For instance, Exodus 22:1 says, "The thief shall restore five oxen for one oxen and four sheep for one sheep." Also, certain sins that are not very grave are punished by severe punishments—e.g., in Numbers 15 a man was stoned because he had gathered wood on the Sabbath. Again, in Deuteronomy 21 it is commanded that an unruly son should be stoned for small transgressions, viz., for spending his time in revelry and feasting. Therefore, punishments were not appropriately instituted in the Law.

Objection 10: As Augustine says in *De Civitate Dei* 21, "Tully writes that there are eight forms of punishment recognized in the laws, viz., fines (*damnum*), incarceration (*vincula*), scourging (*verbera*), retaliation (*talio*), public disgrace (*ignominia*), exile (*exilium*), death (*mors*), and servitude (*servitudo*)."

Some of these were established under the Old Law: fines, as when a thief is fined five times or four times as much as he has stolen; incarceration, as when Numbers 15:34 commands, with respect to someone, that he be incarcerated; scourging, as when Deuteronomy 25:2 says, "If they see that he who has sinned deserves flogging, they shall lay him down, and shall make him to be scourged in their presence." Likewise, the Law imposed public disgrace on anyone who refused to marry the wife of his deceased brother; she was to "take off his shoe and spit in his face." Again, the Law imposed death, as is clear from Leviticus 20:9: "If anyone curses his father or mother, let him die the death." Again, the Law imposed the punishment of retaliation, with Exodus 21:24 saying, "An eye for an eye, a tooth for a tooth." Therefore, it was inappropriate for the Law not to impose the other two forms of punishment, viz., exile and servitude.

Objection 11: There ought not to be a punishment unless there is guilt. But brute animals cannot have guilt. Therefore, it is wrong for punishment to be imposed on them, as in Exodus 21:29 ("An ox shall be stoned if it kills a man or a woman") and Leviticus 20:16 ("If a woman has sexual relations with any beast, she shall be killed along with the beast"). So, then, it seems that things pertaining to the common life of men with one another were inappropriately directed under the Old Law.

Objection 12: In Exodus 21:12 the Lord commanded that homicide should be punished by the death of a man. But the death of a brute animal counts for much less than the death of a man. Therefore, the punishment for homicide cannot be adequately replaced by putting a brute animal to death. Therefore, it was wrong for Deuteronomy 21:1–4 to command that "when the corpse of a slain man is found and no one knows who is guilty of the murder . . . the elders of the nearest city shall take from the herd a heifer that has not drawn a yoke or plowed the ground, and they shall bring her into a rough and stony valley that has never been plowed or sown, and there they shall cut off the head of the heifer."

But contrary to this: Psalm 147:20 counts it as a special blessing that "He has not done thus for every nation, and He has not made His judgments known to them."

I respond: In *De Civitate Dei* 2 Augustine cites the following passage from Tully: "A people is the union of a multitude brought together by consent to the law and by their common welfare." Hence, it pertains to the notion of a people that the interaction of men with one another should be directed by precepts of law that are just.

Now there are two types of interaction that men have with one another: One type is effected by the authority of the rulers, and the other type is effected voluntarily by private persons. Since everyone's will is such that it has the capacity to oversee what is subject to its power, it has to be by the authority of the rulers, to whom men are subject, that judgments between men are enacted and that punishments are imposed on evildoers. By contrast, possessions are subject to the power of private persons, and so with respect to these possessions they are able to interact with one another voluntarily, e.g., in buying, selling, making gifts, and other activities of this sort.

Now the Law gave adequate direction with respect to both types of interaction.

For instance, the Law established judges, as is clear from Deuteronomy 16:18 ("You shall appoint judges and magistrates at all its gates, that they might judge the people with just judgment"). Again, the Law instituted a just order of judgment, as when Deuteronomy 1:16–17 says, "Make a just judgment, regardless of whether the person is a citizen

or a stranger; there will be no difference of persons." Again, as is clear
from Exodus 23:8 and Deuteronomy 16:19, the Law removed an occasion
for unjust judgment by forbidding judges to accept gifts. Again, as is clear
from Deuteronomy 17:6 and 19:15, it fixed the number of witnesses at two
or three. Again, as will be described below, the Law established fixed punishments for various crimes.

With respect to possessions, on the other hand, as the Philosopher says
in *Politics* 2, it is best for possessions to be divided among the people, and
for their use to be partly communal and partly up to the will of those who
possess them. These three points were laid out in the Law.

First, the possessions themselves were divided among the individuals.
For instance, Numbers 33:53–54 says, "I have given the land for a possession, and you shall divide it among you by lot." And since, as the
Philosopher points out in *Politics* 2, many cities are ruined by disparities
in possessions, the Law applied a threefold remedy for regulating possessions. First, the Law stipulated that possessions should be divided equally
according to the number of men; hence Numbers 33:54 says, "You shall
give a larger part to the more and a smaller part to the fewer." The second
remedy is that one's possessions do not fall to others in perpetuity but
revert to their former owners after a fixed period, so that shares of the possessions do not become mixed up with one another. The third remedy,
aimed at removing confusion of the sort just mentioned, is that the relatives
of those who die succeed them in ownership: in order, first, the son; second, the daughter; third, the brothers; fourth, the father's brothers; fifth,
any other relative. And to preserve shares of the possessions, the Law further stipulated in Numbers 36:6 that women who inherit should marry men
of their own tribe.

Second, the Law stipulated to what extent the use of things would be
communal. First, with respect to *taking care of things*, Deuteronomy 22:1
says, "You shall not pass by if you see your brother's ox or his sheep going
astray; but you shall bring them back to your brother," and likewise for
other possessions. Second, with respect to *fruits*, it was generally allowed,
for instance, that anyone, having entered his friend's vineyard, could licitly eat of the fruit, as long as he did not take any fruit away with him. Next,
with respect to *poor people in particular*, according to Leviticus 19:9 and
Deuteronomy 24:19, the leftover sheaves should be left behind for them, as
well as the leftover fruit and bunches of grapes; and according to Exodus
23:11 and Leviticus 25:4, anything grown in the seventh year should be
given to them.

Third, the Law regulated the transfer of possessions by those who owned them. One sort of transfer was a *pure gift*. Deuteronomy 14:28–29 says, "Every third year you shall separate off another tithe, and the Levite and the stranger and the orphan and the widow shall come, and they shall eat and be filled." By contrast, the other sort of transfer was a transfer *with advantageous compensation*—as, for instance, through selling and buying, through leasing and hiring, and through loans and safekeeping, and there are fixed rules in the Law about all of these.

Hence, it is clear that the Old Law appropriately directed the common life of the people.

Reply to objection 1: As the Apostle says in Romans 13:8, he who loves his neighbor has fulfilled the Law, since all the precepts of the Law, especially the ones directed toward one's neighbor, seem to be ordered toward the goal of men loving one another. Now what proceeds from this love is that men share their goods with one another. For as 1 John 3:17 says, "If someone sees his brother suffering from want and closes off his affection from him, then how does the love of God abide in him?" And so the Law intended to make men accustomed to sharing their goods easily with one another, just as the Apostle likewise commands the rich "to give readily and share with others" (1 Timothy 6:18).

Now someone is not quick to share if he does not tolerate his neighbor's taking something modest from him without any great loss on his part. And so the Law stipulated that someone entering his neighbor's vineyard is permitted to eat of the fruit there—though he is not permitted to carry any fruit away, lest this become an occasion for inflicting a large loss on his neighbor and thereby disturbing the peace. Among disciplined people, the taking of a little does not disturb the peace, but rather strengthens friendship and makes men accustomed to being quick to share.

Reply to objection 2: The Law did not stipulate that women should have succession with respect to their father's goods unless there were no male children. In such a case it was necessary that the succession pass to the women in order to console the father, to whom it would have been a grave blow if his inheritance were going to pass in its entirety to outsiders.

However, according to Numbers 26:7–8, the Law did apply a due precaution in this matter, commanding that women who succeeded to their father's inheritance should marry within their own tribes, so that the shares of the tribes would not get mixed up with one another.

Reply to objection 3: As the Philosopher says in *Politics* 2, the regulation of possessions contributes greatly to the preservation of a city or nation. Hence, as he himself points out, in certain Gentile cities there was a rule that "no one could sell a possession except to compensate for an obvious loss" (*nisi pro manifesto detrimento*). For if possessions were sold indiscriminately, then it could happen that all the possessions would end up with just a few people, making it necessary for the city or region to be emptied of inhabitants. And so in order to remove this danger, the Old Law directed matters in such a way that men's needs might be satisfied by permitting the selling of possessions up to a certain point in time, and yet it removed the danger in question by commanding that at a set point in time the possessions that had been sold should revert to the seller. The Law set things up in this way so that the shares would not get mixed up with one another, but instead there would always be the same determinate division of goods among the tribes.

However, since urban houses were not divided by lot, the Law permitted them to be sold in perpetuity in the same way that mobile goods were. For the number of houses in a city had not been mandated in the same way that the Law had mandated a set measure of possessions which could not be added to. Rather, the number of houses in a city could be increased. By contrast, houses that were not in a city but in a village "that has no walls" (Leviticus 25:31) could not be sold in perpetuity. For houses of this sort are constructed only for purposes related to cultivation and for the safekeeping of possessions. And so the Law appropriately established the same rule for both.

Reply to objection 4: As has been explained, the Law's intention was to make men accustomed through its precepts to assisting one another promptly with necessities, since this is especially conducive to friendship. And it mandated such promptness in assisting not only with respect to those goods that are given away freely and without qualification, but also with respect to those goods that are given as loans, since assistance of this sort is the more frequent and the more necessary for the majority of people.

Now the Law prescribed this promptness of assistance in a number of ways:

First, as Deuteronomy 15 shows, the Law prescribed that they should show themselves willing to lend and that they should not withdraw from this practice when a year of remission was approaching.

Second, the Law prescribed that they should not burden the one to whom they lend either with usurious interest or by taking as collateral something that is altogether necessary for his life, and it prescribed that if such things have been taken, they should immediately be given back. For Deuteronomy 23:19 says, "You shall not lend money to your brother unto usury." And Deuteronomy 24:6 says, "You shall not take the lower or upper millstone as collateral, since he has pledged his life to you." And Exodus 22:26 says, "If you take your neighbor's garment as collateral, you shall give it back to him before sunset."

Third, the Law forbade them to be unmannerly in exacting payment. Hence Exodus 22:25 says, "If you lend money to my poor people who live among you, you shall not be exacting with them like an extortioner." And it is because of this that Deuteronomy 24:10–11 likewise says, "When you demand of your neighbor anything that he owes you, you shall not go into his house to take away the collateral, but you shall stand outside and he shall bring out to you what he has"—this because one's home is his safest refuge, and thus it is offensive to a man that his own house should be invaded, and also because the Law does not allow a creditor to take the collateral he wants, but rather allows the debtor to give what he needs the least.

Fourth, the Law prescribed that every seventh year debts would be entirely remitted. For it was probable that those who could easily repay their debts would do so before the seventh year and would not defraud their lender without cause. However, if they were altogether unable to repay, then canceling the debt was owed to them out of love, for the same reason that it should have been given to them from the beginning because of their need.

As regards borrowed animals, the Law prescribed that if, because of the negligence of the borrower, the animals died or were injured in his absence, then he should be forced to make restitution. On the other hand, if the animals died or were injured while he was present and diligently caring for them, then he was not forced to make restitution—especially if they had been rented out for a fee. For they might likewise have died or been injured in the same way under the lender's care (*apud mutuantem*), and so as long as the borrower succeeded in preserving the animal, the lender would already be profiting from the loan, and it would not be a gratuitous loan. This rule had to be observed especially in cases where the animals were rented out for a fee, since in such cases the lender received a set fee for the use of the animals. Hence, the lender was not to get anything extra by way of restitution for the animals—unless there was negligence on the part of the one entrusted with the animals. On the other hand, if the animals were not rented out for a fee, then the lender could have a just claim for at least as much compensation as the use of the dead or injured animal could have been rented out for.

Reply to objection 5: The difference between something that is lent (*mutuum*) and something that is deposited for safekeeping (*depositum*) is that what is lent is handed over for the benefit of the one to whom it is lent, whereas what is deposited for safekeeping is handed over for the benefit of the one who deposits it. And so in certain cases one was more constrained to give back what had been lent than to give back what had been deposited for safekeeping.

What was deposited for safekeeping could be lost in two ways.

First, through an *unavoidable* (i.e., natural) cause, as when an animal deposited for safekeeping died or was disabled, or through an *extrinsic* cause, as when an animal deposited for safekeeping was captured by enemy forces or was eaten by a beast. In this last case, however, one was obliged to return the remains of the slain animal to its owner, whereas in the previous cases one was not obliged to return anything, but was obliged only to take an oath in order to clear away any suspicion of fraud.

The second way in which something deposited for safekeeping could be lost was through an *avoidable* cause, viz., theft. In such a case the guardian was obliged to make restitution if the theft occurred because of negligence on his part. However, as has been explained, one who received an animal on loan was obliged to make restitution even if the animal died or was disabled in his absence. For it took a lesser degree of negligence to make a borrower liable than someone holding a thing in safekeeping, who was liable only in the case of theft.

Reply to objection 6: Laborers who sell their services are poor and seek their daily sustenance by their labors. And so the Law was provident in prescribing that a wage laborer should be paid immediately, lest he fall short of food. By contrast, those who rent out other items tend to be well-off, and they do not need the rental fee for their daily sustenance. Thus, the arguments in the two cases are not parallel.

Reply to objection 7: Judges are appointed among men to clear up possible ambiguities concerning justice among men.

Now there are two ways in which a matter can be ambiguous:

First, it can be ambiguous *to ordinary people* (*apud simplices*). And to remove this sort of doubt, Deuteronomy 16:18 mandates that judges and magistrates should be appointed for each tribe in order to judge the people with just judgments.

In the second way, something can be doubtful *even to the experts* (*apud peritos*). And so to remove this sort of doubt, the Law prescribed that everyone should return to the principal place which had been chosen by

God and in which resided both (a) the *high priest*, who was to clear up doubts concerning the ceremonies of divine worship, and (b) the *high judge* of the people, who was to clear up things relevant to judicial matters among men—just as even in our own time cases are sent from lower judges to higher judges because of appeals (*per appellationem*) or for consultation (*per consultationem*). Hence, Deuteronomy 17:8–9 says, "If you notice among you a difficult and ambiguous judgment and you see that the words of the judges within your gates vary among themselves, then go up to the place that the Lord chooses and you will come to the priests of the Levite race and to the one who is judge at that time." Still, doubtful judicial matters of this sort did not come up very often, and so the people were not burdened because of this.

Reply to objection 8: In human affairs there can be no demonstrative and infallible proofs; rather, what suffices is conjectural probability of the sort that rhetoricians use for persuasion. And so even if it is possible for two or three witnesses to agree in a lie, it is nonetheless not easy for them to conspire in this way or likely that they will do it. And so their testimony is accepted as the truth—especially if they do not vacillate in their testimony or come under suspicion in other ways. Moreover, in order that it might not be easy for witnesses to deviate from the truth, the Law prescribed that witnesses should be examined with extreme care and severely punished when caught in a lie (Deuteronomy 19:16).

However, there was a reason for specifying this number of witness, viz., to signify the infallible truthfulness of the divine persons, who are sometimes numbered as two, with the Holy Spirit as the link between them, and sometimes expressed as three—as Augustine points out in commenting on John 8:17 ("In your Law it is written that the testimony of two men is true").

Reply to objection 9: Severe punishment is imposed not only because of the seriousness of a fault but for other reasons as well:

First, because of the quantity of the sin, since, all other things being equal, the more quantity a sin has, the more severe is the punishment due for it.

Second, because of the sin's degree of habituation, since men are not easily drawn away from habitual sins except through severe punishments.

Third, because of a high degree of concupiscence or pleasure associated with the sin, since men are not easily drawn away from such sins except through severe punishments.

Fourth, because of the ease with which the sin was committed and the ease of hiding the sin, since when sins of this sort are made public, they should be more severely punishment in order to instill fear in others.

As far as the quantity of a sin is concerned, there are four degrees to be noted, even with respect to one and the same deed:

The first occurs when someone commits a sin *involuntarily*. For in such a case, if he acts altogether involuntarily, he is totally exempt from punishment. For instance, Deuteronomy 22:25 says that a girl who is assaulted in the fields is not liable to death, since "she cried out and no one was there to help her." On the other hand, if someone commits a sin that is in some sense voluntary but he sins out of weakness—as, for instance, when someone sins from passion—then the sin is lessened and the punishment should be lessened to the degree that this judgment about it is true. A possible exception occurs when, for the sake of the common welfare, the punishment, as explained above, is made more severe in order to deter men from sins of this sort.

The second degree of sin occurred when someone sinned *through ignorance*. In such a case guilt was in some way assigned because of the sinner's negligence in finding something out. Yet instead of being punished through the mediation of the judges, the sinner expiated his own sin through sacrifices; hence, Leviticus 4:2 says, "The soul that sins through ignorance . . .". However, this should be understood to mean ignorance of a fact and not ignorance of a divine precept, which everyone was expected to know.

The third grade of sin occurred when someone sinned *out of pride*, i.e., out of a fixed choice or out of fixed malice. In such a case he was punished in proportion to the quantity of his crime (*delictum*).

The fourth grade of sin occurred when someone sinned *through impudence* (*protervia*) and *obstinance* (*pertinacia*). In such a case, as a rebel and destroyer of the Law's ordinance, he was to be wholly destroyed (*omnino occidendus erat*).

Accordingly, the reply to the objection is that in punishing theft, the Law took into consideration the frequency with which something could happen. So for the theft of things that could easily be guarded from thieves, the thief was to make twofold restitution. On the other hand, since sheep grazed in the fields, they could not be easily guarded from theft, and so it happened that sheep were very often taken by theft. Hence, the Law imposed a greater punishment, viz., that four sheep were to be given over for every one stolen. Again, oxen are even more difficult to guard, since they are kept in the fields and they do not graze in herds like sheep do. And so the Law imposed a still greater punishment in their case, viz., that five oxen were to be given back for every one stolen. (I mean this except for times when the same animal was found alive with the thief, in which case the restitution was only twofold, as with other thefts; for there could have been a presumption that the thief was thinking about returning the ox and that this is why he had preserved its life.)

An alternative reply, in accord with the Gloss [on Exodus 22:1], is that an ox has five uses—viz., being sacrificed, plowing, being eaten, giving milk, and providing a hide with many uses—and that this is why five oxen were given back for every one stolen. A sheep, on the other hand, has four uses—viz., being sacrificed, being eaten, giving milk, and providing wool.

Now an unruly son was put to death not because he ate and drank, but because of his contumaciousness and rebellious spirit, which were always punished by death, as was explained above.

On the other hand, someone who gathered wood on the Sabbath was stoned as a violator of the Law, which, as was explained above (q. 100, a. 5), prescribed that the Sabbath should be observed in order to call to mind one's faith in the creation of the world. Thus, he was put to death as one who was unfaithful (*tamquam infidelis*).

Reply to objection 10: The Old Law imposed the death penalty in the case of very serious crimes, viz., sins against God, homicide, kidnapping (*furtum hominum*), disrespect for parents, adultery, and incest. For the theft of other things [besides human beings], the Law imposed fines as punishment. For striking or mutilating someone it imposed the punishment of retaliation, and likewise for the sin of false testimony. In the case of other lesser sins, the Law imposed the punishment of scourging or public disgrace.

Now the Law did impose servitude as a punishment in two cases. The first was when, during the seventh year of remission, someone who was a servant refused to take advantage of the Law in order to depart as a free man. In such a case, the punishment imposed on him was that he would remain a servant in perpetuity. Second, servitude was imposed on a thief when he was unable to make restitution (see Exodus 22:3).

However, the Law did not prescribe absolute exile as a punishment. For it was only among this people that God was worshiped, whereas all the other peoples had been corrupted by idolatry. Hence, if someone were absolutely excluded from this people, it would be an occasion of idolatry for him. And so 1 Kings 26:19 reports that David said to Saul, "They are cursed in the sight of the Lord who have cast me out this day, so that I might not dwell in the inheritance of the Lord, saying: 'Go, serve strange gods'."

Still, there was a certain limited exile (*particulare exilium*). For Deuteronomy 19:4 says that if someone struck down his neighbor unknowingly and was proved to have had no hatred against him, then he was to flee to one of the cities of refuge and remain there until the death of the high priest. He was allowed to return to his home at that time because in the face of a general loss for the whole people, particular grievances were normally put to rest, and so those close to the dead man were less likely to kill the man in question.

Reply to objection 11: It was commanded that brute animals should be killed not because of any fault on their part, but as a punishment for their owners, who had not safeguarded the animals from sins of the sort in question. And so an owner was punished more if his ox had already gored people yesterday and the day before, in which case the present danger could have been obviated, than if the ox gored someone all of a sudden.

An alternative reply is that the animals were killed out of hatred for the sin and in order that men should not be struck with terror upon seeing those animals.

Reply to objection 12: As Rabbi Moses points out, the literal reason for the precept in question was that the killer was often from a neighboring city. Hence, the killing of the heifer was done to investigate the unsolved homicide (*homicidium occultum*). This was accomplished in three ways: (a) first, the elders of the city swore that they would overlook nothing in guarding their highways; (b) second, the owner of the heifer suffered a loss when the animal was killed, and if the murder was cleared up first, then the animal would not be killed; (c) third, the place where the heifer was killed remained uncultivated. And so, in order to avoid losses of both sorts, the men of the city would be quick to make the murderer known if they knew who he was, and it would rarely happen that no talk or opinions were voiced about the matter.

An alternative reply is that this was done to instill terror, out of hatred for homicide. For the killing of a heifer, which is a useful animal and very strong—especially a heifer that had not yet labored under the yoke—signified that (a) even if the one who had committed the murder was himself useful and strong, he should nonetheless be killed, and that (b) he should die a cruel death, which was signified by cutting the animal's head off, and that (c) he should be cut off from human society as someone vile and contemptible, which was signified by the fact that the heifer, once having been killed, was left in a wild and uncultivated place to rot away.

Now the mystical reason is that the heifer taken from the herd signifies the flesh of Christ, which did not bear the yoke, since He never sinned. Nor did the heifer ever plow the ground, i.e., Christ never admitted of the stain of rebellion. Now the fact that the heifer was killed in an uncultivated valley signified the disgraceful death of Christ, through which all sins are washed away and through which the devil is shown to be the author of murder.

Article 3

Were appropriate judicial precepts given with respect to outsiders?

It seems that appropriate judicial precepts were not given with respect to outsiders (*extranei*):

Objection 1: In Acts 10:34–35 Peter says, "In truth I have come to see that God is not a respecter of persons, but, in every nation, whoever fears Him and does justice is acceptable to Him." But those who are acceptable to God should not be excluded from the assembly of God (*ecclesia Dei*). Therefore, it was inappropriate for Deuteronomy 23:3 to command, "The Ammonites and the Moabites, even after the tenth generation, shall not enter into the assembly of the Lord forever," while, on the contrary, in the very same place Deuteronomy 23:7 commands with respect to certain of the nations, "You shall not hate the Edomite, because he is your brother, or the Egyptian, because you were an alien in his land."

Objection 2: What is not within our power is not deserving of punishment. But that a man is a eunuch, or that he was born of a prostitute, is not within his power. Therefore, it was inappropriate for Deuteronomy 23:1–2 to command, "The eunuch and he who was born of a prostitute shall not enter the assembly of the Lord."

Objection 3: The Old Law mercifully prescribed that aliens were not to be persecuted; for Exodus 22:21 says, "You shall not molest the alien or persecute him; for you yourselves were likewise aliens in the land of Egypt," and Exodus 23:9 says, "You shall not make trouble for the alien, for you know the souls of aliens, because you were likewise aliens in the land of Egypt." Therefore, it was inappropriate for Deuteronomy 23:19 to permit them to lend money to aliens at a usurious rate.

Objection 4: Men are much closer to us than trees are. But the closer something is to us, the more we ought to show it the affection of love and the effects of love—this according to Ecclesiasticus 13:19 ("Every beast loves what is like it; so every man likewise loves what is closest to himself.") Therefore, it was inappropriate for the Lord to command in Deuteronomy 20:13–19 that they were to slay everyone in the captured enemy cities, and yet were not to cut down the fruit trees.

Objection 5: Everyone should, in accord with virtue, prefer the common good to his own private good. But in a war conducted against enemies, it is the common good that is sought. Therefore, it was inappropriate for Deuteronomy 20:5–7 to prescribe that when battle was imminent, certain men were to be left at home—for instance, whoever had just built a new house, whoever had planted vines, and whoever had just betrothed a wife.

Objection 6: No one ought to profit (*commodum reportare*) from his own faults. But it is a man's own fault that he is fearful and fainthearted, since this is contrary to the virtue of fortitude. Therefore, it was inappropriate for the fearful and fainthearted to be excused from the hardships of battle.

But contrary to this: In Proverbs 8:8 Divine Wisdom says, "All my words are just, there is nothing wicked or perverse in them."

I respond: The relations of men with outsiders can be of two types, viz., *peaceful* and *hostile*. And the Law contained appropriate precepts in directing both types.

There are three ways in which the Jews had occasion to have *peaceful* relations with outsiders:

The first was when outsiders passed through their territory as travelers. The second way was when they came to their land to live as aliens. And with respect to these two ways, Exodus 22:21 says, "You shall not make trouble for the alien," and Exodus 23:9 says, "You shall not molest the traveler."

The third way was when outsiders wished to be admitted fully into their fellowship and rites. And a certain order was followed in such cases. For they were not immediately received as citizens—just as, according to the Philosopher in *Politics* 3, in certain nations it was prescribed that no one would be counted as a citizen except those whose grandparents or great-grandparents had been citizens. The reason for this is that if outsiders, upon arriving, were immediately admitted into deliberations about matters pertaining to the people, many dangers could arise. For instance, outsiders, not yet having a firm love for the public good, might strive for certain goals in opposition to the people. And so the Law prescribed that those from nations that had some connection with the Jews—viz., the

Egyptians, among whom they had been born and raised, and the Edomites, who were the children of Esau, the brother of Jacob—would be received into the fellowship of the people in the third generation. By contrast, others, since they were from nations that had maintained hostile relations with the Jews, e.g., the Ammonites and Moabites, would never be admitted into the fellowship of the people, whereas the Amalekites, who had been even more hostile to them and had no blood relations with them, would be counted as perpetual enemies. For Exodus 17:16 says, "God will war against Amalek from generation to generation."

As for *hostile* relations with outsiders, the Law likewise handed down appropriate precepts.

First, it established that war should be justly undertaken; for instance, Deuteronomy 20:10 prescribes that when they go out to attack a city, they should first make an offer of peace.

Second, the Law prescribed that they should courageously fight the war once it had been undertaken, putting their trust in God. And to make sure that this precept would be observed in the best way, the Law prescribed that when battle was imminent, a priest should strengthen them by promising them God's help.

Third, the Law commanded that impediments to battle should be removed by leaving at home certain men who could present problems.

Fourth, the Law prescribed that they should moderate the advantage of victory by sparing the women and children and also by not cutting down the fruit trees of the region.

Reply to objection 1: The Law did not exclude the men of any nation from the worship of God and from what pertains to the salvation of the soul. For Exodus 12:48 says, "If an alien wants to dwell with you and to keep the Passover of the Lord, all his males shall first be circumcised, and then he shall celebrate the rite in the prescribed manner, and he shall be as one born in the land."

However, in temporal matters, not everyone was immediately admitted into the common life of the people, and this for the reason explained above. Rather, some, viz., the Egyptians and the Edomites, were admitted in the third generation, whereas others were permanently excluded out of hatred for their past sins, e.g., the Moabites, Ammonites, and Amalekites. For just as one man is punished for a sin he has committed in order that others who see this might be afraid and refrain from sinning, so too a nation or city can be punished for some sin in order that other nations and cities might refrain from a similar sin.

However, it was possible, in light of some act of virtue, that someone should be admitted by dispensation into the fellowship of the people. For instance, Judith 14:6ff. says that Achior, the leader of the children of Ammon, "was joined to the people of Israel, and all of his descendants." And the same is true of the Moabite Ruth, who was a woman of virtue. (Still, one could reply here that the prohibition in question extended only to men and not to women, who were not citizens absolutely speaking.)

Reply to objection 2: As the Philosopher says in *Politics* 3, there are two ways in which someone is said to be a citizen, viz., (a) absolutely speaking and (b) in a qualified sense.

A citizen absolutely speaking is one who is able to do those things that properly belong to citizens, e.g., to voice his views or make judgments (*dare consilium vel judicium*) in the assembly of the people.

On the other hand, a citizen in the qualified sense is someone who lives in the city, including lowly people (*viles personae*) and children and the aged, who are not fit to have power in matters pertaining to the common welfare.

Thus, bastards, because of their lowly origin, were excluded from the assembly, i.e., from the tribunal of the people (*collegium populi*), up to the tenth generation.

The same was true of eunuchs, who were unable to have the honor that is owed to fathers—and especially within the people of the Jews, among whom the worship of God was preserved by carnal generation. For as the Philosopher points out in *Politics* 2, even among the Gentiles those who had begotten many sons were given special honor. However, as regards the things having to do with God's grace, eunuchs were not separated off from the others—just as, in they way explained above, outsiders were not separated off, either. For Isaiah 56:3 says, "Let not the son of the outsider that adheres to the Lord speak, saying, 'The Lord will divide and separate me from His people.' And let not the eunuch say, 'Behold, I am a dry tree.'"

Reply to objection 3: It was not the Law's intention that usurious interest should be taken from outsiders; rather, the Law permitted this, as it were, because of the Jews' inclination toward greed and in order that they might relate more peaceably to the outsiders from whom they were making a profit.

Reply to objection 4: A distinction must be drawn with respect to the citizens of enemy lands.

Some of them lived far away and did not belong to those cities that had been promised to the Jews; and in these cities, once conquered, the men who had fought against the people of God were slain, whereas the women and children (*infantes*) were spared.

However, in the nearby cities, which had been promised to them, the command was that everyone should be killed because of their prior iniquities, and it was to punish those iniquities that the Lord sent the people of Israel as the executioners of divine justice. For Deuteronomy 9:5 says, "Because they have acted wickedly, they are destroyed at your coming."

Now it was commanded that the fruit trees be spared because of their usefulness to that people to whose rule the city and its territory were to be subject.

Reply to objection 5: There were two reasons why those who had built new houses, planted new vines, or betrothed a wife were exempted from battle.

The first is that the things a man has just acquired or is just about to acquire are such that he normally loves them more and, as a result, is fearful of losing them. Hence, it was likely that because of this love such men would fear death more and so would fight less courageously.

The second reason is that, as the Philosopher says in *Physics* 2, "It seems to be a misfortune, when one is close to acquiring some good, if he is afterwards prevented from doing so." And so in order that the close survivors would not be more upset by the death of these men who had not gotten to possess the goods awaiting them, and in order that the people would likewise not be horrified, men of this sort were sequestered from the danger of death by being removed from battle.

Reply to objection 6: The fearful were left at home not in order that they themselves might thereby have an advantage, but in order that the people might not suffer a disadvantage from their presence. For because of their fearfulness and their taking flight, others might likewise be incited to become fearful and take flight.

Article 4

Did the Old Law issue appropriate precepts with respect to household members?

It seems that the Old Law did not issue appropriate precepts with respect to household members (*circa dometicas personas*):

Objection 1: As the Philosopher says in *Politics* 1, a servant, in everything he is, belongs to his master. But what belongs to someone is owed to him perpetually. Therefore, it was inappropriate for Exodus 21:2 to command that servants should go free in the seventh year.

Objection 2: Just as an animal, like a donkey or an ox, is a possession of its owner, so too with his servant. But Deuteronomy 22:1–3 prescribes that animals are to be returned to their owners if they are discovered after having gone astray. Therefore, it is inappropriate for Deuteronomy 23:15 to command, "You shall not hand over a servant to his master if he flees to you."

Objection 3: Divine law ought to move one toward mercy even more than human law does. But under human law someone who treats his male or female servants with excessive harshness is severely punished. Now the harshest treatment seems to be that which results in death. Therefore, it is inappropriate for Exodus 21:20–21 to mandate, "If someone beats his male or female servant with a rod . . . and the servant survives for a day . . . then he shall not be subject to punishment, since the money belongs to him."

Objection 4: As *Politics* 1 and 3 say, the rule of a master over his servant is different from the rule of a father over his child. But it pertains to the rule of a master over his servant that the master is allowed to sell his male or female servant. Therefore, it was inappropriate for the Law to permit someone to sell his daughter as a handmaid or servant.

Objection 5: A father has power over his son. But one who has power over a sinner is in a position to punish him. Therefore, it was inappropriate for Deuteronomy 21:19 to prescribe that a father should take his son to the elders of the city to be punished.

Objection 6: In Deuteronomy 7:3 the Lord prohibited them from making marriages with aliens; and as is clear from Esdra 10, He commanded that marriages with aliens that had already been contracted should be dissolved. Therefore, it was inappropriate for Deuteronomy 21:10 to permit them to take women captured from alien nations as their wives.

Objection 7: As is clear from Leviticus 18, the Lord commanded that certain degrees of consanguinity and kinship were to be avoided in the making of marriages. Therefore, it was inappropriate for Deuteronomy 25:5 to command that if a man died without children, then his brother should marry his wife.

Objection 8: Just as there ought to be the greatest degree of familiarity between man and wife, so too there should be the firmest trust. But this cannot be if marriage is dissoluble. Therefore, it was inappropriate for the Lord to permit a man to dismiss his wife with a written decree of divorce (*repudium*) and to prescribe further that he could not take her back as his wife again (Deuteronomy 24).

Objection 9: Just as a wife can break trust with her husband, so too a servant can break trust with his master, and a son with his father. But no sacrifice was instituted in the Law as part of the investigation of a servant's harming his master or of a son's harming his father. Therefore, it seems superfluous for the Law to have established, in Numbers 5, a "sacrifice of jealousy" to investigate a wife's adultery.

Therefore, it seems that the Law did not issue appropriate precepts for household members.

But contrary to this: Psalm 18:10 says, "The judgments of the Lord are true, justified in themselves."

I respond: As the Philosopher says in *Politics* 1, the relation of household members with one another has to do with daily actions that are ordered toward the necessities of life. Now the life of man is preserved in two ways.

First, it is preserved in the *individual*, viz., insofar as numerically the same man remains alive. In the preservation of life in this sense a man is assisted by exterior goods on the basis of which he has food, clothing, and other things of this sort that are necessary for life. And a man needs servants to administer these goods.

Second, the life of man is preserved in the *species* through generation, and for this a man needs a wife in order that he might generate children from her.

So, then, a domestic community involves three sorts of relations, viz., master to servant, man to wife, and father to children. And the Old Law issued appropriate precepts with respect to all of them.

As regards *servants*, the Law prescribed that they should be treated with moderation, both (a) with respect to their work, so that they were not to be burdened with too much work—and this is why Deuteronomy 5:14 says, "The Lord commanded that on the Sabbath day your male and female servants should rest, even as you do"—and also (b) with respect to the punishments imposed on them, so that the Law prescribed that those who mutilated their servants must let them go free (Exodus 21:26–27). The Law prescribed this same freedom in the case of a female servant whom someone took as his wife. Again, the Law specifically prescribed that servants who themselves were members of the Jewish people should be freed in the seventh year, along with everything they had brought with them, including their clothes (Exodus 21:2). In addition, Deuteronomy 15:13 prescribed that they be given provisions for their journey.

As regards *wives*, the Law contained prescriptions about taking a wife.

Specifically, as Numbers 36:6 has it, the Law prescribed that they take wives from their own tribe—and this in order that the shares of the tribes not be conflated with one another. Again, as Deuteronomy 25:5–6 has it, the Law prescribed that a man was to marry the wife of his brother who had died without children—and this in order that someone who could not have descendants according to carnal origin might at least have descendants by a sort of adoption, so that the memory of the dead man would not be totally erased. Again, the Law prohibited them from marrying certain persons, viz., (a) alien women, because of the danger of their being seduced [by alien ways of life], and (b) women who were close relatives, because of the natural reverence owed to them. The Law also prescribed how wives, once taken in marriage, should be treated. Specifically, as Deuteronomy 22 has it, the Law commanded that anyone who falsely accused his wife of a crime should be punished. Again, as Deuteronomy 21 has it, a child was not to suffer harm because of a husband's hatred for his wife. And, as is clear from Deuteronomy 24, a husband was not to persecute his wife because of his hatred for her, but instead he was to dismiss her with a written decree of divorce. Again, in order that even greater love should draw the spouses closer together from the beginning, the Law prescribed that when someone had recently taken a wife, no publicly necessary task should be enjoined on him, so that he might be free to rejoice with his wife.

As regards *children*, the Law prescribed that fathers should give their children discipline by instructing them in the faith. Hence, Exodus 12 says, "When your children ask you, 'What is this rite?', you are to say, 'It is the Passover of the Lord.'" Likewise, the Law prescribed that they should instruct their children in morals. Hence, according to Deuteronomy 21:20, fathers had to say [to the elders], "He dislikes hearing our warnings; he gives himself over to revelry and debauchery."

Reply to objection 1: Since the children of Israel had been freed by the Lord from servitude and had thereby been assigned to serve God, the Lord did not want them to be servants in perpetuity. Hence, Leviticus 25:39 says, "If your brother, constrained by poverty, sells himself to you, you shall not oppress him with the service of servants, but he shall be like a wage laborer and a migrant worker. For they are my servants, and I brought them out of the land of Egypt. Let them not be sold as servants." And so since they were not servants absolutely speaking, they were to be let free.

Reply to objection 2: This commandment should be understood to be speaking of a servant whose master is seeking to kill him or to enlist his help in some sin.

Reply to objection 3: As far as injuries (*laesiones*) inflicted on servants are concerned, the Law seems to have taken into consideration whether or not it was certain [that the injury had resulted from the beating].

If it was certain, then the Law applied a penalty. More specifically, the prescribed penalty for mutilation was the loss of the servant, who was to be granted his freedom, whereas the prescribed penalty for death was that of a murderer, in cases where the servant died while being beaten at the hand of his master.

On the other hand, if it was not certain but had some appearance of being so (*aliquam apparentiam haberet*), then the Law did not impose a punishment in the case of one's own servant, e.g., when the beaten servant did not die immediately, but after a few days. For in that case it was uncertain whether or not he had died from the beating. For if his master had beaten a free man in such a way that the latter did not die immediately but "walked around again with the help of his staff" (Exodus 21:19), then he would not be guilty of homicide, even if the man died afterwards. Still, the master was obligated to assume the expenses which the beaten servant had paid to the doctors. However, this did not apply in the case of a master's own servant, since whatever the servant had—even the very person of the servant—was, as it were, the master's possession. And the reason given for his not being subject to a fine was that the servant's money belonged to him.

Reply to objection 4: As has been explained, no Jew could possess another Jew as a servant absolutely speaking; rather, he was a servant in a qualified sense—something like a wage laborer—for a certain period of time. And it is in this sense that the Law permitted someone, under the duress of poverty, to sell his son or his daughter. This is also shown by the very wording of the Law, which says, "If a man sells his daughter as a servant, she shall not go forth as the handmaids are wont to" (Exodus 21:7). In this same way, a man was able to sell not only his child but even himself, more as a wage laborer than as a servant—this according to Leviticus 25:39-40 ("If, compelled by poverty, your brother sells himself to you, you shall not oppress him with the servitude of servants, but he will be like a wage laborer or migrant worker."

Reply to objection 5: As the Philosopher says in *Ethics* 10, a father's authority extends only to the power to admonish, and he does not have the sort of coercive power by which someone rebellious and stubborn can be constrained. And so in this case the Law commanded that a stubborn child should be punished by the rulers of the city.

Reply to objection 6: The Lord prohibited them from taking foreign women in marriage because of the danger of seduction, i.e., lest they be led into idolatry. And He prohibited this especially with regard to women from those nations that lived close by, where they would be more likely to retain their own rites.

On the other hand, if the woman was willing to abandon idolatrous worship and to make the transition to worship under the Law, then she could be taken in marriage—as is clear from the case of Ruth, whom Boaz took in marriage. Hence, in Ruth 1:16 she had said to her mother-in-law, "Your people will be my people, and your God my God." And so it was permitted to take a captive women in marriage only if she first shaved off her hair, cut her nails, cast off the clothes in which she had been captured, and mourned for her father and mother—all of which signified the everlasting rejection of idolatry.

Reply to objection 7: As Chrysostom says in *Super Matthaeum*, "Because death was an unmitigated evil among the Jews, who did everything with a view to the present life, the Law prescribed that children should be born to the dead man through his brother, and this constituted a certain mitigation of death. However, no one other than his brother or a close relative was ordered to marry the wife of the dead man, since otherwise a child who was to be born from this union would not be regarded as the son of the man who had died. Moreover, an outsider would not be obliged, in the way a brother would be, to sustain the household of the man who had died. For it was a just thing for the brother to do this because of his relationship with the dead man."

From this it is clear that in taking his brother's wife as his own, he was acting in the place of his dead brother.

Reply to objection 8: The Law permitted divorcing one's wife not because this was just absolutely speaking, but because of the Jews' hardness of heart, as our Lord said in Matthew 19:8. We will have to talk about this more fully when we deal with the sacrament of Matrimony.

Reply to objection 9: Wives break the trust of matrimony through adultery, and they do it both easily, because of the pleasure, and covertly, because, as Job 24:15 says, "The eye of the adulterer observes darkness."

However, it is not the case that a similar explanation holds for the case of a son with respect to his father or a servant with respect to his master.

For unfaithfulness of this latter sort proceeds not from a desire for pleasure but rather from malice. Nor can it remain hidden in the way that the infidelity of an adulterous woman does.

The Law of the Gospel, Called the New Law, in Itself

Next we have to consider the Law of the Gospel, which is called the New Law. First, we will consider it in itself (question 106). Second, we will consider it in relation to the Old Law (question 107). Third, we will consider the things contained in the New Law (question 108).

On the first topic there are four questions: (1) What sort of law is it? More specifically, is it a written law or an infused law? (2) As to its power, does it confer justification? (3) As to its beginning, should it have been given from the beginning of the world? (4) As to its end, will it last until the end, or should another law succeed it?

Article 1

Is the New Law a written law?

It seems that the New Law is a written law:

Objection 1: The New Law is the Gospel itself. But the Gospel has been written down; for John 20:31 says, "These things have been written in order that you might believe." Therefore, the New Law is a written law.

Objection 2: An instilled law (*lex indita*) is a law of nature—this according to Romans 2:14–15 ("They do by nature what belongs to the law. . . . They have the work of the law written in their hearts"). Therefore, if the Law of the Gospel were an instilled law, then it would not differ from the law of nature.

Objection 3: The Law of the Gospel belongs only to those who are in the status of the New Covenant. But an instilled law is common both to those in the status of the New Covenant and to those in the status of the Old Covenant; for Wisdom 7:27 says that divine wisdom "conveys herself throughout the nations into holy souls, and she establishes the friends of God and the prophets." Therefore, the New Law is not an instilled law.

But contrary to this: The New Law is the Law of the New Covenant. But the Law of the New Covenant is instilled in the heart. For in Hebrews 8:8–10 the Apostle, citing the authority of Jeremiah 31:31–33 ("Behold the days shall come, says the Lord, and I will consummate a new covenant with the house of Israel and with the house of Judah . . ."), goes on to explain what this covenant is in the following words: "This is the covenant I will make with the house of Israel by putting my laws in their minds, and I will write my laws in their heart." Therefore, the New Law is an instilled law.

I respond: As the Philosopher puts it in *Ethics* 9, "Each thing seems to be that which is most prominent in it." But that which is most prominent in the Law of the New Covenant and in which its power consists is the grace of the Holy Spirit, which is given through faith in Christ. And so the New Law is in the first instance the very grace of the Holy Spirit that is given to those who believe in Christ (*datur Christi fidelibus*).

This is manifestly apparent from the Apostle, who in Romans 3:27 says, "Where, then, is your boasting? It is excluded. By what law? The law of works? No, but by the law of faith." For he calls the very grace of faith a law. And in Romans 8:2 he says even more clearly, "The Law of the Spirit of life in Christ Jesus has freed me from the Law of sin and death." Thus, in *De Spiritu et Littera* Augustine says, "Just as the Law of works was written on tablets of stone, so the Law of faith has been written in the hearts of the faithful." And elsewhere in the same book he says, "What else are the laws of God written by God in our hearts than the very presence of the Holy Spirit?"

Still, the New Law contains certain elements that *dispose* us toward the grace of the Holy Spirit and certain elements that have to do with the *use* of that grace. These elements are, as it were, secondary aspects of the New Law, about which those who believe in Christ have to be instructed, through both the spoken word and the written word, regarding what they ought to believe and what they ought to do. And so one should reply that the New Law is in the first instance an instilled law, but that, secondarily, it is a written law.

Reply to objection 1: The Scriptures of the Gospel contain only things that pertain to the grace of the Holy Spirit, either in the sense that they dispose us toward that grace or in the sense that they direct us in the use of that grace.

In order to dispose our understanding through the faith by which the grace of the Holy Spirit is given, the Gospel contains things that involve the manifestation of either Christ's divinity or His humanity. Again, in order to dispose our affections, the Gospel contains things which involve that hatred of the world through which a man comes to have a capacity for the grace of the Holy Spirit. For as John 14:17 says, "The world [read: lovers of the world] cannot take in (*capere*) the Holy Spirit."

On the other hand, the use of spiritual grace occurs in the works of the virtues, which the Scriptures of the New Testament exhort men to in many ways.

Reply to objection 2: There are two senses in which something is instilled (*inditum*) into a man.

The first sense has to do with human nature, and it is in this sense that the natural law is a law which is instilled in a man.

In the second sense, what is instilled in a man is, as it were, something added to his nature through the gift of grace. And this is the sense in which the New Law is instilled in a man, not only pointing out what is to be done, but also helping him to do it.

Reply to objection 3: No one has ever had the grace of the Holy Spirit except through explicit or implicit faith in Christ. But it is through faith in Christ that a man belongs to the New Covenant. Hence, if anyone has had the Law of grace instilled in him, then he thereby belonged to the New Covenant.

Article 2

Does the New Law confer justification?

It seems that the New Law does not confer justification:

Objection 1: No one is justified unless he obeys God's law—this according to Hebrews 5:9 ("He, viz., Christ, has become to all who obey Him the cause of eternal salvation"). But the Gospel does not always bring it about that men obey it; for Romans 10:16 says, "Not everyone obeys the Gospel." Therefore, the New Law does not confer justification.

Objection 2: In Romans the Apostle proves that the Old Law did not confer justification from the fact that after it came, transgression increased; for Romans 4:15 says, "The Law makes for wrath, since where there is no law, there is no transgression, either." But the New Law increases transgression even more, since one who continues to sin after the New Law has been given is deserving of even more punishment—this according to Hebrews 10:28–29 ("One who invalidates the Law of Moses dies without any mercy at the word of two or three witnesses. How much more, do you think, does he who tramples upon the Son of God deserve worse punishments?"). Therefore, the New Law, like the Old Law, fails to confer justification.

Objection 3: Conferring justification is an effect that belongs properly to God—this according to Romans 8:33 ("It is God who confers justification"). But the Old Law was from God, just as the New Law is. Therefore, the New Law does not confer justification any more than the Old Law did.

But contrary to this: In Romans 1:16 the Apostle says, "I am not ashamed of the Gospel, since it is the power of God for the salvation of all who believe." But salvation comes only to those on whom justification has been conferred. Therefore, the Law of the Gospel confers justification.

I respond: As has been explained (a. 1), there are two elements involved in the New Law.

The first, and principal, element is the very grace of the Holy Spirit, which is given inwardly. And on this score, the New Law confers justification. Hence, in *De Spiritu et Littera* Augustine says, "There, viz., under the Old Covenant, a Law is posited outwardly by which the unjust are made fearful, whereas here, viz., in the New Covenant, a Law is given inwardly by which the unjust are justified."

The other element involves the Law of the Gospel in a secondary way, viz., the documents of the faith and the precepts that direct human affections and human actions. On this score, the New Law does not confer justification. Hence, in 2 Corinthians 3:6 the Apostle says, "The letter kills, but the spirit gives life." In *De Spiritu et Littera* Augustine explains that by 'the letter' is meant any writing that exists exterior to men, even the writing of the moral precepts contained in the Gospel. Hence, even the letter of the Gospel kills unless the healing grace of faith is inwardly present.

Reply to objection 1: This objection goes through in the case of the New Law not with respect what is primary in it, but with respect to what is secondary in it, viz., the documents and precepts that are proposed to man exteriorly either by the spoken word or by the written word.

Reply to objection 2: Even if the grace of the New Covenant helps a man not to sin, it nonetheless does not confirm a man in the good, so that he is unable to sin. For this belongs to the state of glory. And so if anyone sins after having received the grace of the New Covenant, he deserves a greater punishment because he is ungrateful for greater blessings and is not using the help that has been given to him. However, the New Law is not said to "work wrath" because of this, since the New Law of itself gives help that is sufficient for not sinning.

Reply to objection 3: The one God gave both the New Law and the Old Law, but in different ways. For He gave the Old Law as written on stone tablets, whereas He gave the New Law as written on "the fleshy tablets of the heart," as the Apostle puts it in 2 Corinthians 3:3.

Furthermore, as Augustine says in *De Spiritu et Littera*, "The Apostle calls *that* letter, written outside of man, both a ministration of death and a ministration of damnation. *This* letter, however, viz., the Law of the New Covenant, he calls a ministration of the Spirit and a ministration of justification, since it is through the gift of the Spirit that we work justice and are freed from the damnation of transgression."

Article 3

Should the New Law have been given from the beginning?

It seems that the New Law should have been given from the beginning:

Objection 1: As Romans 2:11 says, "There is no respecting of persons with God." But as Romans 3:23 says, "All men have sinned and need the glory of God." Therefore the Law of the Gospel should have been given from the beginning of the world, in order that all might have been helped by it.

Objection 2: Just as different men live in different places, so too they live at different times. But God—who, as 1 Timothy 2:4 says, wills all men to be saved—commanded that the Gospel should be preached in all places, as is clear from Matthew 28:19 and Mark 16:15. Therefore, the Law of the Gospel should have been present at all times, with the result that it should have been given from the beginning of the world.

Objection 3: Spiritual salvation, which is eternal, is more necessary for man than is corporeal salvation, which is temporal. But as is clear from Genesis 1, from the beginning of the world God provided man with those things necessary for corporeal salvation by giving him power over all the things that had been created for the sake of man. Therefore, the New Law, which is especially necessary for spiritual salvation, should have been given to man from the beginning of the world.

But contrary to this: In 1 Corinthians 15:46 the Apostle says, "That which is spiritual was not first, but instead that which is animal." But the New Law is more spiritual than anything else is. Therefore, the New Law should not have been given from the beginning of the world.

I respond: Three reasons can be cited for why the New Law should not have been given from the beginning of the world.

The first is that, as has been explained (a. 1), the New Law is in the first instance the grace of the Holy Spirit, which could not have been given in abundance until the obstacle of sin had been removed from the human race by the consummation of redemption through Christ. Hence, John 7:39 says, "The Spirit had not yet been given, because Jesus had not yet been glorified." And this is the reason clearly stated by the Apostle in Romans 8, where, after having begun by talking about the "law of the Spirit of life," he added, "God, in sending His own Son in the likeness of sinful flesh and for the sake of sin, condemned sin in the flesh in order that the justification of the Law might be fulfilled in us."

The second reason that can be given is based on the perfection of the New Law. For a thing is not brought to perfection immediately from the beginning; rather, it is brought to perfection with a certain temporal order of succession, in the way that someone is first a boy and later a man. The Apostle cites this reason in Galatians 3:24–25: "The Law was our teacher in Christ, in order that we might be justified by faith. But when faith arrives, we are no longer under the teacher."

The third reason is based on the fact that the New Law is a law of grace, and so it was first required that man should be left to himself in the state of the Old Law, in order that, falling into sin and seeing his own weakness, he might recognize that he needed grace. It is this reason that the Apostle cites in Romans 5:20, where he says, "The Law entered in so that sin might abound; but where sin abounded, grace did more abound."

Reply to objection 1: Because of the sin of its first parent, the human race deserved to be deprived of the assistance of grace. And so as Augustine says in *De Perfectione Iustitiae*, "If grace is not given to someone, this is out of justice, whereas if grace is given to someone, this is out of mercy (*ex gratia*)." Hence, the fact that God did not confer the Law of grace on everyone from the beginning of the world does not involve His being a respecter of persons. For as has been explained, grace had to be conferred in due order.

Reply to objection 2: A diversity of locations does not change the status of the human race; rather, this status varies through temporal succession. And so the New Law is proposed to all locations, but not at all times, even though, as was explained above (a. 1, ad 3), at every time there have been some who belong to the New Covenant.

Reply to objection 3: Things having to do with corporeal salvation aid man with respect to his nature, which is not destroyed through sin. By contrast, things having to do with spiritual salvation are ordered toward grace, which is lost through sin. And so the arguments in the two cases are not parallel.

Article 4

Will the New Law last until the end of the world?

It seems that the New Law will not last until the end of the world:

Objection 1: In 1 Corinthians 13:10 the Apostle says, "When that which is complete (*perfectum*) has come, then that which is partial will be done away with." But the New Law is partial (*ex parte*); for in the same place the Apostle says, "We know in part, and we prophesy in part." Therefore, the New Law will have to be done away with when another, more complete, state succeeds it.

Objection 2: In John 16:13 our Lord promised His disciples that they would know "all truth" at the coming of the Holy Spirit, the Paraclete. But the Church does not yet know all truth within the state of the New Covenant. Therefore, another state is to be expected in which all truth will be manifested through the Holy Spirit.

Objection 3: Just as the Father is other than (*alius a*) the Son, and the Son is other than the Father, so too the Holy Spirit is other than the Father and the Son. But there was a status corresponding to the person of the Father, viz., the status of the Old Law, in which men tended toward generating children. Similarly, there is likewise a status corresponding to the person of Son, viz., the status of the New Law, in which the leaders are clerics tending toward wisdom, which is appropriated to the Son. Therefore, there will be a third status of the Holy Spirit, in which spiritual men will lead.

Objection 4: In Matthew 24:14 our Lord says, "The Gospel of the kingdom will be preached in the whole world, and then the consummation will come." But the Gospel of Christ has long since been preached in the whole world, and yet the consummation has not yet come. Therefore, the Gospel of Christ is not the Gospel of the kingdom; rather, there will be another Gospel, the Gospel of the Holy Spirit—another Law, as it were.

But contrary to this: In Matthew 24:34 our Lord says, "I tell you that this generation will not pass away until all these things have been accomplished." Chrysostom explains that this refers to "the generation of those who believe in Christ." Therefore, the status of those who believe in Christ will remain until the consummation of the world.

I respond: There are two senses in which the status of the world can vary.

One sense corresponds to the differences among the *laws*. And in this sense there will be no other status succeeding the present status of the New Law. For the status of the New Law succeeded the status of the Old Law in the way that the more perfect succeeds the less perfect. But no status of the present life can be more perfect than the status of the New Law. For there can be nothing closer to the ultimate end than that which immediately leads up to the ultimate end. But this is what the New Law does; hence, in Hebrews 10:19–22 the Apostle says, "And so, brothers, having confidence in our entry into the Holy of Holies through the blood of Christ, a new way that He has opened for us . . . let us draw near to Him." Hence, there can be no more perfect state of the present life than the status of the New Law, since the more perfect a given thing is, the closer it is to the ultimate end.

Second, the status of *men* can vary in a way corresponding to the different ways in which men are related to the same law, be it a more perfect or a less perfect law. And in this sense the status of the Old Law changed quite often. For sometimes the laws were kept very well, whereas at other times they were completely ignored. In this sense, the status of the New Law varies as well in a way corresponding to different places and times and persons, insofar as the grace of the Holy Spirit is had in a more perfect or less perfect way by given individuals.

However, one should not expect there to be some future status in which the grace of the Holy Spirit is had in a more perfect way than it has been had up to now—especially by the apostles, who received the first fruits of the Spirit, i.e., who "received them first in time and more abundantly than others," as the Gloss on Romans 8:23 puts it.

Reply to objection 1: As Dionysius says in *De Ecclesiastica Hierarchia*, there are three statuses: first, the status of the Old Law; second, the status of the New Law; the third status comes afterwards, not in this life, but in heaven (*in patria*). But just as the first status is figurative and imperfect with respect to the status of the Gospel, so too the latter status is figurative and imperfect with respect to the status of heaven. When this last status arrives, the present status will be done away with, just as we read in the same place, "Now we see darkly through a mirror, then we shall see face to face."

Reply to objection 2: As Augustine reports in *Contra Faustum*, Montanus and Priscilla claimed that our Lord's promise to give the Holy Spirit was brought to fulfillment not in the apostles, but in themselves. Similarly, the Manicheans claimed that it was brought to fulfillment in Manes, whom they claimed to be the spirit Paraclete. And so in both cases they refused to accept the Acts of the Apostles, in which it is manifestly

shown that this promise was brought to fulfillment in the apostles, just as
our Lord promised them again in Acts 1:5 ("You shall be baptized in the
Holy Spirit, not many days from now") and which Acts 2 says was fulfilled.

But these falsehoods are ruled out by the fact that John 7:39 says, "The
Spirit had not yet been given, because Jesus had not yet been glorified."
From this it is understood that the Holy Spirit was given immediately upon
Christ's being glorified in His resurrection and ascension. This also rules
out the empty notions of anyone who claims that another era of the Holy
Spirit is to be expected.

Now the Holy Spirit taught the apostles all truth concerning those
things that are necessary for salvation (*quae pertinent ad necessitatem
salutis*)—more specifically, what is to be believed and what is to be done.
However, He did not teach them about all future events, since this was not
relevant to them—this according to Acts 1:7 ("It is not for you to know the
times or moments which the Father has reserved for His own power.")

Reply to objection 3: The Old Law belonged not only to the Father
but also to the Son, since the Old Law was a figure of Christ. Hence, in
John 5:46 our Lord says, "If you believed Moses, you would perhaps
believe me as well, since he wrote about me."

Similarly, the New Law belongs not only to Christ but also to the Holy
Spirit—this according to Romans 8:2 ("The Law of the Spirit of life in
Christ Jesus," and so on). Hence, another law which is a law of the Holy
Spirit is not to be expected.

Reply to objection 4: Since it was at the very beginning of the preaching of the Gospel that Christ said, "The kingdom of heaven is at hand," it
would be utterly stupid to claim that the Gospel of Christ is not the Gospel
of the kingdom.

However, there are two possible meanings of 'the preaching of the
Gospel of Christ':

The first sense has to do with spreading the knowledge about Christ,
and in this sense, as Chrysostom points out, the Gospel was preached in
the whole world even during the time of the apostles. Accordingly, what is
then added, viz., ". . . and then the consummation will come," should be
understood to be speaking about the destruction of Jerusalem, about which
He was speaking literally at that time.

In the second possible sense it means the preaching of the Gospel in
the whole world with its full effect, with the result that the Church is firm-

ly fixed (*fundetur*) in every nation. And as Augustine points out in his letter to Hesychius, in this sense the Gospel has not yet been preached in the whole world; but once this is done, the consummation of the world will come.

QUESTION 107

The Relation between the Old Law and the New Law

Next we have to consider the relation of the New Law to the Old Law. And on this topic there are four questions: (1) Is the New Law a law different from the Old Law? (2) Does the New Law bring the Old Law to fulfillment? (3) Is the New Law contained within the Old Law? (4) Which is the more burdensome, the New Law or the Old Law?

Article 1

Is the New Law different from the Old Law?

It seems that the New Law is not different from the Old Law:

Objection 1: Both Laws are given to those who have faith in God, since, as Hebrews 11:6 says, "Without faith it is impossible to please God." But the faith of the ancients is the same as the faith of the moderns, as the Gloss on Matthew 21:9 says. Therefore, the Laws are the same as well.

Objection 2: In *Contra Adimantum Manichaei Discipulum* Augustine says, "Briefly put, the difference between the Law and the Gospel is fear and love." But the New Law and the Old Law cannot be differentiated with respect to fear and love. For precepts of charity are proposed even in the Old Law. Leviticus 19:18 says, "You shall love your neighbor," and Deuteronomy 6:5 says, "You shall love the Lord your God." Similarly, they cannot be differentiated by the other distinction that Augustine proposes in *Contra Faustum*: "The Old Covenant made temporal promises, the New Covenant makes spiritual and eternal promises." For even in the New Covenant certain temporal things are promised—this according to Mark 10:30 ("You will receive a hundred times as much in this present age, houses and brothers . . ."). Moreover, even in the Old Covenant hope was placed in spiritual and eternal promises—this according to Hebrews 11:16, which says of the ancient fathers: "But now they desire a country, i.e., a celestial country." Therefore, it seems that the New Law is not different from the Old Law.

Objection 3: In Romans 3:27 the Apostle seems to be distinguishing the two Laws, calling the Old Law a 'law of works', while calling the New

Law a 'law of faith'. But the Old Law was likewise a law of faith—this according to Hebrews 11:39, which says of the fathers of the Old Covenant: "All were approved by the testimony of faith." Similarly, the New Law is likewise a law of works; for Matthew 5:44 says, "Do good to those who hate you," and Luke 22:19 says, "Do this is memory of me." Therefore, the New Law does not differ from the Old Law.

But contrary to this: In Hebrews 7:12 the Apostle says, "When the priesthood is transformed, it is necessary for a transformation of the Law to be made." But as the Apostle proves in the same place, the priesthood of the New Law is different from the priesthood of the Old Law. Therefore, the Laws are likewise different.

I respond: As was explained above (q. 91, a. 4), all law directs human interaction in relation to some end. Now there are two ways in which things that are ordered to an end can be differentiated with respect to the notion of an end. First, they can be differentiated by the fact that they are ordered to diverse ends, and this is a difference in species, especially if the end is a proximate one. Second, they can be differentiated by their closeness to or distance from the end itself. For instance, it is clear that two movements differ in species insofar as they are ordered to different termini; on the other hand, to the extent that one part of a given movement is closer to the terminus than another part, there is a difference within the movement with respect to the perfect and the imperfect.

So, then, two laws can be differentiated in two ways.

In one way, they are differentiated in the sense of being wholly diverse, insofar as they ordered toward diverse ends. In the case of cities, for instance, a law that was ordered toward rule by the common people (*populus*) would be different in species from a law that was ordered toward rule by the aristocrats (*optimates*) in the city.

In the second way, two laws can be differentiated by the fact that the one of them orders things more closely to the end, while the other orders things more remotely. For instance, in one and the same city, a law imposed on grown men (*viri perfecti*), who are capable of immediately doing what contributes to the common good, is different from a law meant to teach children, who have to be instructed in how to perform the acts of men later in life.

Therefore, one should reply that, according to the first way of differentiating laws, the New Law is not different from the Old Law, since both have the same end, viz., that men should submit to God, and there is just one God for both the New Covenant and the Old Covenant—this according to Romans 3:30 ("There is one God who justifies circumcision on the basis of faith and the lack of circumcision through faith").

According to the second way of differentiating laws, the New Law is different from the Old Law. For the Old Law is, as it were, a teacher of children, as the Apostle says in Galatians 3:24, whereas the New Law is a law of perfection, since it is a law of charity. On this score, the Apostle says in Colossians 3:14 that the New Law is a "bond of perfection."

Reply to objection 1: The oneness of faith in both covenants attests to the oneness of the end. For it was explained above (q. 62, a. 2) that the object of the theological virtues, one of which is faith, is the ultimate end. Still, though, faith had one status in the Old Covenant and another in the New Covenant. For they believed in what was to come; we believe in what has been accomplished.

Reply to objection 2: All of the ascribed differences between the New Law and the Old Law are taken in a way corresponding to the perfect and the imperfect. For the precepts of any law are given concerning acts of virtue. But the imperfect, who do not yet have the habit of a virtue, are inclined toward doing the acts of virtue in a way different from those who have been perfected through the habit of the virtue.

Those who do not yet have the habit of a virtue are inclined toward doing the works of the virtue by some extrinsic cause, e.g., the threat of punishment or the promise of some extrinsic reward such as honor or wealth or something of this sort. And so the Old Law, which was given to the imperfect, i.e., to those who had not yet attained spiritual grace, was called a 'law of fear' insofar as it induced one to the observance of its precepts by threatening certain punishments. Again, it is said to contain certain temporal promises.

By contrast, those who have a virtue are inclined toward performing acts of that virtue out of love of virtue and not because of any extrinsic punishment or reward. And so the New Law, which consists principally in the spiritual grace poured into our hearts, is called a 'law of love'. And it is said to contain spiritual and eternal promises, which are the objects of virtue, especially of charity. And thus the perfect are inclined *per se* toward those objects of virtue—not in the sense of being inclined toward something extrinsic, but in the sense of being inclined toward something that is their own.

Moreover, the reason why the Old Law is said to "restrain the hand and not the mind" is that someone who refrains from sinning out of a fear of punishment is such that his will does not abstain from sin absolutely speaking, as does the will of someone who abstains from sin out of a love of righteousness (*amore iustitiae*). And it is for this reason that the New Law, which is a law of love, is said to restrain the mind.

To be sure, there were some individuals in the status of the Old Law who, having charity and the grace of the Holy Spirit, looked toward spiritual and eternal promises. And to that extent, they belonged to the New Law. Similarly, even in the New Covenant there are some carnal men who have not yet attained the perfection of the New Law and who, even in the New Covenant, have to be induced to acts of virtue through the fear of punishment and through certain temporal promises.

Moreover, even if the Old Law hands down precepts of charity, it is still the case that the Holy Spirit was not given *through* that Law—and, as Romans 5:5 says, it is through the Holy Spirit that "charity is diffused in our hearts."

Reply to objection 3: As was explained above (q. 106, a. 1), the New Law is called a 'law of faith' insofar as it principally consists in the very grace which is given inwardly to those who have faith (*credentes*), and hence this grace is called the 'grace of faith'. To be sure, the New Law secondarily contains certain moral and sacramental deeds, but the principal aspect of the New Law does not consist in these deeds in the way that the principal aspect of the Old Law did consist in them.

Now someone who was acceptable to God through faith under the Old Covenant belonged in that respect to the New Covenant. For he received justification only through faith in Christ, who is the author of the New Covenant. Hence, in Hebrew 11:26 the Apostle says even of Moses that "he thought of the reproach of the Christ as greater riches than the treasures of the Egyptians."

Article 2

Does the New Law bring the Old Law to fulfillment?

It seems that the New Law does not bring the Old Law to fulfillment:

Objection 1: *Being fulfilled* (*impletio*) is a contrary of *being made void* (*evacuatio*). But the New Law makes void, or rules out, the observances of the Old Law; for in Galatians 5:2 the Apostle says, "If you get circumcised, Christ will profit you nothing." Therefore, the New Law is not a fulfillment of the Old Law.

Objection 2: One contrary does not fulfill another. But in the New Law our Lord proposed certain precepts that are contrary to the precepts of the Old Law; for Matthew 5:31–33 says, "You have heard it said to the ancients, 'Whoever dismisses his wife, let him give her a written decree of divorce.' But I say to you, whoever divorces his wife makes her commit adultery." And the same thing is clear with oaths, as well as with the prohibition of retaliation and with the hatred of enemies. Similarly, in Matthew 15:11 ("It is not what enters into the mouth that defiles a man . . .") our Lord also seems to have ruled out those precepts of the Old Law that have to do with the distinction among foods. Therefore, the New Law is not a fulfillment of the Old Law.

Objection 3: If anyone acts contrary to a law, he does not fulfill that law. But in certain cases Christ acted contrary to the Law. For instance, as Matthew 8:3 reports, He touched a leper—which was contrary to the Law. Again, He seems to have violated the Sabbath many times, and this is why the Jews said of Him in John 9:16, "This man is not from God, for He does not keep the Sabbath." And so the New Law given by Christ is not a fulfillment of the Old Law.

Objection 4: As was explained above (q. 99, a. 4), the Old Law contained moral, ceremonial, and judicial precepts. But in Matthew 5, where He brought fulfillment to the Law in certain respects, He seems to make no mention of the judicial or ceremonial precepts. Therefore, it seems that the New Law does not completely fulfill the Old Law.

But contrary to this: In Matthew 5:17 our Lord says, "I have come not to destroy the Law, but to fulfill it." And later on He adds, "Not one iota or one letter of the Law will pass away until each of them is fulfilled."

I respond: As has been explained (a. 1), the New Law is related to the Old Law as the perfect to the imperfect. Now everything perfect supplies what the imperfect lacks. Accordingly, the New Law brings the Old Law to fulfillment insofar as it supplies what the Old Law lacked.

Now there are two possible things to consider in the Old Law, viz., its *end* and the *precepts* contained in the Law:

As was explained above (q. 92, a. 1), the *end* of any type of law is that men should be made just and virtuous. Hence, the end of the Old Law was likewise men's becoming justified (*iustificatio hominum*). The Law was unable to accomplish this, but it prefigured it in certain ceremonial actions and promised it in words.

In this respect, the New Law brings the Old Law to fulfillment by conferring justification through the power of Christ's passion. This is what the

Apostle is talking about in Romans 8:3–4: "What the Law could not do . . . God, sending His own Son in the likeness of sinful flesh, has condemned sin in the flesh, in order that the justification of the Law might be fulfilled in us." In this respect, the New Law accomplishes what the Old Law had promised—this according to 2 Corinthians 1:20 ("All the promises of God are in Him," i.e., in Christ).

Again, the New Law likewise brings to completion what the Old Law was a figure of. Hence, Colossians 2:17 says of the ceremonial precepts that "they were shadows of things to come, but the body is Christ's," i.e., the reality (*veritas*) belongs to Christ. Hence, the New Law is called the 'law of reality' (*lex veritatis*), whereas the Old Law is called the 'law of shadows' or 'law of figures'.

On the other hand, Christ fulfilled the *precepts* of the Old Law both by His deeds and by His teaching.

He did this by His deeds in the sense that He willed to be circumcised and to observe all the legal regulations that were supposed to be observed at that time—this according to Galatians 4:4 (". . . made under the Law").

Moreover, there were three ways in which He fulfilled the precepts of the Law by His teaching:

First, by expressing the true meaning of the Law. This is clear in the case of homicide and adultery, in the prohibition of which the Scribes and the Pharisees had understood only the prohibited exterior act. Hence, our Lord brought the Law to fulfillment by showing that interior acts of sin also fall under the prohibition.

Second, our Lord fulfilled the precepts of the Law by giving directions about how what the Law had prescribed might be more securely observed. For instance, the Old Law had prescribed that a man should not perjure himself, and this is more securely observed if he abstains from oaths altogether, except in the case of necessity.

Third, our Lord fulfilled the precepts of the Law by adding to them certain counsels of perfection, as is clear from Matthew 19:21, where our Lord, speaking to an individual who claims that he has observed the precepts of the Old Law, says, "One thing you are lacking. If you wish to be perfect, then go and sell all that you have."

Reply to objection 1: As was established above (q. 103, a. 3), the New Law does not make the observance of the Old Law void except with respect to the ceremonial precepts. But those precepts were figures of future realities. Hence, the ceremonial precepts are not to be observed any longer precisely because they have been fulfilled by the perfect things that they were figures of. For if they were observed, then something would still be signified as future and unfulfilled—just as there is no longer room for a promise of a future gift once the promise has already been fulfilled by the giving of the gift. And it is in this sense that the ceremonies of the Law are done away with when they are fulfilled.

Reply to objection 2: As Augustine explains in *Contra Faustum*, the cited precepts of our Lord are not contrary to the precepts of the Law: "For instance, what our Lord prescribed about not divorcing one's wife is not contrary to what the Law prescribed. For the Law does not say, 'If anyone wishes to, he may divorce his wife', the contrary of which would be 'Do not divorce your wife'. To the contrary, the Law did not want a wife to be divorced by her husband and proposed a delay in order that a mind bent on divorce might desist when confronted with the writing of the bill of divorce. Hence, in order to emphasize that a wife is not to be easily divorced, He makes an exception only where the cause is fornication."

The same thing should be said about the prohibition of oaths, as has been explained.

Again, the same thing is clear in the case of the prohibition of retaliation. For the Law set a limit to vengeance by prescribing that a man should not pursue it to the point of immoderate revenge. But our Lord removed him more perfectly from immoderate revenge by warning him to refrain from vengeance altogether.

Again, as regards hatred of one's enemies, He corrected the inaccurate understanding had by the Pharisees, warning us that it is the sin, and not the person, that should be held in contempt.

And as for the distinctions concerning food, which were ceremonial, our Lord did not prescribe that these distinctions should not be observed at that very time. Rather, as has been explained (q. 102, a. 6), He showed that food is unclean not by its nature, but only figuratively.

Reply to objection 3: As was explained above (q. 102, a. 5), touching a leper was forbidden under the Law because from it a man incurred a sort of uncleanness of irregularity, as was also the case with touching the dead. But our Lord, who was a cleanser of lepers, could not incur uncleanness.

Now by the things He did on the Sabbath He did not in reality break the Sabbath. The Master Himself showed this in the Gospel, by the fact that (a) He worked miracles by divine power, which is always active in things, and also by the fact that (b) He performed works that contributed to man's health, given that the Pharisees provided for the health even of animals on the Sabbath day; and also by the fact that (c) by reason of necessity He excused the apostles when they were collecting grain on the Sabbath.

To be sure, He did seem to break the Sabbath according to the superstitious understanding of the Sabbath had by the Pharisees, who believed that one should abstain even from health-giving works on the Sabbath—a belief that was contrary to the intention of the Law.

Reply to objection 4: The ceremonial precepts were not mentioned in Matthew 5 because, as has been explained, the observance of those precepts is entirely ruled out by their fulfillment.

As for the judicial precepts, He did mention the precept of retaliation in order that what was said about this precept should be understood to apply to all the others. In the case of this precept, He taught that the Law's intention was not that the penalty of retaliation should be sought for the sake of vengeful spite, which He forbade, warning that a man should be ready to suffer even grave injuries. Instead, the Law's intention was that retaliation should be sought only out of a love for justice—something that still remains under the New Law.

Article 3

Is the New Law contained within the Old Law?

It seems that the New Law is not contained within the Old Law:

Objection 1: The New Law consists principally in faith, and this is why it is called a 'law of faith', as is clear from Romans 3:27. But there are many things proposed for belief in the New Law which are not contained in the Old Law. Therefore, the New Law is not contained within the Old Law.

Objection 2: A certain Gloss on Matthew 5:19 ("Whoever breaks one of the least of these commandments . . .") says that the commandments of the Law are lesser, whereas the commandments in the Gospel are greater. But what is greater cannot be contained within what is lesser. Therefore, the New Law is not contained within the Old Law.

Objection 3: Anything that is contained within another is such that it is had when the latter is had. Therefore, if the New Law were contained within the Old Law, then when the Old Law was had, the New Law would be had as well. Therefore, once the Old Law was had, it was redundant for the New Law to be given again. Therefore, it is not the case that the New Law is contained within the Old Law.

But contrary to this: As Ezechiel 1:16 says, "There was a wheel within a wheel"—that is, as Gregory explains, the New Covenant was contained within the Old Covenant.

I respond: There are two ways for one thing to be contained within another. In one way, it is *actually* contained, as in the case of something that is located in a place. In the second way, it is *virtually* contained, in the way that an effect is contained within its cause, or in the way that what is complete is contained within what is incomplete, as a genus contains its species in potentiality or as a whole tree is contained within its seed.

It is in this second way that the New Law is contained within the Old Law. For, as has been explained (a. 1), the New Law is related to the Old Law as the perfect to the imperfect. Hence, Chrysostom, in commenting on Mark 4:28 ("The earth for its part brings forth fruit: first, the blade, and then the ear, and then the full ear of corn") says, "First, He brings forth the herb in the law of nature; then He brings forth the blade in the Law of Moses; and then He brings forth the full ear of corn in the Gospel." So, then, the New Law is in the Old Law in the way that the full ear of corn is in the blade.

Reply to objection 1: Everything that is explicitly and openly proposed for belief in the New Covenant is proposed for belief in the Old Covenant, but implicitly through figures. And it is in this sense that the New Law is contained with in the Old Law even with respect to what is proposed for belief.

Reply to objection 2: It is with respect to explicit manifestation that the precepts of the New Law are said to be greater than the precepts of the Old Law. But with respect to the very substance of the precepts of the New Covenant, all of them are contained within the Old Covenant. Hence, in *Contra Faustum* Augustine says, "Almost all the things our Lord warned about or commanded when He added the phrase, 'But I say to you', are found in those old books as well. But because they understood homicide to be nothing other than the slaying of the human body, our Lord disclosed that every evil impulse toward harming one's brother is to be assigned to the genus of homicide."

It is in light of disclosures of this sort that the precepts of the New Law are said to be greater than the precepts of the Old Law. But nothing prevents the greater from being contained virtually within the lesser in the way that a tree is contained within a seed.

Reply to objection 3: That which was given implicitly had to be made explicit. And so after the Old Law was handed down, the New Law likewise had to be given.

Article 4

Is the New Law more burdensome than the Old Law?

It seems that the New Law is more burdensome (*gravior*) than the Old Law:

Objection 1: In commenting on Matthew 5:19 ("Whoever breaks one of the least of these commandments . . .") Chrysostom says, "The commandments of Moses are easy to enact: 'You shall not kill', 'You shall not commit adultery'. By contrast, the commandments of Christ—i.e., 'You shall not be angry', 'You shall not lust'—are very difficult to enact." Therefore, the New Law is more burdensome than the Old Law.

Objection 2: It is easier to take advantage of earthly prosperity than to endure tribulations. But as is clear from Deuteronomy 28, in the Old Covenant temporal prosperity followed upon the observance of the Old Law. By contrast, many adversities follow for those who observe the New Law—just as 2 Corinthians 6:4 says: "Let us show ourselves to be God's ministers in great patience, in tribulations, in necessities, in distresses," and so on. Therefore, the New Law is more burdensome than the Old Law.

Objection 3: What results from addition to something else seems to be more difficult. But the New Law results from addition to the Old Law. For as is clear from Matthew 5, following Augustine's commentary, the Old Law prohibited bearing false witness (*periurium*), whereas the New Law prohibited even the taking of oaths; the Old Law prohibited divorcing one's wife without a written decree of divorce, whereas the New Law prohibited divorce altogether. Therefore, the New Law is more burdensome than the Old Law.

But contrary to this: Matthew 11:28 says, "Come to me all you who labor and are burdened." In commenting on this passage, Hilary says, "He calls to Himself those who labor under the difficulties of the Law and all who are burdened with the sins of the world." And later on, concerning the yoke of the Gospel, our Lord adds: "My yoke is easy and my burden is light." Therefore, the New Law is a lighter burden than the Old Law.

I respond: It is with respect to works of virtue that precepts of law are given, and there are two types of difficulty that can attend works of virtue.

One sort of difficulty involves the *exterior works*, which are in a way difficult and burdensome in their own right. On this score, the Old Law is much more burdensome than the New Law, since the Old Law obligated one to many more exterior actions in the many ceremonies than does the New Law, which in the teaching of Christ and the apostles adds very little beyond the precepts of the law of nature—even though afterwards some additional things were instituted by the holy Fathers. Even with respect to these additions, Augustine says that moderation should be observed in order that the way of life of the faithful not be rendered onerous. For in *Ad Inquisitiones Januarii* he says of certain individuals, "Our religion, which God's mercy wanted to be free, with very clear and very few sacramental celebrations, these people load up with servile burdens, to such an extent that the situation of the Jews is more tolerable, since they were subject to the sacraments of the Law and not to human presumption."

The second sort of difficulty involves the works of virtue in *interior acts*, i.e., that one should perform a virtuous work promptly and with pleasure. And in this respect virtue is difficult, since for someone who does not have a virtue it is very difficult; however, it is made easy by the virtue. On this score, the precepts of the New Law are more burdensome than the precepts of the Old Law, since in the New Law there are prohibitions against interior movements of the mind that were not explicitly prohibited in the Old Law. (Even if they were prohibited in some cases, there was no penalty attached to what was prohibited.) But this is extremely difficult for one who does not have a virtue; hence, in *Ethics* 5 the Philosopher says that it is easy to do the things that the just man does, but to do them in the way in which the just man does them, viz., with pleasure and promptly, is difficult for one who is not just. So, too, 1 John 5:3 says, "His commandments are not burdensome"—which Augustine comments on by saying that they are not burdensome for one who has love, but that they are burdensome for one who does not have love.

Reply to objection 1: The passage in question is expressly talking about the difficulty of the New Law with respect to the explicit constraint on interior movements.

Reply to objection 2: The adversities suffered by those who observe the New Law are not imposed by the Law itself. However, it is because of love, which the New Law consists in, that they are borne easily. For as Augustine says in *De Verbis Domini*, "Love renders easy and almost null all the things that are harsh and frightful."

Reply to objection 3: As Augustine says, the additions to the precepts of the Old Law are ordered toward making what the Old Law commanded easier to fulfill. And so the objection shows not that the New Law is more burdensome, but rather that it is easier.

QUESTION 108

The Contents of the New Law

Next we have to consider what is contained in the New Law. And on this topic there are four questions: (1) Should the New Law command or prohibit certain exterior works? (2) Does the New Law adequately command or prohibit exterior acts? (3) Does the New Law appropriately direct men with respect to interior acts? (4) Is it appropriate for the New Law to add counsels over and beyond its precepts?

Article 1

Should the New Law command or prohibit any exterior acts?

It seems that the New Law should not command or prohibit any exterior acts:

Objection 1: The New Law is the Gospel of the kingdom—this according to Matthew 24:14 ("This Gospel of the kingdom will be preached in the whole world"). But the kingdom of God consists not in exterior acts, but only in interior acts—this according to Luke 17:21 ("The kingdom of God is within you") and Romans 14:17 ("The kingdom of God is not meat and drink, but justice and peace and joy in the Holy Spirit"). Therefore, the New Law should not command or prohibit any exterior acts.

Objection 2: As Romans 8:2 says, the New Law is "the Law of the Spirit." But as 2 Corinthians 3:17 says, "Where the Spirit of the Lord is, there is freedom." But there is no freedom where man is obligated to do or to avoid certain exterior works. Therefore, the New Law does not contain any commands or prohibitions with respect to exterior acts.

Objection 3: All exterior acts are thought of as involving the hand, just as interior acts involve the mind. But the difference posited between the New Law and the Old Law is that "the Old Law restrains the hand and the New Law restrains the mind." Therefore, in the New Law prohibitions and precepts ought to be posited not with respect to exterior acts, but only with respect to interior acts.

But contrary to this: Through the New Law men are made children of the light; hence, John 12:36 says, "Believe in the light, in order that you might be children of the light." But it is fitting for children of the light to do works of light and to cast aside works of darkness—this according to Ephesians 5:8 ("You were once darkness, but now you are light in the Lord. Walk as children of the light"). Therefore, the New Law should prohibit some exterior works and should command others.

I respond: As has been explained (q. 106, a. 1), the New Law is principally the grace of the Holy Spirit, which is manifested in faith working through love. But men attain this grace through the Son of God made man; for grace filled His humanity in the first instance, and from there it flowed to us. Hence, John 1:14 says, "The Word was made flesh," and later adds, "He was full of grace and of truth," and further on, "Of His fullness we have all received, and grace for grace." Later on, John 1:17 adds, "Grace and truth were made by Christ."

And so it is appropriate that (a) the grace flowing from the incarnate Word comes down to us through certain exterior and sensible things and that (b) from this interior grace, through which the flesh is made subject to the spirit, certain sensible works are produced.

So, then, there are two possible ways for exterior works to involve grace.

First, they lead us in a some way to grace. These are the works of the sacraments instituted under the New Law, such as Baptism, the Eucharist, and others of this sort.

Second, there are the exterior works produced by the prompting of grace. And among these works there is a distinction to be noted.

For some of them have a necessary agreement with or necessary opposition to the interior grace that consists in faith working through love. Exterior works of this sort are commanded or prohibited in the New Law. For instance, the confession of one's faith is commanded and the denial of one's faith is prohibited. For Matthew 10:32–33 says, "If anyone acknowledges me before men, I will likewise acknowledge him before my Father. But if anyone denies me before men, I will likewise deny him before my Father."

By contrast, there are other works that do not have a necessary opposition to or agreement with faith operating through love. Such works were not commanded or prohibited in the New Law at the first institution of the Law; instead, the Lawgiver, viz., Christ, has left them up to each individual, to the extent that he is charged with the responsibility. And so with respect to such works, each individual is free to determine what is expedient for him to do or to avoid, and each individual who has responsibility for others (*praesidens*) is free to direct his subordinates with regard to what they should do or avoid in the case of such works. Hence, in this respect the Law of the Gospel is also called a 'law of freedom', since the Old Law determined many things and left few things to be determined by the freedom of men.

Reply to objection 1: The kingdom of God consists principally in interior acts, but, as a result, all the things without which interior acts cannot exist are likewise relevant to the kingdom of God. For instance, if the kingdom of God is interior justice and peace and spiritual joy, then all the exterior acts which are incompatible with justice or peace or spiritual joy must be incompatible with the kingdom of God. And so all such acts have to be forbidden in the kingdom of God.

By contrast, acts that are related neutrally to interior justice and peace and spiritual joy, e.g., eating this or that food, are such that the kingdom of God does not consist in them. And this is why the Apostle prefaces [the reference to justice and peace and joy] by saying, "The kingdom of God is not meat and drink."

Reply to objection 2: According to the Philosopher in *Metaphysics* 1, "the free is what is a cause of itself." Therefore, someone acts freely when he acts 'from himself' (*ex seipso*). Now when a man does something from a habit that agrees with his nature, he does it from himself, since a habit inclines one in the manner of a nature. By contrast, if the habit ran contrary to his nature, then the man would not act insofar as it is he himself, but instead he would act in accord with a certain corruption that had supervened on him. Therefore, since the grace of the Holy Spirit is like an interior habit infused into us and inclining us toward acting uprightly, it makes us do freely those things that agree with grace and to avoid those things that are contrary to grace.

Thus, there are two senses in which the New Law is called a 'law of freedom':

First, because it does not restrict us in doing or avoiding things except for those that are of themselves (*de se*) either necessary for salvation or incompatible with salvation; these things fall under a either a commandment of the Law or a prohibition of the Law.

Second, because it makes us fulfill even these precepts or prohibitions freely, insofar as we fulfill them because of the interior prompting of grace.

It is for these two reasons that the New Law is called a "law of perfect freedom" (James 1:25).

Reply to objection 3: In restraining the mind from disordered movements, the New Law must also restrain the hand from disordered acts, since these acts are the effects of interior movements.

Article 2

Does the New Law give adequate direction to exterior acts?

It seems that the New Law does not give adequate direction to exterior acts:

Objection 1: The New Law seems principally to involve faith working through love—this according to Galatians 5:6 ("In Christ Jesus neither circumcision nor lack of circumcision counts for anything; rather, it is faith that works through love"). But the New Law made explicit certain beliefs (*credenda*) that were not explicit in the Old Law, e.g., the belief in the Trinity. Therefore, it should likewise have added some exterior moral acts that had not been specified in the Old Law.

Objection 2: As was explained above (q. 102, a. 4), under the Old Law it was not only sacraments that were instituted, but also sacred things. But under the New Law, even if certain sacraments have been instituted, still, no sacred things seem to have been instituted by our Lord—e.g., things having to do with the sanctification of a temple or of vases, or even things having to do with the celebration of sacred feasts. Therefore, the New Law has not given adequate direction concerning exteriors.

Objection 3: Just as under the Old Law there were certain observances involving ministers of God, so too there were certain observances that involved the people—as was explained above (q. 102, a. 6) when the ceremonial precepts of the Old Law were being discussed. But under the New Law certain observances seem to have been handed down to the ministers of God, as is clear from Matthew 10:9 ("Do not take with you gold or silver or money in your wallets," and so on, along with the other things that follow in that place and other things that are said in Luke 9 and 10). Therefore, there should have also been some observances involving the lay faithful (*populus fidelis*) instituted under the New Law.

Objection 4: In the Old Law there were judicial precepts in addition to the moral and ceremonial precepts. But no judicial precepts are handed down in the New Law. Therefore, the New Law did not give adequate direction to exterior works.

But contrary to this: In Matthew 7:24, "Everyone who hears my words and keeps them is like a wise man who built his house on rock." But the wise builder did not overlook anything that was necessary for his building. Therefore, everything that involves salvation is adequately set down in the sayings of Christ.

I respond: As has been explained (a. 1), in the case of exterior acts the New Law should command or prohibit only (a) acts through which grace is introduced or (b) acts which necessarily involve the correct use of grace.

Because we are able to obtain grace only through Christ and not on our own, our Lord Himself instituted by Himself the sacraments through which we obtain grace, viz., Baptism, the Eucharist, the Ordination of ministers of the New Law (by appointing the apostles and the seventy-two disciples), Penance, and indissoluble Matrimony. He also promised Confirmation through the mission of the Holy Spirit. In addition, we read that, by His institution, the apostles cured the sick by anointing them with oil (Mark 6:13). These are the sacraments of the New Law.

Now the correct use of grace occurs through works of charity. Insofar as such works have a necessary connection with virtue, they pertain to the moral precepts, which were also handed down in the Old Law. Hence, on this score, it was not appropriate for the New Law to add anything to the Old Law with respect to exterior acts. On the other hand, as was explained above (q. 99. a. 4), the specification of exterior works in relation to the worship of God pertains to the ceremonial precepts of the Law, whereas the specification of such works in relation to one's neighbor pertains to the judicial precepts. And so, since these specifications are not in themselves necessarily connected with interior grace, which the New Law consists in, they do not fall under a precept of the New Law, but are instead left up to human discretion. Some of these specifications are left up to the lower ranks and have to do with each individual taken one by one, whereas others are left up to temporal or spiritual authorities (*ad praelatos temporales vel spirituales*) and have to do with the common welfare.

So, then, the only exterior works that the New Law ought to determine by commands and prohibitions are (a) the sacraments and (b) moral precepts that of themselves involve the essence (*ratio*) of virtue, e.g., 'Do not kill', 'Do not steal', and others of this sort.

Reply to objection 1: The things that pertain to faith lie beyond human reason; hence, we are unable to arrive at them except through grace. And so when a more abundant grace comes along, more beliefs need to be made clear.

By contrast, we are directed to the works of the virtues by our rational nature, which, as was explained above (q. 19, a. 3 and q. 63, a. 2), is a measure (*regula*) of human action. And so in the case of these works there is no need for any precepts to be given beyond the moral precepts of the Law, which come from the dictate of reason.

Reply to objection 2: The grace given in the sacraments of the New Law is from Christ alone, and so the sacraments had to be instituted by Him.

By contrast, no grace is given in the sacred things, e.g., in the consecration of a temple or of an altar or of other things of this sort, or even in the very celebration of solemn feasts. And so because such things do not have a necessary relation to interior grace, our Lord left it up to the faithful to institute them by their own choice.

Reply to objection 3: Our Lord gave the precepts in question to the apostles not as ceremonial observances, but as moral statutes. There are two possible ways to understand this.

First, according to Augustine in *De Consensu Evangelistarum*, they were given not as precepts, but as permissions (*concessiones*). For instance, he permitted them to undertake the role of preaching without a wallet or a staff or other things of this sort, since they had the authority to receive the necessities of life from those to whom they preached; this is why he added, "For the laborer is deserving of his food." However, one who has the role of preaching does not sin, but instead goes beyond his duty (*supererogat*), if, as Paul did, he brings along with him what he will live on and does not receive supplies from those to whom he preaches the Gospel.

The second way to understand these precepts, following the explanation of other saints, is that they are temporary statutes given to the apostles for that time during which they were being sent forth to preach in Judea before Christ's passion. For the disciples, still like little ones under Christ's care, needed to receive special instructions from Christ, in the way that subordinates need instructions from their superiors—and this mainly because they had to practice little by little at abandoning temporal cares, so that they might thereby become fit for preaching the Gospel throughout the whole world. And given that the status of the Old Law still persisted and that they had not yet attained the perfect freedom of the Spirit, it is not surprising that our Lord instituted certain determinate modes of living. When the passion was imminent, He abrogated these statutes, since the disciples had by that time been adequately trained through them. Hence, at Luke 22:35–36 our Lord said, "When I sent you without a sack or wallet or shoes, were you lacking anything?" And they replied, "No." And then He said to them, "But now let one who has a sack take it, and the same with a wallet." For the time of perfect freedom was already imminent, and so they were left entirely to their own judgment in those matters that did not of themselves have a necessary connection with virtue.

Reply to objection 4: Likewise, the judicial precepts, considered in themselves, have a necessary connection with virtue only with respect to the general nature of justice and not with respect to the particular specifications. And so our Lord left it up to those who were going to have spiritual or temporal care of others to specify the judicial precepts. However, as will be noted below (a. 3), He did explain certain of the judicial precepts of the Old Law because of the Pharisees' defective interpretations of them.

Article 3

Does the New Law give man adequate direction with respect to interior acts?

It seems that the New Law does not give man adequate direction with respect to interior acts:

Objection 1: There are ten precepts of the Decalogue ordering man toward God and neighbor. But our Lord brought only three of them to perfection, viz., the prohibition of homicide, the prohibition of adultery, and the prohibition of bearing false witness (*periurium*). Therefore, it seems that He gave man inadequate direction by failing to bring the other precepts to perfection.

Objection 2: In the Gospel our Lord gave no direction concerning the judicial precepts except for those having to do with divorcing one's wife, the punishment of retaliation, and the persecution of enemies. But as was explained above (q. 105), there were many other judicial precepts in the Old Law. Therefore, in this respect He gave inadequate direction to the lives of men.

Objection 3: In the Old Law there were ceremonial precepts in addition to the moral and judicial precepts. Our Lord gave no direction at all concerning ceremonial precepts. Therefore, it seems that He has given inadequate direction.

Objection 4: Having a good interior disposition of mind involves a man's not doing good works for the sake of temporal ends. But there are many temporal goods other than human respect, and there are likewise many good works other than fasting, almsgiving, and praying. Therefore, it was inappropriate for our Lord to teach, concerning just these three good works, that we ought to avoid the glory of human respect, without mentioning any other earthly goods.

Objection 5: It is naturally instilled in man that he should be solicitous about those things that are necessary for him to live, a solicitude that other animals also share in common with man; hence, Proverbs 6:6–8 says, "Go to the ant, O sluggard, and consider her ways. . . . She prepares her food in the summer and stores up provisions in a harvest." But every precept that is given in opposition to an inclination of nature is evil, since it is contrary to the natural law. Therefore, it seems inappropriate for our Lord to have prohibited solicitude about food and clothing.

Objection 6: No act of virtue should be prohibited. But judgment is an act of justice—this according to Psalm 93:15 (". . . until justice be turned into judgment"). Therefore, it seems inappropriate for our Lord to have prohibited judgment.

And so it seems that the New Law has given inadequate direction with respect to interior acts.

But contrary to this: In *De Sermone Domini in Monte* Augustine says, "Notice that when He said, 'Whoever hears these words of mine . . .', this is a sufficient indication that our Lord's sermon is complete, containing all the precepts by which the Christian life is shaped."

I respond: As is clear from the passage cited from Augustine, our Lord's Sermon on the Mount contains a comprehensive instruction for the Christian life in which the interior movements of man are perfectly directed. For after declaring beatitude to be the end and commending the authority of the apostles, through whom the doctrine of the Gospel was to be promulgated (Luke 6:12–17), He gives directions for the interior movements of man, first with respect to oneself and then with respect to one's neighbor.

As regards oneself, He does this in two ways, corresponding to man's two interior movements with respect to action (*de agendis*), viz., (a) willing the action and (b) intending the end. Hence, he first directs man's willing of an action in accord with the different precepts of the Law. More specifically, He directs that one should abstain not only from exterior works that are evil in themselves (*secundum se mala*), but from evil interior acts of will as well, and also from occasions for evil acts of will. He then directs man's intentions, teaching that in the good acts we do, we should seek neither human glory nor worldly riches, i.e., we should not seek to build up our treasure on earth.

Now after this He directs man's interior movement with respect to his neighbor. More specifically he directs that we should not pass judgment rashly or unjustly or presumptuously; nor, on the other hand, should we be remiss toward our neighbor in such a way that we entrust him with sacred things when he is unworthy.

Lastly, He teaches us the manner in which the Gospel doctrine should be fulfilled, viz., by imploring God's help, by making the effort to enter through the narrow gate of perfect virtue, and by exercising caution in order that we not be corrupted by those who would seduce us (*a seductoribus*). And He teaches us that observing His commandments is necessary for virtue, and that it is not sufficient merely to make a confession of faith, or to work miracles, or merely to hear His word.

Reply to objection 1: Our Lord brought to perfection those precepts of the Law which the Scribes and Pharisees had an incorrect understanding of. This occurred mainly with respect to three precepts of the Law. For in the case of the prohibitions against adultery and homicide, they thought that the exterior act alone was prohibited, and not the interior desire. They believed this more with regard to homicide and adultery than with regard to stealing and bearing false witness, because the movement of anger that leads to homicide and the movement of concupiscence that leads to adultery seemed to them to be somehow in us by nature, whereas this was not the case with the desire to steal or to bear false witness.

Still, they had a false understanding of perjury. To be sure, they believed that bearing false witness is a sin, but they believed that taking oaths was desirable in itself and should frequently be done, since it seems to involve reverence for God. And so our Lord showed that the taking of oaths is not to be desired as a good, but that it is better to speak without oaths unless necessity compels one to.

Reply to objection 2: There were two ways in which the Scribes and the Pharisees were mistaken about the judicial precepts.

First, there were certain acts handed down as *permissible* in the Law of Moses which they took to be *righteous* in themselves, viz., divorcing one's wife and taking usurious interest from outsiders. And so our Lord prohibited divorcing one's wife (Matthew 5:32), along with the taking of usurious interest, saying "Lend without expecting something in return" (Luke 6:35).

The second way in which they were mistaken was in believing that certain things that the Old Law had directed to be done for the sake of justice were to be done out of either (a) an appetite for revenge or (b) a desire for temporal things or (c) a hatred of one's enemies. And this involved three precepts.

For they believed that the desire for revenge was licit because of the precept that had been given concerning retaliation as a punishment. However, this precept had been given to preserve justice and not so that a man might seek revenge. And so our Lord, in order to exclude this interpretation, teaches that a man's mind ought to prepared so that, if necessary, he will be ready to suffer many things.

Again, they considered the movement of sense desire licit because of those judicial precepts in which, as was explained above (q. 105, a. 2, ad 9), the restitution of a thing that had been stolen (*restitutio rei ablatae*) had to be made along with something additional. Now the Law commanded this in order to maintain justice, and not in order to make room for greed (*cupiditas*). And so our Lord teaches that we should not demand what belongs to us out of greed, but that we should be ready, if necessary, to hand over even more.

Again, they believed that the impulse to hatred was licit because of those precepts of the Law that had been given about the killing of enemies. As was explained above (q. 105, a. 3, ad 4), the Law prescribed this in order to fulfill justice and not in order to fully satisfy one's hatred. And so our Lord teaches that we should have love for our enemies and that we should be ready, if necessary, even to do good to them.

As Augustine explains, these precepts are to be taken "as a preparation of the mind."

Reply to objection 3: It was fitting for the moral precepts to remain in their entirety under the New Law, since they involve the essence of virtue in themselves. The judicial precepts, on the other hand, did not necessarily remain in the manner in which the Law specified; instead, it was left up to the judgment of men whether they should be specified in the same way or some other way. And so our Lord gave us adequate direction concerning these two kinds of precepts.

However, the observance of the ceremonial precepts was completely done away with because of the fulfillment of the reality. And so in His general teaching He did not give any direction with respect to precepts of this sort. However, in other places He shows that the entire corporeal worship which had been specified under the Law had to be changed into spiritual worship. This is clear from John 4:21–23, where He said, "The hour is coming when you will worship the Father neither on this mountain nor in Jerusalem, but true worshippers will worship the Father in spirit and in truth."

Reply to objection 4: All worldly things fall under three headings, viz., honors, riches, and pleasures. This is in accord with 1 John 2:16, "All that is in the world is concupiscence of the flesh"—which has to do with pleasures of the flesh—"and concupiscence of the eyes"—which involves riches—"and pride of life"—which pertains to the ambition for fame and honor.

Now the Law did not promise superfluous pleasures of the flesh; rather, it prohibited them. On the other hand, it did promise lofty honor and an abundance of riches; for with respect to the former, Deuteronomy 28:1 says, "If you listen to the voice of the Lord your God, He will exalt you above all the nations," and with respect to the latter, it adds a little later, "He will make you abound with every kind of good." The Jews understood these promises perversely (*prave*) to mean that they should serve God for the sake of these things as an end.

And so our Lord excluded this understanding. He taught, first of all, that the works of virtue should not be done for the sake of human glory. And He proposed three such works, which all the others fall under. For all the things that someone does to restrain himself in his sense desires fall under *fasting*; and whatever is done because of love of one's neighbor falls under *almsgiving*; and all the things done for the sake of worshiping God fall under *prayer*. Now He posits these three works in particular because they are the principal ones and the ones through which men are especially wont to strive for glory.

Second, He taught that we should not set up riches as our end when He said, "Do not store up for yourselves treasures on earth" (Matthew 6:19).

Reply to objection 5: Our Lord did not prohibit necessary solicitude, but instead prohibited disordered solicitude. Now there are four types of disordered solicitude concerning temporal goods that should be avoided.

First, we should not take temporal goods as our end, and we should not serve God for the sake of necessary food and clothing. Hence, He says, "Do not store up for yourself treasures . . ."

Second, we should not be solicitous about temporal goods in a way that involves our despairing of God's help. Hence, our Lord says, "Your Father knows that you need all these things" (Matthew 6:32).

Third, our solicitude should not be presumptuous, as when a man becomes confident that he himself, through his own solicitude, can procure the necessities of life without God's help. Our Lord rules this out by saying that a man cannot add to his own height (Matthew 6:27).

Fourth, a man anticipates the time of solicitude, so that he is solicitous at the present moment about what pertains to the cares of the future and not to the cares of the present moment. Hence, He says, "Do not be solicitous about tomorrow" (Matthew 6:34).

Reply to objection 6: Our Lord did not prohibit the sort of judgment that belongs to justice, without which what is sacred could not be taken away from those who are unworthy. Rather, He prohibits disordered judgment, as has been explained.

Article 4

Is it appropriate for certain determinate counsels to be proposed in the New Law?

It seems that it is inappropriate for certain determinate counsels (*consilia aliqua determinata*) to be proposed in the New Law:

Objection 1: As was explained above when we talked about counsel (q. 14, a. 2), counsels are given about things that are expedient for an end. But it is not the case that the same things are expedient for everyone. Therefore, certain determinate counsels should not have been proposed for everyone.

Objection 2: Counsels are given with respect to a better good. But there are no determinate grades of better goods. Therefore, determinate counsels ought not to be given.

Objection 3: Counsels have to do with the perfection of a life. But obedience has to do with the perfection of a life. Therefore, it is inappropriate that in the Gospel a counsel is not given for obedience.

Objection 4: Among the precepts there are many that pertain to the perfection of a life, such as our Lord's saying, "Love your enemies," along with the precepts He gave to the apostles in Matthew 10. Therefore, it is inappropriate for counsels to be given in the New Law, both because not all of them are posited, and also because they are not distinct from the precepts.

But contrary to this: The counsels of a wise friend afford great assistance—this according to Proverbs 27:9 ("Ointments and various perfumes delight the heart, and the good counsels of a friend gladden the soul"). But Christ especially is wise and a friend. Therefore, His counsels have the greatest usefulness and are appropriate.

I respond: The difference between a counsel and a precept is that a precept implies necessity, whereas a counsel is left up to the choice of the one to whom it is given. And so it was appropriate that counsels should be added to the precepts in the New Law, which is a law of freedom, but not in the Old Law, which was a law of servitude. Therefore, the precepts of the New Law must be understood to have been given about things that are necessary for attaining the end of eternal beatitude, toward which the New Law directly leads one. By contrast, the counsels have to concern things through which a man is able to attain the end in question in a better and more expeditious manner.

Now man is situated between the things of this world and the spiritual goods in which eternal beatitude consists, so that the more he clings to the one, the more he withdraws from the other, and vice versa. Therefore, someone who totally clings to the things of this world, in the sense that he sets them up as his end and takes them as the reasons for and measures of his actions, falls away entirely from spiritual goods. And so it is a disorder of this sort that is excluded by the precepts. However, a man need not totally cast off the things of the world in order to attain the end of eternal beatitude, since a man who makes use of the things of this world can attain eternal beatitude as long as he does not set them up as his end. And it is about this matter that the counsels of the Gospel are given.

Now as is clear from 1 John 2:16, the goods of this world that are involved in the practice of human life are of three types, viz., (a) the riches of exterior goods, which pertain to the concupiscence of the eyes; (b) carnal pleasures, which pertain to the concupiscence of the flesh; and (c) and honors, which pertain to pride of life. The evangelical counsels involve giving up all three of these in their entirety, to the extent that this is possible. Every sort of religious life (*religio*) that professes the state of perfection is based on these three counsels. For wealth is given up through *poverty*, carnal pleasures are given up through *perpetual chastity*, and pride of life is given up through *obedience*.

Now when these three are observed absolutely speaking, then they pertain to the proposed counsels in an unqualified way. On the other hand, the observance of any of them in a special case involves the counsels in a qualified way, viz., in that particular case. For instance, if a man gives alms to someone who is poor when he is not obligated to do so, then he is following the counsel with respect to that deed. Similarly, when someone abstains from carnal pleasures for a fixed period of time in order to make room for prayer, then he is following the counsel during that time. Similarly, when someone does not follow his own wishes with respect to some action that he could licitly perform, then he is following the counsel in that particular case—if, say, he does good to his enemies when he is not obligated to, or if he forgives an offense for which he could justly demand retribution (*vindicta*).

And in this way all the particular counsels fall under the three general and perfect counsels.

Reply to objection 1: The counsels mentioned above are of themselves expedient for everyone, but because some individuals lack the right disposition, it happens that the counsels are not expedient for a given individual, since his affections are not inclined toward them. And so when our Lord proposes the evangelical counsels, he always mentions the fitness of men for observing the counsels. For instance, when He is giving the counsel of perpetual poverty in Matthew 19:21, He begins by saying, "If you wish to be perfect . . . ," and then He adds, ". . . go and sell all that you have." Similarly, when He was giving the counsel of perpetual chastity, after He had said, "There are eunuchs who have castrated themselves for the sake of the kingdom of heaven," He immediately added, "Let him who can take it, take it." Similarly, in 1 Corinthians 7:35 the Apostle, having given the counsel of virginity, says, "I am telling you this for your benefit, and not to set a trap for you."

Reply to objection 2: It is not determinate just which particular goods are better in each case. But it is determinate which general goods are better simply and absolutely speaking. And, as has been explained, it is these goods that all the particular goods fall under.

Reply to objection 3: Our Lord is understood to have given the counsel of obedience when He said, ". . . and let him follow me" (Matthew 16:24). We follow Him not only by imitating His works, but also by obeying His commandments—this according to John 10:27 ("My sheep listen to my voice and follow me").

Reply to objection 4: If the things our Lord says about genuine love of enemies and other such things in Matthew 5 and Luke 6 are taken to refer to *the preparation of the mind*, then they are necessary for salvation— viz., that a man be ready to do good to his enemies and to do other things of this sort when necessity requires it. And in this sense they are counted as precepts.

On the other hand, as has been explained, it pertains to the counsels that a man should promptly do good to his enemies in actuality, where there is no special necessity for doing so.

Now as was explained above, the things that are posited in Matthew 10 and Luke 9 and 10 were certain precepts of discipline for that time, or certain permissions. And so they are not taken to be counsels.

Index